Encyclopedia of World Pop Music, 1980–2001

Encyclopedia of World Pop Music, 1980–2001

Stan Jeffries

An Oryx Book

Greenwood Press
Westport, Connecticut   London

Library of Congress Cataloging-in-Publication Data

Jeffries, Stan.
   Encyclopedia of world pop music, 1980–2001 / Stan Jeffries.
    p. cm.
   Includes bibliographical references (p.) and index.
   ISBN 0–313–31547–7 (alk. paper)
  1. Popular music—1981–1990—Bio-bibliography—Dictionaries. 2. Popular
music—1991–2000—Bio-bibliography—Dictionaries. I. Title.
ML102.P66 J44 2003
781.63'03—dc21   2002021627

British Library Cataloguing in Publication Data is available.

Library of Congress Catalog Card Number: 2002021627
ISBN: 0–313–31547–7

First published in 2003

Greenwood Press, 88 Post Road West, Westport, CT 06881
An imprint of Greenwood Publishing Group, Inc.
www.greenwood.com

Printed in the United States of America

∞™

The paper used in this book complies with the
Permanent Paper Standard issued by the National
Information Standards Organization (Z39.48-1984).

10 9 8 7 6 5 4 3 2 1

This book is dedicated to the memory of Alison Ewbank,
whom I never met but with whom I exchanged phone calls,
and who was responsible, in the spring of 1999,
for setting me along the path to the completion of this book.

Contents

Acknowledgments

The author would like to thank the following individuals, without whose help and advice this book would have taken even longer to complete: Debby Adams, Rob Kirkpatrick and Megan Belanger at Greenwood, Lisa Buckley, Sarah Beighton, Delphine Planes, Amy Good, Mei-Ling Stubbs, Amy Lander, Sarah Leiberman, Polly Woodbridge, James "Turbulence" Smith, Stelios Vahaviolos, Lena Holman, "French" Ben Farvaque, Anjelika Dykstra, Aurelio Alonso-Cortes, Luisa Strani, Holger Braun, Manasvini Prabhat, Csaba Piller, Gianluigi Borotti, Wirachai Roynarin, Maija Bissett, Giles Tongue, Jayne Ducker, Elizabeth Lydon, Jen Hart, Christie Carter, and Gilly Allcock.

Introduction

When Robin Scott and his group M released the single "Pop Muzik" in 1979, they took it to the top of the charts across the world with the help of a simple refrain that stated people across the world, be they in London, Paris, New York or Munich, would always talk about pop music. What they stated was a simple truth: that pop music has always been and will always be talked about. Be it by musicians, by journalists, by governments, or most important, by the fans, the merits or otherwise of popular music and the artists that make it are discussed whenever music fans come together.

It is the fans, the people who buy the music, who decide what acts are going to be the heroes of a new generation. Pop music has always created heroes. From Johnny Ray in the 1950s (the decade of the birth of pop as we know it today) to the boy/girl bands of today, pop stars have forged new fashions and new genres of music. Many have faced government indignation; some have even forced governments to re-think certain policies.

In the period covered by this book, trends in pop music changed dramatically. By the late 1970s the influence of deejays and their treatment of records on the turntable created a new musical force, as they mixed different, seemingly inappropriate songs together to produce a hybrid that soon added new genres to the musical lexicon. Acid-house, techno, and hip-hop were all created by deejays experimenting with existing forms of music fueled by their desire for new and challenging sounds. Deejay culture was beginning to grow, and by the end of the twentieth century some deejays had become fixtures in charts across the world. In Britain deejay artists such as Fatboy Slim and Judge Jules had become stars. However, although the rise in popularity of the deejay cannot be ignored, bands and singers are the ones who attain true superstar status. In Asia, for example, the deejay has yet to emerge as a serious artist; charts are dominated either by rock acts, which play a more traditional Western style of music, or by "manufactured" boy/girl bands, created by record companies and entrepreneurs who choose group members for their physical attraction and vocal and dancing ability, as opposed to the traditional band that forms through friendship and a mutual love of music. Likewise in eastern Europe, rock is the predominant musical genre in pop music.

Pop is such a wide-ranging term that an absolute definition is almost impossible. For the purposes of this book, pop is the music that makes up the contents of a country's main popular music charts. Although many nations have a myriad of charts (a glance through the British music industry magazine *Music Week* shows twelve different charts in the United Kingdom, including Urban, Club, and Garage), usually only one is seen as the definitive list of bestselling artists nationally of any particular week. It is this chart, the chart based solely on national record sales from major music stores rather than genre-specific independent stores, that I have taken as the benchmark for entries. Thus I consider indie, grunge, rock, electronica, and metal to be all "pop" music in that they have a massive widespread appeal, appearing regularly in the major charts of any country. Of course, many popular bands are not featured in this book. Although many other artists fulfill the criteria employed for inclusion, my aim was not to simply re-introduce acts to a new audience in the United States, but to show the depth of music across the world that has barely grazed the U.S. charts, to show how groups that may have been one-hit wonders (and no-hit wonders) in America have enjoyed success in their own countries. Therefore U.S. acts, and acts that have had substantial popularity in the United States, have been omitted in favor of artists that hold a strong position at home without gaining long-lasting fame in America.

It is worth mentioning that many of the entries from Asia, particularly those from India and Pakistan, verge on what might in the West be termed *world music;* that is, they employ the traditional instruments, instrumentation, and musical styles of that particular country. However, the artists presented in this book have all added a modern twist, be it through instrumentation, lyrics, or style. Through this modernization, or westernization, of their music, they have come to be seen as pop musicians in their own countries, rather than musicians playing traditional music in a traditional style.

Aside from chart success, some artists were included because they have influenced other artists far beyond what their sales figures would indicate. Switzerland's Yello, for example, has won respect from inside the industry for its continual desire to experiment with musical boundaries, but is rarely seen on the popular charts. However, when the deejay Afrika Bambaataa first began sampling Yello's music in the 1970s, he was tentatively promoting the first examples of a music that has evolved into one of the most popular genres in the world today. Thus the eccentric Swiss duo Yello influenced the birth of hip-hop.

Several themes keep recurring throughout this book: artists who have come close to being dropped by their record companies but have survived to become superstars; other bands that were together for many years, or came close to splitting up, before achieving recognition. The nature of the music industry, however, demands constant change. New acts are discovered and take the place of established ones. Famous names suddenly fall from grace and are sometimes seldom heard of again. This is the essence of being a fan of pop music: the thrill of discovering a new talent, and the salacious satisfaction we sometimes feel when a star's career bites the dust.

Although some of the artists featured in these pages are happy to remain respected figures in their home market, many others have attempted to break into more international arenas, most noticeably the United States. A few have succeeded, and some have been noticeable failures.

I have not judged the artistic merits of any artists in this book, as individuals' tastes in pop music vary widely. This is one of the fundamental joys of pop music. It is always better to judge for oneself. To enable you to do this I have listed one Web site address (in English, where available) for each entry; however, many of the artists do not have English-language sites, and in this instance I have listed a site in their native language. I have also included other sources, book titles, magazine articles, and the like. Although every effort was made to find these in English, where that was not possible I have included a source in a different language (not necessarily the artist's native language).

The book is organized alphabetically by the artist's surname or, in the case of a band, the first letter of its name (groups using the prefix *The* are organized by the initial letter of the next word; e.g., The Stone Roses are listed under S). Each listing provides an overview of the artist's career, a discussion of his or her recorded output and chart placings (primarily in the native country), and his or her influence on other artists. Some of the artists you will have heard of; others you most definitely will not. I sincerely hope that at least one of the artists in this book will fire your imagination enough to find out more about them, to see into a different culture's tastes, and to find a new hero for yourself.

A

Abel, Morten (Norway)

Morten Abel Knutsen was born on October 15, 1962, in Stavenger, Norway. After a less-than-happy school life, Abel spent three years at college studying marketing before becoming a scaffolder on the oil platforms in the North Sea. Abel also taught himself guitar and in 1980 formed the band Mods, which through a series of critically well-received concerts earned a recording contract with PolyGram. The band's first album, *Revansj!*, was released in 1981 and consisted of eleven songs, all in Norwegian. The album earned little recognition, and Mods found themselves abandoned by PolyGram but soon signed with a small Norwegian label, Slagerfabrikken, with which they released another guitar-driven album, *Amerika*, in 1982. This album was also largely ignored, and Abel left the band to reconsider his career in music. (In 1984 the band released one more album, *Time Machine*, without Abel.)

In 1987 Abel resumed his career when he formed The September When with two former Mods members, Helge Hummervoll and Tor Øyvind Syvertsen. The band's first eponymous (self-named) album was recorded in London and released in 1989. Unlike Mods records, the album was written and sung entirely in English, and the change resulted in sales of over 25,000 copies. By 1991 Syvertsen had left the band but The September When had expanded into a five-piece with the addition of Morten Molster (guitar), Stene Osmundsen (drums), and Gulliev Wee (bass). A second album, *Mother I've Been Kissed*, was released in 1991, and the band's growing fan base helped it top the Norwegian chart with sales in excess of 80,000 copies. The band toured Scandinavia before returning to the studio and, in 1992, releasing their third album, *One Eye Open*. Similar in content to the group's previous releases, consisting of tight pop sings backed by a traditional guitar/bass/drums arrangement, it too reached #1 in Norway.

In 1993 Abel ventured into motion pictures when he starred in the Norwegian romantic drama *Hodet Over Vannet* and released a single from the soundtrack. At the same time he began another musical project and named the new band Peltz, after a doctor who had treated him for a throat infection. Three years later, in 1996, the band released its debut album, *Coma*, the delay owing to Abel's previous commitments in The September When. The experimental, electronic sound of *Coma* was a marked change from the musically traditional sound of The September When.

Despite Abel's focus on his acting and his work with Peltz, The September When steadily gained popularity, and in 1994 it released the guitar-driven *Hugger Mugger*, which became the band's bestselling album. It sold over 100,000 copies and gave the band a double platinum disc. Although the group was highly popular in Norway, no new material was forthcoming; and after releasing a best-of album, *Prestige de la Norvége 89–96* (1996), the band split up. Abel then released his debut solo album, *Snowboy*, in 1997. Despite the album's use of the pop sound that had been so successful for Abel in the past, it struggled to sell 40,000 copies. After the relative failure of the record, Abel retreated from the public eye to concentrate on new material.

Two years later Abel released *Here We Go Then, You And I* (October 1999). The introspective album was recorded in various studios in England during the winter of 1998, and by March 2000 it had sold over 100,000 copies. Abel was named best pop solo artist by the Norwegian music industry, and Norwegian TV aired one of his concerts. He now began working with other artists and by the end of the year had written tracks for fellow Norwegian singer **Sissel** and newcomer **Espen Lind**.

In September 2000 the Norwegian Hit Awards named Abel best Norwegian male artist. By the end of the year he was in England playing small pub and club venues as a solo artist and writing new material. After he returned home for Christmas, the Norwegian magazine *Café!* voted Abel the best-dressed man in Norway in February 2001. In June he appeared at festivals across Europe, including the Norwegian Wood festival in Oslo and the Nattjazz festival in Bergen, Germany, where he performed with a brass band. The appearances were a prelude to the release of a new album that entered the Norwegian chart at #1. This album, *I'll Come Back and Love You Forever*, was more optimistic than *Here We Go Then* but was equally intensely personal; it was released in November while a single of the same name also reached the top of the chart. By the end of 2001 *Here We Go Then, You And I* had spent over a year on the local album chart.

References

www.mortenabel.com

Ace of Base (Sweden)

Jonas Berggren (b. March 21, 1967) was born and raised in Gothenburg, Sweden, with his younger sisters, Malin (b. October 31, 1970) and Jenny (b. May 19, 1972). All the family members showed musical traits, as Jonas learned keyboards and the sisters sang in the local church choir. When Jonas was a teenager he began writing songs with his school friend Ulf Ekberg (b. December 6, 1972).

Ace of Base
Pictorialpress Ltd., London, UK

Berggren and Ekberg called themselves Tech Noir and began to record fast techno songs during the late 1980s but could not find a record label willing to release their material. In the early 1990s the duo introduced pop and reggae into their style. They also began to audition singers but had no luck until Berggren asked his sisters if they were interested. The foursome became Ace of Base and began rehearsing in a room they shared with a car repair company on the outskirts of Gothenburg. Although the band was recording demos, it received no interest from Swedish labels. Jonas Berggren then sent a tape to a Danish company, Mega, in Copenhagen. The company signed the band and released a single, "Wheel of Fortune," in 1992. The single was released twice but never won any airplay. Mega and the band both believed the single had hit potential and continued to promote it. After it was released for a third time, it suddenly found itself on the playlist of local radio stations and reached #2 in Denmark. The band already had its follow-up planned and released "All That She Wants" the week after "Wheel of Fortune" hit #2. The second single, a catchy pop song with a vaguely reggae feel, overtook the group's debut single and reached #1. Despite success in Denmark, the rest of Europe showed little interest in the band until a German company, Metronome Musik, released "All That She Wants" in Germany, where it became #1. The band followed the success of its singles by releasing an album, *Happy Nation*, that was a collection of songs featuring a jaunty reggae feel. The record reached #1 in Germany, achieving a platinum disc, and then made #1 across most of mainland Europe as MTV heavily promoted the singles.

The band's breakthrough in the United States came later in 1992 when the video for "All That She Wants" was seen by Clive Davis, the president of Arista Records. Davis signed the band, and *Happy Nation* was renamed *The Sign* for the U.S. market. "All That She Wants" was released as a single and reached #1 on the Billboard chart in 1993 as it turned platinum. Within a year *The Sign* had sold 2 million copies in the United States and over 20 million worldwide, as two more singles, "Don't Turn Around" (a cover version of a tune by British reggae band Aswad) and "The Sign," were released in the United States. The band toured the world as the album sold millions elsewhere, including eight times platinum in Malaysia. In 1994 the trade magazine *Music & Media* named "All That She Wants" the bestselling European single between 1984 and 1994. In the same year Gothenburg made the band members Honorary Citizens of their home city. Ace of Base's second album, *The Bridge* (1995), followed the same formula that had earned the band so much popularity. It went platinum in Scandinavia in the first six months of its release and went on to sell over 5 million copies world-wide. During this period the band was crowned the biggest-selling Scandinavian act at the World Music Awards for four consecutive years.

By now the pressure to produce new material to match their initial successes was immense. In 1998 the band released its third album, *Flowers*. Still unashamedly pop, it was less reggae-inspired than the group's previous releases. Although the band released a number of singles, among them a cover of English trio Bananarama's 1984 hit song "Cruel Summer," neither the singles nor the album had sales like their debut. Later a greatest-hits album, *Singles of the '90s* (retitled *Greatest Hits* in the United States), sold well in Denmark but very poorly elsewhere. Although Ace of Base has not officially split up, Ekberg now lives in Marbella, Spain, while the Berggrens continue to live in Gothenburg. Currently there are no plans to release any new material.

References

www.aceofbase.net
MTV-Cyclopedia by Nick Duerden, Ian Gittens, and Shaun Phillips (London: Carlton, 1997). ISBN 185868336x

A-Ha (Norway)

A-Ha broke onto the European pop scene in 1985, but although the group continued as a band for nearly a decade, its commercial and critical success lasted only until 1988. Based heavily around vocalist Morten Harket's falsetto voice, Pal Waaktaar and Mags Furuholmen's songs helped the band become the first major Scandinavian pop success since Abba in the 1970s. Waaktaar (b. September 6, 1961) and Furuholmen (b. November 1, 1962) had been friends since childhood in Oslo, Norway, when they formed the rock band Spider Empire in

A-Ha
Pictorialpress Ltd., London, UK

1977. The band was heavily influenced by U.S. rock stars Jimi Hendrix and The Doors, but as success eluded it the group evolved into Bridges in 1979. Although Bridges had the same personnel as Spider Empire, the music they created began to assimilate the sounds of the New Romantic movement prevalent in England at the time. The band's songs were now based around a strong keyboard melody rather than guitars. In October 1980 the group released the single "Fakkeltog" on its own Vekenalt label. Vekenalt released only 1,000 copies of the single, and the band struggled to sell any of them. Believing success was to be found in England, the group moved to London but soon became disillusioned and, after running out of money, returned to Norway. It continued performing across the country, and it was during this period that Harket (b. September 14, 1959) first saw the band play. Over time Waaktaar and Furuholmen got to know Harket as he continued to appear at Bridges' shows. After discovering that Harket could sing, they invited him to join the band, by now renamed A-Ha by Furuholmen, who thought the name would be easily remembered in any language.

In January 1983 the trio returned to London. After six months the band members once again found themselves with no money and no record contract and, again, returned to Norway. Shortly thereafter they secured a small record deal with WEA (a subsidiary of Warner) and recorded a song, "Take on Me," which they were convinced would be a hit. It flopped completely, selling only 300 copies in the United Kingdom. Undeterred, they re-recorded the song, using a mechanical drum beat and synthesizers, and re-released it. It flopped again, and the band then agreed to split up.

At this point Waaktaar decided to visit his girlfriend in America. While he was living in Boston, he decided to call WEA, and learned that the label was beginning to take A-Ha seriously. As popular music began to take a more electronic direction with the heavy use of synthesizers by bands such as Depeche Mode and Ultravox, A-Ha's style was becoming fashionable. As Harket's good looks were seen by the company to be an ideal selling point for the band, the label was planning to invest heavily in the group. In 1985, having gotten back together, the group released "Take on Me" for a third time. The single was now accompanied by a state-of-the-art video combining live action with a black-and-white, storyboard-style cartoon. The single was an immediate success, reaching #2 in the United Kingdom and #1 in the United States, launching the band members as teen heartthrobs across the world. By now the band had released its first album, *Hunting High and Low* (1985). Soon it released three more top ten singles, including a United Kingdom #1 with "The Sun Always Shines on TV" (the video for which showed Harket preaching in a church to a congregation of shop mannequins). A second album, *Scoundrel Days*, was released in 1986. Like their debut album, the songs were uptempo pop numbers highlighting Harket's falsetto, exemplified by the #5 hit, "Cry Wolf." The band was now appearing on TV and in magazines across Europe. In 1987 it joined the elite group of stars invited to record the theme song to a James Bond movie. *The Living Daylights* (both the song and the film) was released in 1987. *Stay on These Roads* (1988) was A-Ha's third album; the title track reached #5 later in the year, and another single, "Touchy," made #11. In 1989 Harket appeared in his first movie, *Kamilia and the Thief.*

All began solo careers but delivered little in terms of commercial success until, in 1998, A-Ha re-formed specifically to perform at a concert celebrating the Nobel Peace Prize. In April 2000 the band released a new album, *Minor Earth/Major Sky*. The new songs followed in the same vein as the group's earlier material but had a more downbeat feel. A-Ha's first single as a band in ten years, "Summer Moved On," became a top ten hit around Europe, including #1 in Norway and Germany. A-Ha began a thirty-three-date world tour in Oslo, Sweden, in June 2002 which kept them on the road until October.

References

www.a-ha.com

A-Ha: Memorial Beach by (International Music Publications, 1994). ISBN 185909077x

Aksu, Sezen (Turkey)

Sezen Aksu was born in the town of Saraykoy in the Denizli province of Turkey in 1953. When she was three years old her parents moved to the bigger town of Izmir on the eastern coast. After school she went to agricultural college but also took lessons in painting, drama, and dance. In the early 1970s she joined the Izmir Arts Association and began to learn about the history of Turkish music and art. In 1975 she released her first single, "Haydi Sansim Gel Barna." It won little attention from the public, but her second single, supplied by the record company, "Yasanmamis Yillar Kusura Bakma," released the following year, began to build a profile for the new singer. At this time Turkish women artists had to sing material presented to them by their record companies, which commissioned professional songwriters. Aksu began to be frustrated by the material she was being offered and decided to write and release her own songs. The songs became more biographical in content as she wrote of her feelings both as a Turkish woman and as a Turkish woman artist. The record company allowed her to release her own songs and her first self-penned effort, "Olmaz Olsun Vurdumduyma," a heartfelt ballad, was an instant success and reached #1 in Turkey in 1976. The next year she released two more of her own songs, "Kac Yil Gecti Arada" and "Kaybolan Yillar," both of which also reached #1. Aksu was, at the time, the only Turkish woman artist who wrote her own material.

In 1978 her first album, *Serçe*, spent most of the year in the Turkish national chart. Aksu began performing the album across Turkey. In 1981 she released *Aglamak Güzeldir*, and the album spent over twelve months on the charts. The tracks on *Aglamak Güzeldir* contained a mix of traditional Turkish melodies and rhythms combined with sentimental ballads that became a trademark of Aksu's writing. Over the next few years Aksu released a series of three Greek-language albums that showcased her delicate but powerful voice and blended traditional Greek rhythms with a more western style of instrumentation. All the albums—*Firuze* (1982), *Sen Aglama* (1984), and *Git* (1986)—reached #1 as her voice matured and gave the music warmth and depth.

Although she was nicknamed "The Little Sparrow" on account of her diminutive size, Aksu became the biggest star in the country. After she released her next two albums—*Sezen Aksu* (1988) and *Sezen Aksu Söylü Yor* (1989)—she began to write material for other artists. Askin Nur Yengi had been Aksu's backing vocalist, and in 1990 she released *Sergiliye*, an album of songs written by Aksu, that sold almost a million copies. Yengi's second album the following year, *Hesapver*, sold 900,000 copies.

Aksu was still writing for herself and in 1992 released *Gülümse*. The album found international release via a German label, Ariola, and began to sell well in that country as well as in Holland and Belgium. Aksu then embarked on a number of promotional dates across Europe. Still prolific with her writing, which doggedly held to the Aksu musical formula, she released an album each year between 1995 and 1997: *Isik Dogudan Yükselir, Düs Bahçleri*, and *Dügün of VE Cenaza*, respectively. In 1998 she performed a few live shows, and in 1999 she released her thirteenth album, *Adi Bende Sakli*. Relying on her well-tested formula of ballads and mid-tempo rhythmical numbers, the album shot to the top of the Turkish charts and sold relatively well in Holland and Belgium (where Aksu performed a short tour of each country) and reached the top twenty in Germany. Late in the year she released another #1 single, "Sari Odalar," which was a prelude to a new album. In June 2000 *Deliveren* became another #1 album typical of Aksu's style, combining Turkish rhythms with a lush production. Aksu once again played concerts across the country to sold-out audiences. Although 2001 was a quiet year for Aksu in May 2002 she was at the top of the charts once again. The single "Kiss Kiss," co-written by Aksu and originally a Turkish hit for fellow Turkish artist Tarkan, was recorded in English by Australian soap opera actress Holly Valance, who made it a #1 in the national charts across Europe. Aksu is currently the most successful female singing star that Turkey has ever produced.

References
http://members.tripod.com/~Saksu/

A-Mei (Taiwan)

Chang Hui-Mei (b. August 9, 1972) was born and raised among mountain tribes in the Taidong region of Taiwan. Although by birth a princess, Chang and the tribes of the region are officially recognized as Yuanzhuming ("ethnic minority") and are often considered on the outside of Taiwanese society. When Chang was an infant her mother would often leave the village and record herself singing on a tape player before returning home and playing the tape to her children. Although music was always a part of Chang's life, it wasn't until she entered the Five Lights Singing Contest (to fulfill the wish of her ill father) that Chang first performed in public. A-Mei, as she had renamed herself in an effort to make her name more memorable, won first prize. The young singer then moved to Taipei at the request of her cousin, who played in a rock band and needed a singer. A-Mei supplemented her income during these years by performing in the pubs and bars of the Taiwanese capital, presenting a combination of Western pop songs and traditional Taiwanese folk songs. She continued singing in bars for over five years, until she won a little fame singing the title song of a popular TV show that aired nightly on the Flying Disc channel. Forward Music, a local record label, decided to sign her on the strength of the song, and in 1996 she was invited to record a song with Zhang Yusheng, an established artist and producer. The ballad "The One Who Loved Me Most, Hurt Me the Most" focusing on A-Mei's warm, deep voice, was an instant hit with the Taiwanese public, and A-Mei returned to the studio to begin recording her first album.

Insisting that her family be part of the recording process, A-Mei released *Sisters*, a series of keyboard-driven pop/dance songs featuring her mother, brothers, and sisters singing on tracks. Within two weeks of its release in March 1997 the album reached #3 on the Taiwanese charts, and then it went to #1, where it remained for another fifteen weeks. Zhang Yusheng wasted no time in following up the triumph of *Sisters*, and by June he had written and produced A-Mei's second album, *A-Mei II: Bad Boy*, which quickly followed its predecessor to the top of the charts. The album was similar in content to her debut, the songs being driven by simple keyboard melodies, but with a more Western rock influence and elements of hip-hop. The albums officially sold one million and 850,000, respectively, but it is estimated that in China, Taiwan's close neighbor, there can be up to forty bootleg copies for every official album sale.

A-Mei's career was soon overshadowed, however, when Zhang Yusheng was involved in a traffic accident. He was in a coma for a month before he died, on November 11, 1997. Shortly after Yusheng's death, A-Mei released *Tribute to Zhang Yusheng*, featuring downbeat but romantic love songs. By 1998, although the political tension between Taiwan and China was escalating daily, A-Mei was performing to huge crowds in both countries as well as in other Asian territories. During a concert in Singapore in June, she was fined by the Malaysian government after she touched the hands of her ecstatic audience members. Fearing the effect it would have on the excitable crowd, the government had already warned A-Mei not to have physical contact with her fans.

More albums of up-tempo pop songs followed as A-Mei was dubbed "the Madonna of China" by the media. Although her albums showed little progression in their musical development, her fans were unconcerned and her popularity reached a frenzied peak. In fact, tickets for a concert in the Chinese capital of Beijing sold on the black market for $250, more than ten times the face value. Over 45,000 fans attended the event, accompanied by 2,000 local policemen; the scoreboard in the stadium reminded fans to "observe discipline, maintain order."

In 2000 A-Mei became the "face" of Sprite and her face was seen daily on TV all over Asia. Her popularity earned her an invitation to sing at the inauguration of the new Taiwanese president, Chen Shui-Bian, on May 20. The gesture angered the Chinese government, which then banned A-Mei from performing in China and took her advertisements off TV, resulting in her losing the Sprite contract. The Taiwanese government was outraged by the action, but so too were A-Mei's Chinese fans, who bombarded newspapers and music magazines with letters condemning the action. Thus in June 2000 the Chinese government rescinded the order and A-Mei was again a staple on TV. By the end of the year she released another album, a collection of her previous singles, *Best of 1995–2000*. A-Mei is still one of the most recognized women artists in Asia, and continues to perform across the Asian continent, although no new recordings are immediately planned.

References

www.isle.net/~dude/amei.htm

Anggun (Indonesia)

Anggun Cipta Sasmi was born in Djakarta, Indonesia, on April 29, 1974, Her father, Darto Singo, was a famous Indonesian singer and producer while her mother came from a noble Javanese family. Anggun's parents sent her to a Catholic school in the country, where she learned to speak English, a language she would later use when performing and recording. At age seven she had already decided to follow in her father's footsteps and she recorded an album of songs for children, and at age twelve recorded her first rock album, *Dunia Aku Punya*. Thereafter she returned to her schooling, and in 1990 she released her second album. Now simply known as Anggun (her name means "grace born out of a dream"), her second album, *Tua Tua Keladi*, moved away from her rock beginnings and was a more polished production of strings and ethereal ballads. The album reached the top of the local charts. The follow-up, *Anak Putih Abu Abu*, won Anggun Indonesia's most popular singer award for 1991. She continued to fill auditoriums across Asia and remained at the top of the charts with subsequent albums *Noc Turno* (1992) and *Anggun C. Sasmi . . . Lah!* (1993). The albums continued in the same vein, as Anggun confirmed her status as a singer of rock ballads and pop tunes.

Although she was now a well-respected and bestselling artist, Anggun craved more international recognition, and in the following year she married and left for London. However, the experience did not bring her the recognition she wanted, and she felt uncomfortable with the music industry in the English capital. Within a year she had moved to Paris, where she found the international break that she had been searching for. While in the French capital she met writer/producer Erick Benzi, who had already gained a reputation for his early work with Celine Dion. Together they began to write powerful ballads, relying heavily on Benzi's lush production style and Anggun's powerful vocals, influenced by artists from the West such as The Police, Bon Jovi, and Guns N' Roses. It was the strong vocal performances of Sting, Jon Bon Jovi, and Axl Rose that helped influence her own singing style. The album *Au Nom de la Lune* followed, and Anggun sang in French (in which she was now fluent), English, and Indonesian. The album initially sold poorly until Anggun released the song "La Neige au Sahara." The single bore all the Benzi trademarks, with an orchestral backing and Anggun's up-front yet delicate vocal performance. The single reached #1 in France and renewed interest in *Au Nom de la Lune*, which sold 150,000 copies in France and Belgium. The album, re-titled *Anggun*, was also released in Indonesia, where she maintained her popularity and where it sold another 100,000 copies.

Anggun's experience working with Benzi lead to her being invited onto the bill for 1998's Lilith Fair, the music festival that crosses the U.S. and whose lineup is made primarily of women performers. This led to Anggun's appearance on the TV talk show *The Rosie O'Donnell Show* and interviews in *Rolling Stone* magazine. During Christmas 2000 Anggun sang at the Vatican. She then returned to France to play her first French concerts during the opening months of 2001. The rest of the year was spent recording new material that emerged in April 2002. The album *Désirs contraires* continued Anggun's love affair with the rock ballads and uptempo pop songs that have seen her become Indonesia's foremost musical star.

References

www.anggun.com

Aquarium (Russia)

Boris Grebenshikov was born in St. Petersburg, Russia, on November 27, 1953. After studying mathematics at Leningrad State University he turned his attentions to rock music, which he had loved as a child after hearing recordings of The Beatles that had entered the Soviet Union. He formed Aquarium in the former Soviet Union in 1973 and, over the next twenty years, released over seventy albums. Throughout the latter part of the 1970s Aquarium began to develop a unique style that blended drums and guitars with flutes and cellos that had not been heard in the Soviet Union previously. Although the band's line-up was that of a traditional rock group, its lyrical content set Aquarium apart from its contemporaries. Grebenshikov did not directly challenge the authorities; instead, he used his songs to communicate on a more personal and philosophical level about the hardships of life in the Soviet Union.

Aquarium had its first release, *The Blue Album*, in 1981. (At the time Aquarium's music was only available in cassette form.) Two more albums appeared later in the year, all recorded and produced by the band with money raised from concerts throughout the Soviet Union. Altogether ten albums were released in this way, gaining Aquarium a huge fan base throughout Russia and its neighboring areas. (Aquarium also released nine "live" albums.)

In 1987, as the Russian government began to relax its attitudes to Western rock music under the influence of President Gorbachev, the Soviet authorities offered Aquarium financial help in the recording process. The result was the *White Album*, which took months to finish as the band was allowed in the studio for only four hours every other day, giving the record a "live" feel as the group raced against time. Although sponsored by the government, Grebenshikov continued his lyrical polemic and the album sold out immediately. It earned the band the chance to record again and *Equinox*, also released in 1987, became the first Aquarium album to be recorded without time or budget constraints. Helped by the political upheaval of the time as President Gorbachev introduced *glasnost*, a freeing of social mores and political ideas, Aquarium went from being the most important "underground" rock band in Russia to simply being the most important rock band in Russia. The new openness that *glasnost* invited led to Grebenshikov and Aquarium leaving their home country in 1989 and touring the West, where they released an English-language album, *Radio Silence*, and played with The Eurythmics and Chrissie Hynde. Another album in English, *Radio London*, was released in 1990.

After returning home, Grebenshikov moved back to his roots in folk culture and used many traditional instruments. The result was the *Russian Album* (1991), which has been credited with changing Russian rock music through its combination of tradition and modernity. The band released several more studio albums throughout the decade, including one a year from 1993 to 1996 (*Favourite Songs of Ramses IV, Kostroma Mon Amour, Navigator*, and *Snow Lion*, respectively), and two in 1997 (*Hyperborea* and *Lilith*). The latter album signaled another change in style, as Grebenshikov recorded it with an entirely different group of musicians: Bob Dylan's backing group The Band. The album reflected a new folk rock sound that Grebenshikov had been developing throughout the 1990s. In 1997, he also released a compilation, *Aquarium 25—The History*, which contained some of the most important recordings the band had been involved in. By the end of 1999 Aquarium had toured the United States and Japan and was preparing to release an anthology, *Territory,* that covered its music from 1983 to 2000. The album was released in October 2000 and a new album of typical Aquarium rock, *Black Box*, followed in 2001. A new album of Aquarium's folk-rock, *Sister Chaos,* was released in February 2002. In June the band toured across the United States, beginning in Boston and ending in Seattle.

References

www.planetaquarium.com

Arbelo, Rosana (Spain)

Born on the Spanish Canary Island of Lanzarote just off the coast of Africa in 1963, Rosana Arbelo was the youngest of eight children. Presented with a guitar when she was five years old, she wrote her first song within three years. Despite playing music from such an early age, it wasn't until she was thirty-two that Arbelo became known in Spain as an artist in her own right.

At age twenty Arbelo left Lanzarote and went to Madrid to study. During this time in the Spanish capital she made her debut in the music industry, as a writer for other artists. But then, finding herself frustrated at simply giving other people her songs, she recorded a demo in 1994, and two of the tracks were broadcast on a local radio station. The songs' sparse, acoustic-based arrangement reflected a traditional take on folk music and became an immediate success as the public tried to buy an album that did not exist. Returning to the studio, Arbelo re-recorded the tracks professionally with the help of producer José A. Romero. In 1996 she released a single, "El Talismán," that soon made the top of the Spanish charts. The album *Lunas Rotas* followed shortly thereafter and entered the chart at #4, selling over 25,000 copies in the first ten days of its release. The album was a collection of songs steeped in the musical history of the Canary Islands, which borrows heavily from the rhythms of its neighbor Africa, while still based on the Latin/flamenco guitar rhythms of Spain. Within weeks it became a million seller and reached #1 on the local chart. (Current sales for the album stand at two and a half million.) At the end of the year the album won two "Premios Ondas," presented by the Spanish music industry for best newcomer and best album. Arbelo had become the first artist whose debut went double platinum in Spain. The singles "El Talismán" and "Lunas Rotas," taken from the album, were later chosen by film director Quentin Tarantino for his movie *Curled*.

After a major tour of Spain, Arbelo released a re-mix album of her earlier recordings; and a single, "A Feugo Lento," consolidated her position at the top of the charts. Having been working on new material, in October 1998 she released *Luna Nueva*. A more assured and polished effort that showed Arbelo was growing as a songwriter, the album became even more popular in Spain than her debut and turned platinum eight times within a year. More concerts followed as she began to perform with other major European artists, including **Zucchero**. In 2000 Arbelo returned once again to the studio to begin work on a third album, as well as performing in major theaters across Spain. The results of her studio work were released in September 2001. Simply called *Rosana*, her third album once again reflected the rhythms of Africa as well as incorporating a distinctly Latin feel. A single, "Pa' Ti No Estoy," reached the top end of the chart as Arbelo set out once again to tour across Spain from October to December 2001. In May 2002 *Rosana* was nominated for a Premios Ondas in the best album category.

References

www.rosana.net

Axelle Red (Belgium)

Fabienne Demal was born in Hasselt, a small town in the Flemish-speaking area of Belgium, on February 15, 1968. The young Demal took dancing classes from the age of three. In 1983, when she was fifteen, she had a top thirty hit in Belgium with "Little Girls" under the name Axelle. Two years later she was invited to go to London by Mick Ronson (guitar player for David Bowie in the 1970s), but within the year she had returned to Belgium after failing to settle in the English music industry.

In 1989, after she met songwriting brothers Daniel and Richard Seff, the newly named Axelle Red re-entered the charts with the inoffensive keyboard driven pop song "Kennedy Boulevard." An immediate success, the single became a platinum record. In 1990 "Aretha et Moi," a tune that was the first intimation of Axelle Red's love of 1960's U.S. soul music, also reached the top ten in Belgium. For the next three years, however, Axelle Red did not record. She left the music industry and attended drama school, at the same time studying law at the Flemish University of Brussels, graduating in 1993.

In 1993 she released her debut album, *Sans Plus Attendre*. The album confirmed her love of the work of Otis Redding and James Brown, among others, and went quadruple platinum in her home country as well as staying in the charts for over a year in France, where she received a platinum disc. A single, "Sensualité," became her first #1 in Belgium and reached the top spot in Switzerland and France, where it became the bestselling single of the year. During the winter of 1994–95, she played over 100 concerts around Europe to sold-out crowds. Later in 1995 she visited Nashville to begin recording her second album with the help of soul legends Steve Cropper (who played guitar for Otis Redding) and Roger Hawkins (Aretha Franklin's drummer). The album, *A tâtons*, was released in 1996 and turned double platinum in Belgium and France and gold in Switzerland. The single "Rester femme," taken from the album, became her second chart topper, and another song from the album, "A Quoi ça Sert," was used by director Alain Corneau in his 1997 movie *Le Cousin*.

In 1998 Axelle Red recorded *Con Solo Pensarlo*. The album was a mixture of songs from her previous two albums, re-recorded in Spanish. Although it did well in her native country, the Spanish were less than enthusiastic and it barely made the local chart. The same year she sang at the opening ceremony of the soccer World Cup in France. Fully 80,000 people watched her performance in the stadium, and an estimated TV audience of one billion people watched worldwide. The year 1998 proved to be an eventful year away from music as Axelle Red announced she was pregnant and was also named UNICEF ambassador to Haiti. The year ended with two concerts, in Antwerp and Paris, titled "The Soul of Axelle Red," which featured U.S. soul stars Eddie Floyd and Percy Sledge.

By 1999, she had released her third French-language album, *Toujours Moi*, this time writing all the songs herself as well as producing the record. Still based on her passion for soul music, the album entered the French charts at #1, where it quickly turned platinum. The record gave her another double platinum album in Belgium and a second gold in Switzerland. A single from the album, "Parceque c'est toi," became her third #1 as she began a tour of Europe that lasted for most of the year. Toward the end of 1999 she performed at a concert for Amnesty International, organized by fellow Belgian singer **Arno Hintjens**. During the year she was presented with France's most prestigious award, the Victoire de la Musique.

As she took time off with her baby, Axelle Red released a live album. *Alive* reached the top ten during 2000, with the single "Aretha et Moi," originally released in 1990, hitting the charts in early 2001. Axelle Red is currently preparing for concerts in Brussels and Paris scheduled for 2003.

References
www.axelle-red.com

B

Bashung, Alain (France)

Alain Bashung was born in Paris on December 1, 1947. His family soon moved to the Alsace region of the country, where by the age of five the young Bashung was singing in choirs and was learning the harmonica. By 1960 he learned to play the guitar and within three years left the family home to form the first of his many bands. In 1966 he released his first single, "Porquoi révez-vous des Etats-Unis," and in the following year he appeared at the first Festival of French Pop, alongside Cream and The Walker Brothers. Bashung continued to play in various R&B and bluegrass groups before he won a part in the acclaimed rock opera "La Révolution Français" in 1973. In 1977, over a decade after the release of his single, he released his first album, *Roman-Photos*. The record showcased Bashung's love of American music and was heavily influenced by the R&B he had heard during the 1960s. It was another two years before a second album, *Roulette Russe*, also heavily indebted to U.S. R&B, was released.

Although Bashung was becoming well known in musical circles, it wasn't until 1980 that the wider public caught its first glimpse of him. In February he released "Gaby Oh Gaby," which stayed in the charts for fifty-four weeks. In the following year he released two albums, *Pizza* (which won him the Grand Prix du Rock Français) and *Vertiges l'amour*, both of which became gold in France. In June he began his first major tour of France, and in July he appeared in his first feature film, *D'Arrabal*. In 1982 Bashung fulfilled a lifelong dream when he collaborated with French legend Serge Gainsbourg on the album *Play Blessures*. Two singles from the album, "S.O.S. Amour" and "Touché pas a mon pote," both reached #1. By September *Roulette Russe* had won Bashung another gold album.

Bashung's career took another turn in 1984 when he was asked to write the music for the movie *Nestor Burma détective de choc*, in which he also played a small role. In the same year he once again toured the country and in June 1985 performed for a crowd of 300,000 people at the Place de la Concorde, a major thoroughfare in the center of Paris. Later he wrote the music for another film, *Le Ouatrième pouvoir*. Bashung released another album in 1986, *Passé le Rio Grande*, in which he began to experiment with a more lush style of production. He also wrote the music for the movie *Le Beauf*, in which he starred. It was another three years before he released any new material, but the album *Novice*, in 1989, won him an album-of-the-year award in France. Although Bashung's first love was for American R&B, his experience of writing film scores helped him develop into a more complete songwriter; he began to introduce more orchestral backings to his music, moving away from the traditional rock arrangement.

In 1990 he performed for a crowd of 200,000 at an anti-racism concert, and in the following year he released *Oysez Joséphine*, a series of songs about the lover of the Emperor Napoleon Bonaparte. The record was a concept album in that all the tracks followed the same theme and told a loose story concerning Joséphine's life. The album earned him praise from critics and the public: He was nominated in five categories at the Victoires de la Musique, winning two of them—best male singer and best video—in February 1992. In the same year Bashung appeared in three films—*Déshabillès fatals, Des comichons au chocolat*, and *L'ambre du doute*—the last of which was shown at the Venice Film Festival. After the release of his next album, *Chatterton*, in 1994, he toured France and Belgium and visited Canada for a short series of concerts. A live album of the concerts, *Confessions*, was released a year later. The year 1995 also saw the release of his eleventh feature film, *Le jeu de la clé*.

In October 1998 Bashung appeared on *Aux Suivants*, a tribute album to well-known French singer Jacques Brel. In February of the following year he was named artist of the year in France. Thereafter he appeared in two movies, *Je veux tout* and *Mon pére, ma mère, mes fréres et mes soeurs*, and wrote the music for both. In 2000 he won an award for the music to another film, *Ma petite enterprise*, and in May released a "best of" double album, *Climax 2000*. Thirty-six years after the release of his debut single, Bashung is still regarded as one of France's foremost artists, both on record and on screen. His latest album, *X52*, was released in the summer of 2002.

References

www.alainbashung.com.fr

Bazoo (Thailand)

Suaradec "Joey" Tuptimsai was born in Thailand on July 31, 1968, to an American father and a Thai mother. After his parents divorced, Tuptimsai lived with his grandmother in the northern province of Udon Thani. By age sixteen he was singing in hotels and restaurants to earn money, and eventually he joined City Beat, a Thai pop group that released one album to little effect. While he was appearing with City Beat, Tuptimsai joined the U.S. band 911 after auditioning in America, and initially sang for both groups until their respective commitments required him to make a choice. He chose 911, which had success worldwide as one of the music business's prototype modern boy bands, and stayed with them for five years. After the members of 911 decided to take a year off, Tuptimsai began a small music school in Thailand. It was while teaching there that he received a call from RS Promotions, the biggest record label in the country, to "help out" with the writing and recording of one its artists, Ruangsak Loychusak. Although he was invited to tour with Loychusak, Tuptimsai was still contracted to 911 and so declined. Within three months 911 broke up. Tuptimsai then went back to RS Promotions, which was looking to put together a boy/girl duo. He convinced the label to create a trio, Deborah "Debbie" See (b. June 12, 1982) was attending the Ruamrudee International School when she attended the auditions. Already known to Tuptimsai through a mutual friend, See was chosen to be the female part of the band. Another male singer was still required, and Tuptimsai remembered Eakprapant "Gumpan" Panidpong (b. May 11, 1977), who had been involved in the music scene while Tuptimsai was in City Beat. The newly formed trio of singers went into the studio early in 1998, and in December the group emerged as Bazoo.

The band was an immediate success. Its live appearances, complete with what became its signature energetic dance routines, brought the youth of Thailand to the concert halls in record numbers. The eclectic mix of Thai instruments and Western dance beats created a new genre; the band's album *Ho Le Ho Le* was released in July 1999 and reached the top of the national charts. Toward the end of the year the group signed with Rock Records in Taiwan and released singles in the Chinese language. In this endeavor the band had limited success, with some fans criticizing it for "selling out" by recording songs in Mandarin for the Taiwanese market. This was only a small concern for the band, as its next album, *Bazoo in the Mix Non Stop*, a re-mix album of the group's previous hits, again went to the top of the charts.

A new album, *Phee Fah Party*, released in March 2000, continued to feature the group's formulaic pop music, and after its release the band began a promotional tour of Thailand and Taiwan. The title track became Thailand's entry in the MTV Asia Video Music Awards. The band then released an album, *Bazoo 2000*, in Taiwan that was sung entirely in Mandarin. At this time Tuptimsai enrolled at university to begin a course in business studies, admitting that when he fulfilled his contractual obligations he would leave Bazoo to concentrate on the business side of music. In December 2000 an album of new if not different material, *Bazoo 2001*, was released in Thailand, and the band played concerts across the country and appeared on TV music shows. Auditions were launched to replace Tuptimsai.

With Tuptimsai forming a music and promotional company, International Music Consulting, and continuing his studies, the future of Bazoo is unclear. In its brief career to date the band has taken the Thai music scene by storm with its collection of music that fuses traditionalism with modernism, and it is beginning to have an influence on a new generation of Thai artists. In February 2002 Bazoo released another album, *Yo!* Many of the songs were slower in tempo than the band's usual hi-energy efforts but were still very much disco influenced numbers.

References

www.geocities.com/bazoo;llonline

Beautiful South, The (England)

The Beautiful South was formed by singer/songwriter Paul Heaton (b. May 9, 1962; Berkenhead, Merseyside) from the remains of his previous band, The Housemartins, in 1989. Already popular from his past endeavors, Heaton began to write with an old friend, guitarist Dave Rotheray (b. February 9, 1963), and created a body of work that was uniquely English in topics and sentiments. Concentrating on the foibles of the English and his own passion for alcohol, Heaton became one of the most celebrated songwriters in Britain. The Beautiful South's combination of gentle, acoustic music and Heaton's bitter, cynical lyrics won the band a place in the hearts of Britain's music lovers, especially the "thirtysomethings" who identified with Heaton's themes of lost opportunity and everyday frustration in the home and workplace.

Heaton invited Dave Hemingway (b. September 20, 1960), drummer in The Housemartins, to join The Beautiful South as a second vocalist. In 1989, after recruiting Sean Welch (b. April 12, 1965) on bass, David Stead (b. October 15, 1966) on drums, and Brianna Corrigan as a third vocalist, the band released its first single, "Song for Whoever," taken from its debut album, *Welcome to The Beautiful South*. The song, a scathing and satirical attack on romantic songwriters, reached #2 in the charts. Another single, the up-tempo "You Keep It All In," was released in the same year and also reached the top five. It wasn't until 1990, however, after the release of the band's second album, *Choke*, that the group reached the #1 position in the singles chart. "A Little Time" was a duet between Corrigan and Hemingway centering on the breakdown of a relationship. This was a topic that Heaton returned to again and again in songs such as "I'll Sail This Ship Alone" and "We Are Each Other." In 1990 the band toured the United States for the first time, playing to small numbers of fans in small venues.

Two more albums followed—*0898* (1992) and *Miaow* (1994)—that showed Heaton becoming even more world-weary than before; this was reflected in his lyrics to singles such as "Dumb" and "How Long's a Tear Take to Dry?" Also in 1994 the band released a compilation album of its singles to date: *Carry On Up The Charts* became the fastest-selling album of the year in the United Kingdom and the third fastest of all time, behind Michael Jackson (*Thriller*) and Phil Collins (*But Seriously*). It sold three million copies and stayed at #1 for six weeks. By now Heaton and Rotheray had become Britain's most successful songwriters since Lennon and McCartney. Several tours followed, with the band selling out 15,000-capacity stadiums throughout the British Isles.

The group's next studio album, *Blue Is the Colour* (1996), saw the introduction of Jacqueline Abbot (b. November 10, 1973), who replaced Corrigan as vocalist; the band released its version of Harry Nilsson's "Everybody's Talkin'" to showcase her talents. The change in lineup did not affect the continued success of The Beautiful South, as the album went platinum, selling more than 2 million copies. Another single, "Rotterdam," reached the top ten. It conveyed Heaton's twisted lyrical sense: What appeared to be a gentle song about the Dutch city was in fact an attack on federal Europe and the single currency, as Heaton worried that countries within Europe would lose their national identities with the acceptance of the Euro. More singles followed, including "Don't Marry Her," which introduced Abbott as a lead singer as the popularity of the band continued. In 1999 the group was nominated for best single ("Perfect 10") and best group at the prestigious Brit Awards. Both nominations came on the back of the group's 1998 album, *Quench*.

In 2000 the band released *Painting It Red*, which presented Heaton in a more downbeat and exasperated mood than ever even though the music remained mellow. This album also went to the top of the charts in the United Kingdom. In the summer of 2002 The Beautiful South were put on hold as Heaton released his debut solo album, *Fat Chance*. The album was a continuation of The Beautiful South's sound based on guitars with added brass and strings but featured a harder edged, less polished feel to the music. In July Heaton embarked on a short U.K. tour to promote the album. Another "best of" album, *Solid Bronze*, was released in November 2001 and entered the U.K. charts at #10. Since its inception, The Beautiful South has released twenty-four singles and nine albums, selling more than 8 million records.

References

www.beautifulsouth.co.uk
Last Orders at the Liar's Bar: The Official Story of the Beautiful South by Mike Pattenden (London: Victor Gollancz, 1999). ISBN 057506739x

Belolo, Henry (France)

Frenchman Henry Belolo, born in 1936 in Casablanca, Morocco, has been the driving force behind a succession of pop acts that have sold millions of records all over the world. Often credited as one of the brains behind the invention of disco, he was first exposed to music through the U.S. armed forces stationed in Casablanca at the end of World War II. By 1970 he had moved to America and become head of Polydor Records; he subsequently formed his own company, Carabine Music. It was, however, his 1975 meeting with French writer/producer Jacques Morali that propelled both writers to the top of the charts. After Morali went to Belolo with a clutch of songs, the pair decided to create a group to record the material. Named The Ritchie Family, the band made a series of albums that featured the fledgling genre of disco, pre-dating the style's massive popularity after the release of the movie and album *Saturday Night Fever*. The albums, *Brazil* (1975), *Arabian Nights* (1976), and *African Queens* (1977), introduced the swirling strings and skipping hi-hat sounds that are now commonplace but at the time were almost revolutionary. *Brazil* was the first disco record to make the top five in the Billboard chart. The band sold over

10 million records across Europe until the group's demise at the end of the decade.

Next, Belolo and Morali put together a disparate group of American singers and dancers and, in doing so, created one of the first boy bands. Named The Village People, the group went on to sell over 65 million records worldwide. Initially targeted at the gay community (even though only one of the band members was gay), The Village People suddenly found themselves at #1 all over the world with the single "YMCA." The song was the epitome of a disco number and contained a sing-along chorus and a video shot on the streets of New York that won the band a huge following. Belolo and Morali followed this with another chart topper, "In the Navy." The song followed the formula of "YMCA" and was accompanied by a video filmed on board a U.S. Navy aircraft carrier. The video was initially meant to be included in a Navy recruitment drive, but after criticisms arose for using taxpayers' money to finance a pop video, the idea was scrapped. The Village People still had a "big money" video on their hands, and the single benefited from the exposure and became a huge hit. A feature film, *U Can't Stop the Music*, was released before the appeal of The Village People, much like the appeal of disco, began to wane in the mid-1980s. At the start of the decade Morali's health was beginning to decline, and the pair began to work on separate projects. On November 15, 1991, Morali died from an AIDS-related illness.

Belolo's next project was the band Break Machine. The group's 1984 single, "Street Dance," was one of the first hip-hop songs to reach the mainstream charts; in fact, it opened the door for the genre to become a major force in world music. Belolo was also responsible for the re-launch of the career of Eartha Kitt. A popular singer and actress from the 1950s and 1960s (she had played Catwoman in the original TV series *Batman*), Belolo gave her a disco-tinged hit in "Where Is My Man" (1983), after which Kitt became a doyenne of the gay club scene in Europe.

Having launched his own label, Scorpia Records, Belolo continued to produce Eurodance mixes of songs for the newly emerging house music scene that had grown out of New York and was being made by young deejays. (The Eurodance/Europop style is a pumped-up, modernized disco sound for the new millennium.) Spending his summers talent-spotting on the Spanish island of Ibiza (a major source of new talent on the dance scene), he is currently the force behind the Vengaboys, a band from Scandinavia consisting of two young women and two young men in their early twenties. The Vengaboys have released a series of singles tinged with a Eurodisco beat and have reached #1 all over Europe with songs including "Uncle John from Jamaica" and "We're Going to Ibiza."

References

www.disco-disco.com/tributes/henri.html
Saturday Night Forever: The Story of Disco by Alan Jones and Jussi Kantonen. (London: Mainstream Publishing, 1999). ISBN 184018177x

Blur (England)

Singer and keyboard player Damon Albarn (b. London, March 28, 1968) and guitarist Graham Coxon (b. Hannover, Germany, March 12, 1969) met in 1980 at school in Colchester, England, where they both sang in the school choir. Toward the end of the decade they moved to London and began studying at Goldsmiths College, where they met bassist Alex James (b. Bournemouth, November 21, 1968) and drummer Dave Rowntree (b. Colchester, May 8, 1964). After forming the band Seymour, they played the pubs and clubs of London until 1989, when they changed their name to Blur; by the end of the year they signed with Food Records. The group's first single, "She's So High," released in October 1990, was the epitome of early Blur songs, being driven by Coxon's fierce guitar riffs. It reached only #43 on the charts but earned the band some positive reviews in the music press. A second single was released the following April: "There's No Other Way" employed the slipsnare beat that was becoming prevalent across the country in the wake of "Madchester" and **The Stone Roses**; coupled with another highly memorable Coxon riff, it took the band into the top ten. Although the group's next single, "Bang," failed to make the top twenty, its subsequent album, *Leisure*, released in August, reached #7. Successful tours around the United Kingdom followed, but the band's major critical success followed the release of its second album, *Modern Life Is Rubbish*, in May 1993. Although reaching only #15 in the chart, the band was touted as the heir to a quintessentially British style of songwriting that had begun with The Kinks in the 1960s.

The band compounded this reputation with the release of the single "Girls & Boys" in March 1994, and the album *Parklife*, released the following month, entered the chart at #1. The album signaled the beginning of the so-called Britpop movement, which encompassed bands such as Menswear, Supergrass, and Sleeper and concentrated on guitar-driven pop songs about quintessentially English subjects such as pubs, and the class system. Britpop took over the United Kingdom during 1994 and 1995, which led to the Union Jack flag becoming a popular symbol (it had lost popularity after being synonymous with right-wing political movements in the 1970s and 1980s). The newly introduced phrase "Cool Britannia" described this new generation of musicians alongside artists like Damian Hirst and writers like Nick Hornby. Blur won four prestigious Brit awards in 1995, including best band and best album. The culmination of Britpop was highlighted in a well-publicized feud between Blur and fellow British band Oasis, as each group swapped personal and musical insults. Oasis was seen as northern working class while Blur were middle-class southerners. The music press played on these differences, helped by the British obsession with class and the north/south divide. (Southern England is widely regarded as being financially wealthier while the north is regarded as a poor cousin.)

The confrontation with Oasis came to a head in August 1995, when both bands released singles on the same day. The competition made headline news across the United Kingdom. Blur's "Country House," a quirky, almost cartoon-like song about London commuters and their unreachable goals of space and freedom from work, entered the charts at #1. It was the first of three successive #1's that included "The Universal" (November 1995) and "Stereotypes" (February 1996). The band's next album, *The Great Escape*, showed them moving away from the "jokey" feel of *Parklife* to a more downbeat style of songwriting, but it did not stop the album from entering the charts at #1 in September 1995. The band toured the United Kingdom and Europe repeatedly before traveling to the United States. Known in America mainly on account of the Oasis "affair," the band's unwillingness to grant interviews and its reluctance to undertake a heavy touring schedule, coupled with the overwhelming "Englishness" of its lyrics and songs, won the band few friends. The trip to the United States, however, appeared to affect the group's songwriting. Returning to the studio, the band released the album *blur* in February 1997. The lo-fi effort took its cue from U.S. bands such as Pavement, of whom Graham Coxon was a big fan. The production was keyed down to a minimum with scratchy guitars and spartan use of bass and drums. The album repeated the success of Blur's previous two albums when it reached #1. A single, "Beetlebum," also reached #1. The second single from the album, "Song 2," became the group's biggest hit in the United States as well as worldwide. The song was known for its brevity (under two minutes) and the distinctive "woo-hoo" refrain that Albarn shouted over the intro.

By now the members of Blur began to embark on solo projects. James formed the band Fat Les and produced a #1 single to commemorate the English soccer team's entry in the 1998 World Cup competition. Albarn took on his first acting role in the movie *Face*. Coxon formed his own record label, Transcopic, and Rowntree learned to fly airplanes. It wasn't until 1999 that the band returned to celebrate ten years together with the release of *13*, which entered the chart at #1. *Blur: The Best of*, featuring all Blur's singles, was released later in the year.

In 2001 Albarn became the voice of the band Gorillaz, which features rap and hip-hop over sampled beats, far different from the sound of Blur. Initially seen only as cartoon characters in videos, the band members have since played live, albeit from behind a curtain. Their debut album was nominated for the 2001 Mercury Music prize, although the band stated it had no interest in the competition and called the other contenders "muppets." Although the members of Blur continue with their own projects, both inside and outside of music, the band still writes and records together.

References

www.blur.co.uk
Blur: 3862 Days by Stuart Maconie (London: Virgin, 1999). ISBN 0753502879

Bohlen, Dieter (Germany)

Born in Oldenberg, Germany, on February 7, 1954, Dieter Bohlen is the son of a hydraulic engineer who owned a construction company and expected his son to follow him into the business. A decade later, though, Bohlen fell in love with The Beatles' music and set about learning to play the guitar; within months, he had written his first song, "Viele Bomben Fallen." At this time Bohlen was having problems in school. Marked as a troublesome child, he was sent to a boarding school some eighty miles from the family home. The change of scenery had little effect on Bohlen, and it wasn't until he moved to the coastal town of Hamburg and lived with his uncle, who was the harbor master, that Bohlen settled down to schooling and began to learn the keyboards.

When he was seventeen years old he enrolled at the university at Göttingen and began playing with rock bands Da Capo, Aorta, and Mayfair. Bohlen was soon the chief songwriter for the bands and began sending demos to record companies and publishing houses, but they showed no interest. In 1977 he recorded two songs under the pseudonym Monza, but neither had any success. In the following year he graduated and returned to Hamburg, where he found a job at the Intersong publishing firm as a songwriter. Intersong let Bohlen use the studio whenever it was free, and he soon released a single under the pseudonym Steve Benson. "Don't Throw My Love Away" was a rock ballad that again failed to sell, but did get Bohlen noticed as a producer and he subsequently began working with other artists.

In 1983 he had his first breakthrough when an album he had been recording with singer Roland Kaiser, *Gefühle sind frei*, went gold in Germany. Later in the same year Bohlen was introduced to singer Thomas Anders, who already had a fairly successful single. Bohlen gave him the song "Wovon traüst du denn," and it reached the lower end of the charts. In 1984 the duo became Modern Talking and released "You're My Heart, You're My Soul." Although it initially failed to reach the charts, interest in the song began to grow from radio stations in Germany who began to play the song over the air until, in January 1985, it was broadcast on the TV program *Formal Eins*. Then the single reached #1. Although Bohlen was still using guitars, he was moving toward keyboard-driven pop songs. The album *Modern Talking* was released soon thereafter. Then Bohlen released one of the songs from the record, "The Night Is Yours, The Night Is Mine," as a solo single under the pseudonym Ryan Simmons. The song's vocal had originally been sung by Anders on the album, and it was the first sign that Bohlen was keen to take on all musical responsibility for Modern Talking.

Although Bohlen was working constantly on material for Modern Talking, he found the time to begin another project with singer Caroline Muller, whom he had discovered singing in a bar in Hamburg. Naming the project C.C. Catch, in 1985 he released a single with a vague disco feel, "I Can Lose My Heart Tonight," which reached the top ten in Germany. Bohlen now found himself in a vast creative period. Two Modern Talking albums of Bohlen's trademark pop songs were released in 1986, *Ready for Romance* and *In the Middle of Nowhere*, both of which went platinum in Germany. In the same year two C.C.Catch albums in much the same vein as Modern Talking were also released, *Catch the Catch* and *Welcome to the Heartbreak Hotel*. Also in 1986, Modern Talking had its biggest international hit when "Brother Louie," based on Bohlen's love of synthesizer-based guitar songs, reached the top ten all over Europe. Rifts were beginning to appear, however: Anders failed to arrive for a TV show, and then Bohlen pulled out of a tour because of illness and Anders completed it on his own. At the end of the year, after a short series of concerts, the two were never seen together, either on stage or on TV. Modern Talking, however, continued to make records and released *Romantic Warriors* in 1987. The album was more lightweight synth pop, typical of Modern Talking, and it became another multi-platinum album across Europe. The band was now among the most popular in the country, but tensions were increasing and by the end of the year Modern Talking had split up. Bohlen wasted no time in forming a new band and within months was writing under the name Blue System.

Bohlen's new band was similar to Modern Talking, with the only difference being that Bohlen sang. Blue System's debut album, *Walking on a Rainbow* (1987), followed the Modern Talking formula and reached the top of the charts in Germany. As Bohlen was still writing for C.C.Catch, three more albums of Euro Synth pop were released: *Diamonds, Big Fun*, and *Classics*. Then, in 1989, Muller decided that she wanted to take more creative control of the band and split from Bohlen. Bohlen took Muller to court over the use of the name C.C.Catch but lost the case. Muller continued as C.C.Catch but failed to have any more substantial hits without Bohlen at the controls. Blue System, however, was still topping the charts with each new release. The band released nine solid pop albums between 1990 and 1996, including two in 1991 (*Seeds of Heaven* and *Déjà Vu*) and two in 1994 (*21ˢᵗ Century* and *X-Ten*). Although the band was hugely popular in Germany and had recently played to crowds of 30,000 in Russia, in 1996 Bohlen split the group and invited Anders to reform Modern Talking. In 1998 the band released its first album in nine years, *Back for Good*. Although the record broke no new ground musically, it proved that the band still had a major following in Germany as it reached the top ten. Bohlen continued his prolific songwriting for the group, in the same vein as his previous material for Modern Talking and it released *Alone* (1999), *Year of the Dragon* (2000), and *America* (2001). Bohlen has now sold in excess of 42 million albums, and Modern Talking is still performing across Europe, mainly in Germany and Russia.

References
www.fr.ee/bohlen

Bomfunk MC's (Finland)

Raymond Ebanks, although born in London (in 1970), grew up in the capital of Finland, Helsinki. Immersed in the hip-hop culture that was appearing in the United States and being exported to Finland, he began to promote the music in clubs around Helsinki. Ismo Lappalainen was born in 1976 in the small town of Kokkola on the eastern coast of Finland but moved as a child to Turku in the south. Lappalainen began working as a deejay when he was fifteen years old, playing techno and house music, and soon became a regular around the clubs of Turku before he left for the bigger scene in Helsinki.

Although throughout the 1990s they were each building separate careers and Ebanks began recording with various artists, in 1998 Ebanks became MC B.O.W. ("Brother of Word") and Lappalainen because deejay Gismo; collectively they became Bomfunk MC's. It was two years before they released a debut single, "Freestyler," on the Sony Music Finland label. Produced by Jaakko Salovaara (who was known as JS16 and who had become widely known as the third Bomfunk MC), the song threw the band into the spotlight when it was released in October. "Freestyler" took its influences from hip-hop, house, and techno and became a gold record in Finland. It also reached #1 in Australia and New Zealand (selling double platinum and platinum, respectively) and hit the top ten in many other countries across Europe and Scandinavia, earning the band a release in the United States. In the next two months the single sold over 2 million as it was named the biggest-selling single in Europe for 2000 and won a TMF award in the Benelux countries (Belgium, Netherlands, and Luxembourg). It was also named best international dance single at the German Echo Awards and sold triple platinum in Sweden. "Freestyler" eventually made #1 in twelve countries. An album, *In Stereo*, was released on the back of the single and spent ten weeks at #1 in Finland, selling triple platinum. The album also went gold in both Australia and New Zealand, where the group toured and played in front of huge audiences. Another single, "B-Boys & Flygirls," was released before the end of 2000. Although it went gold in Australia, it struggled to match the massive impact of "Freestyler." At the beginning of 2001 the band won Emma awards for best newcomer, best debut album, best song ("Freestyler"), and best producer (JS16). *In Stereo* has since become Sony Music Finland's best-selling album of all time.

Ebanks was subsequently invited to become a presenter of TV music shows, promoting hip-hop to the Finnish people as the Bomfunk MC's played a series of concerts across the country accompanied by a live band and dancers. In December 2001 the band released its third single, "Super Electric." The song was another hit across Scandinavia and mainland Europe but lost ground to the group's previous releases. Although the Bomfunk MC's career is little over three years old and the group's success is based on a single album, the band has earned itself a place in Finnish music history regardless of the outcome of its future career.

References

www.bomfunk.net

Botha, Piet (South Africa)

Born on July 18, 1955, in South Africa, Piet "Hammer" Botha began his musical career while still at school, writing songs and playing in bands with school friends. In 1979 he formed a rock band, Raven, and in the same year the band released its only single, "Wheel of Fortune." After Raven split up, Botha put together the band Wildebeest and released an album, *Bushrock 1*, in 1981. It won critical acclaim with its rock sound underpinned by traditional South African rhythms, and critics speculated that Botha would soon become an influential figure on the South African music scene. Although the band remained together for another two years, it released only one single, "Horings Op Die Stoep," (1983). Thereafter Botha put together another group, Jack Hammer; but in 1984, before the group had a chance to release any material, Botha relocated to the United States to explore the possibilities of a music career in America.

In America he met Billy Bob Thornton (later an Oscar winner for his role in *Slingblade*), who played drums and sang on the first Jack Hammer album. The record, *Jack of All Trades*, was released in 1987 after Botha returned home; It was a basic rock album employing the traditional rock line-up of guitar, bass, and drums supporting Botha's powerful vocals, and it became a bestseller. The band then released two popular rock albums, *The Judas Chapter* (1990) and *Ghosts on the Wind* (1994), in which Botha's lyrics began to reflect on South African culture. In 1995 the group toured as part of the Masters of Rock series of concerts with Uriah Heep and Deep Purple. Jack Hammer also toured the country with the U.S. rock band ZZ Top, one of Botha's biggest influences. Although the band was gaining a reputation internationally among fellow artists, the public outside of the group's native South Africa was less impressed by Jack Hammer. A fourth album, *Death of a Gypsy*, released in the following year, proved to be the band's swansong.

Botha then became involved in a new South African record company, Wildebeest Records, which released his first solo album, *'n Suitcase Vol Winter* (1997). The songs were of a more personal nature than those of Jack Hammer and were recorded in Afrikaans, the language of white South Africa. The album won such critical and public plaudits that Botha released a second Afrikaans album, *Jan Skopgraaf*, in November 1999. Botha once again toured with Jack Hammer, playing old material as well as his new solo songs, but the group was more sedate with only Jonathan "The Kid" Martin on guitar and Tertius du Plessis on bass. After the success of the tour a Jack Hammer compilation album, *Anthology*, was released in January 2000. Toward the end of the year Botha began to tour with Martin as Piet and the Kid, as well as performing with Jack Hammer.

In February 2001 another compilation was released: *Bootleg* covered Botha's career to date, including his pre–Jack Hammer work, as Botha himself continued to tour South Africa both as a solo artist and in bands. In June he visited London and performed with other South African artists at the African Ambush series of concerts. This was the prelude to another compilation, *The Hits*, released in October. This album soon went platinum as Botha began rehearsing for more live dates across South Africa during November and December.

References

www.pietbotha.com

History of Contemporary Music of South Africa by Garth Chilvers and Tom Jasiukowicz (TOGA Publishing, 1994). ISBN 0620181214

C

Casal, Luz (Spain)

Luz Casal was born on November 11, 1958, in the La Coruña region of Spain. As a child she studied classical ballet and dreamed of a career in dance. Her first experience in music was playing with rock band Los Fannys, but by 1977 she had moved to Madrid and found work singing for recording studios and in stage musicals. In 1980 she secured a record deal with the local Zafiro label and released a single, "El Ascensor." The following year she became vocalist for the group Leño and recorded a live album with the group. At the end of 1982 her first solo album was released: A contemplative album that was more folk than rock, *Luz* was a moderate success. Thereafter Casal embarked on a tour with Leño and artist Miguel Rios, visiting thirty-five cities in Spain.

Immediately after the tour Casal began recording her next album in Spain, Germany, and Belgium. After the release of *Los Ojos del Gato* in 1984, Casal began to make an impression in other parts of Europe with her modern, polished folk style, although the album also featured more rock-oriented songs that showed the direction Casal was beginning to explore. She was invited to perform at a festival in the former Czechoslovakia and to take part in a German ecological campaign along with artists such as Dire Straits' Mark Knopfler. A single released in 1987, "Quiereme Aunque te Duela," earned Casal an appearance on TV, but it was not enough for her to keep her record contract with Zafiro, which expired in January 1988.

Always popular in her home country, Casal signed with EMI in 1988 and released *Luz V* in 1991, consolidating her position in Spanish music. The album, a collection of songs that featured Casal's powerful vocals in front of driving rock beats, went double platinum. A subsequent run of singles, including the massive hit "No Me Importa Nada," made Casal one of Spain's most important rock personalities and the country's number one woman rock artist. Because of her new position in the country's music pantheon, the public showed interest in her previously released albums, all of which became platinum. Between 1991 and 1993 Casal embarked on a number of high-profile concerts, including an appearance at Amnesty International in Chile alongside Sting and U2, and at the New York Music Seminar. Casal also began to attract interest in South America, appearing on TV in Argentina, Paraguay, and Chile, where *Luz V* turned platinum.

Casal spent 1994 touring and appearing at festivals around the world and ended the year with the release of *Como la Flor Prometida*, which followed the success of her previous albums and permanently established her rock credentials. Another successful album, *Pequenos y Grandes Exito*, appeared in 1996, after which Casal decided to take a break from touring and recording.

It was three years before the release of *Un Mar de Confianza*. Featuring more mature rock songs that showcased a confident artist in the prime of her career, the album included the song "Mi Confianza," which was later released as a single and went on to win the Premio Ondas of 1999 for best song. A compilation album, *Luz*, was also released and sold a quarter of a million copies. At the end of 1999, Spanish TV recorded a program dedicated to Casals called "The Queen of Spanish Pop." After a quiet two years, Casal visited the United States in 2002 and performed with the rock band Spin Doctors in New York and Philadelphia before returning to Spain to begin recording new material.

References

www.luzcasal.es

Chage & Aska (Japan)

Shuji Shibata (Chage) and Shigeaki Miyazaki (Aska) were born within weeks of each other in 1958, the former in Kitakyushu, the latter in Fukuoka, Japan. As a child, Chage moved to Fukuoka after his parents opened a restaurant there. In high school he formed his first band and retained a keen interest in music after enrolling at Fukuoka Dai-Ichi Economics University, showing little interest in anything except the school music club. Aska, meanwhile, after spending time in the city of Sapporo, returned to Fukuoka to attend senior high school and began playing in a band. Later, he too joined the music club at Fukuoka Dai-Ichi Economics University. Entering the Yamaha Popular Song Contest (Pop-con), Aska failed to win but was hooked and continued entering any contest that he could find. In 1978, the pair entered as separate artists; Chage won the grand prize while Aska won best singer for the Fukuoka area. Although only the grand prize-winner could go through to the next round of competition, Chage was suitably impressed and invited Aska to join him.

Although the duo performed as often as possible anywhere they could secure a booking, they felt their efforts were being wasted. In the summer of 1979, in a last attempt to make a career for themselves, they relocated to Tokyo. By August they had found themselves a record deal and released their first single, "Hitorizaki," a synthesizer-driven pop song. Focusing on a basic electronic sound, their debut album, *Kazemai*, preceded a string of concerts in April 1980 featuring the duo, but the Japanese public was slow to notice the fledgling songwriters. It was only after the release of "Neppu" in February 1981 that the band won acclaim, and a concert in Den'en in August attracted 6,000 fans.

For the next few years Chage & Aska continued to release albums at an astonishing rate: two in 1981, 1982, 1983, and 1987, and three in 1986—all based on the pop formula of keyboard-driven songs. The duo followed these releases with tours of the country, playing up to seventy dates each time. By now the two were releasing books and videos, as the Japanese public continued to support them in ever-increasing numbers. Their popularity resulted in a live TV broadcast of a concert in March 1983. In September of the following year, Aska made his acting debut in a TV drama, "Tomoyo," and released a collection of poetry, "Only Lonely," in November. By 1985 the band had changed record label, from Warner to Canyon, but the change did not interfere with their prolific work rate or with the style they had made their own, as they released three more albums and undertook another series of live shows in 1986.

In 1987 Chage released his first solo single, "My Mr. Lonely Heart," shortly after making his own acting debut in the drama *Shinsengumi*. Although the band released two more electronic albums in 1988, *Rhapsody* (March) and *Energy* (November), Aska still found time to release his own debut solo effort, *Scene*. In September 1989 the duo released a video collection celebrating ten years together. Chage now decided to explore other areas of music and formed another band, Multi Max, and released a single, "Some Day," in October. The side project was not a radical departure in style and did not interfere with Chage & Aska's career. In fact, in 1990, another two albums were released. Although the band was now firmly established as the biggest pop act in the country, it wasn't until the 1991 release of *Tree* that the group became the seminal band they are today. Although the album still focused on melody and rhythm, and reflected no real departure in style, *Tree* broke all Japanese sales records and catapulted the pair even farther up the pop hierarchy. They won a string of awards at the Japan Golden Discs awards, including "bests" for songwriter, single, lyrics, album, and group, as well as bestselling single for "Say Yes."

When 1992's follow-up, a compilation called *Superbest II*, surpassed *Tree*, selling over 3 million copies, the group was named Japan's record sales winners with an overall total of over 18 million records sold. In charts all over Asia, Chage & Aska original songs competed with cover versions by other artists. To commemorate fifteen years together, the band wrote its first song in English for the Jean-Claude Van Damme movie *Streetfighter*.

Although the two were becoming heavily involved in their own projects, Chage and Aska continued to record together. Following 1995's *Code Name 1 Brother Sun*, they played sixty concerts in nine cities to over half a million people before taking the tour to Taiwan, Hong Kong, and Singapore. In the following year they were the first Asians to appear on *MTV Unplugged*.

In 1997, Aska embarked on his first major solo tour, playing to 40,000 people in Shanghai in May, and in 1998 the artists both released solo albums. The next year another Chage & Aska record was released, but this time a definite division was evident. The single contained two songs; "Kono Aino Tameni" was an Aska solo number while "Vision" was entirely Chage's number, each artist having no input in the other's song. Although commercially successful, it was a short-lived experiment, as the band released a new single together in November 2001. The duo introduced new dance-based rhythms given a Japanese twist, with traditional arrangements and instrumentation fighting for space against the modern backing. "Yume no Tubute" was the first release from the album *Not At All*, released the following month. The album hit the charts as Chage & Aska was beginning a 73-date tour of Japan that kept the group on the road until April 2002.

References

www.ryo-aska.com

Cheng, Sammi (Hong Kong)

Born in the former British colony of Hong Kong on August 19, 1972, Cheng Sau Man was sixteen years old when she first began singing in the clubs there. After leaving school she was signed to a small local record label. She had a less-than-remarkable career for the next eight years. Taking the name Sammi in the tradition of Asian singers adopting English names, in the early 1990s she released a series of commercial pop albums that had English titles but were sung in Mandarin: *Sammi* (1990), *Holiday* (1992), and *Never Too Late* (1992). All three were largely ignored, as was her appearance in the first of a string of motion pictures, *Best of the Best*. It wasn't until she signed with the Warner label in 1996 and the company gave her extensive backing, providing her with professional videos and a more polished, if similar, recording sound that Asia found themselves a new favorite and she became an "overnight" star. A series of eight concerts between November 10 and 17, 1996, sold out over a month in advance, as her old recordings began to appear on the country's charts.

Cheng continued to act in movies, being regularly cast as the love object in both comedies and dramas, including *Feel 100%* (1996) and the comedy *Killing Me Tenderly* (1997). Then, in 1998, Cheng's star rose out of all proportion to her early popularity. Still featuring catchy pop tunes, during 1998 her albums *Waiting for You, Sammi X Live, Passion, Sammi Mastersonic 24K Gold (Part 1)*, and *Our Theme Song* sold gold, platinum, double platinum, double platinum, and double platinum, respectively. Cheng also appeared in one of the country's most popular movies, *The Lucky Guy*. As a result of her success, in 1999 Cheng received an award for best woman singer as well as the Silver Award for bestselling singer and best-dressed woman.

By now a star of TV who was regularly featured in teen magazines, Cheng was christened "Queen of Canto Pop" as her albums climbed charts across Asia and made her the bestselling woman artist from Hong Kong ever. After a relatively quiet 1999, events in the year 2000 reaffirmed Cheng's status in Asia. In June the movie *Needing You* was released, in which she co-starred as the love interest of Hong Kong's most popular actor, **Andy Lau**. *Needing You* became the top-grossing film of the year and earned Cheng a nomination in the 37th Golden Horse awards. In July a magazine poll named her 12th Sexiest Asian in the World, and she won a most-outstanding-actress award for her second film of the year, *Ming Pao*.

Although her singing career was taking a back seat to her movie career, the pace of filming in Hong Kong allowed enough time for Cheng to release the award-winning single "On the Palm Line of Love," which reached the top of the charts. The song, another pop ballad, was also named most popular female karaoke song and best Chinese song in the world. The song also won Cheng the titles of most popular woman artist, most popular Hong Kong singer in Taiwan, and most outstanding woman singer. The year 2001 began in much the same vein, as her album *To Love* became a top ten Mandarin record. Continuing to reflect the style that had proved so successful in Cheng's earlier releases, *To Love* was a commercial mix of ballads and dance tracks. In February 2001 Cheng was named most popular woman singer in the Hong Kong region.

Cheng performed in Australia during Easter 2002 and is rumored to be appearing in her first English language film, although there has been no official news. *Tender,* a new album of polished pop songs, was released in May 2002. With her popularity as a singer firmly established, Cheng appears destined to continue her reign as Queen of Canto Pop.

References

www.popsquare.com/sammi

Cheung, Jacky (China)

Cheung Hok-Yau was born in China on July 10, 1961. During his high school years, Cheung played in various bands and entered any singing contest that he could. After finishing his education he became a computer clerk for the Hong Kong Trade Development Council and then Cathay Pacific Airlines. Always more interested in singing than computing, Cheung was singing in karaoke bars when he entered the 18 Districts Amateur Singing Contest in 1984. Employing the experiences gained at school and in the bars of Hong Kong, Cheung won the competition. Immediately thereafter he signed with Polygram and took the name Jacky.

Although he released his first album, *Jacky Cheung*, a blend of east/west synthesizer pop, in 1987, Cheung's music was initially overlooked in favor of his acting career. His debut movie, *As Tears Go By* (1988), won him a Hong Kong Academy best supporting actor award. Because of the rapid turnover in movie making in Hong Kong, over the next seven years Cheung was able to star in twenty-one motion pictures. After this success he decided to concentrate on his singing and began to release pop records. In 1991 "Love You More Each Day" was a huge hit that reached #1, a position that his follow-up single, "Uncontrolled Passion," also achieved. Both powerful ballads, the songs laid the foundation for much of Cheung's future work, as orchestral arrangements on songs about love and loss became his staple material.

Christened one of the "Four Music Kings" (or, alternatively, "Four Heavenly Kings") by the Hong Kong media (with **Andy Lau, Leon Lai** and **Aaron Kwok**) Cheung released the album *True Love Expression* in 1992; it was the bestselling Mandarin album of the 1990s, selling over 400,000 copies. The album spawned eight hit singles, four of which were ballads. "Love You More Than You Do," "Crush on You," "True Love Expressions," and "Breaking Up on Rainy Days" all reached #1, the most hit singles of any album in Hong Kong pop history to date. In the same year Cheung's *Sparks of Love* sold 250,000 copies on the first day of its release.

Still relying on boldly orchestrated ballads, in 1993 Cheung had success in Taiwan when *Goodbye Kiss* sold more than 3 million copies. In fact, he became the bestselling Asian artist in the world for 1993, 1994, and 1995. In 1993 he began a world tour of more than twenty countries, including the United States and Europe. As a result the World Music Awards created the category of bestselling Chinese artist; Cheung was presented with this award in Monte Carlo in May 1996, performing with Celine Dion and Vanessa Mae. This led to an invitation from the Hong Kong Philharmonic Orchestra to perform a special concert, making Cheung the first Chinese pop artist to perform with any orchestra. In 1997 Cheung's production company created a musical, "Snow Wolf Lake," based on traditional Chinese stories and folklore. The show played a run of forty-three sold-out engagements at the Hong Kong Coliseum before Cheung took it to Singapore.

As Cheung's popularity soared across Asia, a body of young professionals and entrepreneurs, the Junior Chamber International, named him one of the top ten outstanding young persons in the world. Bolstered by his new stature, Cheung took a course of action almost unheard of by artists in the region and spoke out on politics. He condemned the riots that were occurring in Indonesia in 1998 as rebels reacted against the military government. The Chinese government refused to comment on this new political stance preferring not to become embroiled in arguments with one of China's biggest stars as Cheung continued to release albums, all of which reached #1. His massive popularity earned him the chance to present a plaque to Hong Kong customs officials who were responsible for cutting the piracy rate in bootleg CDs. Cheung's recordings all had English as well as Mandarin titles, in common with many other Asian artists, and he then began work on an English-language album to be recorded through his own record company, although there is no release date yet.

In 2001, Cheung remained relatively quiet, although he performed at the Touch of Love concert in Hong Kong in February, had appearances in May in Singapore, and staged a show to celebrate his fortieth birthday in July.

References

www.jackyfans.com

Chinai, Alisha (India)

As the daughter of a classically trained singer, Alisha Chinai was surrounded by music since her birth in the 1960s. It soon began to affect her studies, and she subsequently dropped out of college in her hometown of Bombay, India, after only one year. She studied light Hindustani classical music for six months before turning to modeling and acting, which won her a place in an Indian stage version of *Evita*. While she was working on the show the label HMV offered her a record contract, and in 1985 she released *Jadoo*. The album, a series of songs that blended Indian traditional music with Western dance rhythm, was an immediate success and turned platinum.

Chinai's next two albums, *Aah! Alisha* and *Baby Doll*, were both multi-platinum sellers, as Chinai began to be called "India's Madonna" in the press. Although she attempted to play down this image, her next album reinforced it: *Madonna* (1989) turned three times platinum as its up-tempo, bright and energetic dance numbers and memorable melodies won the nation's heart. Later in 1989 she released *Kamasutra*, an album that was very similar to *Madonna* and that earned the singer a double platinum disc. Chinai was also appearing in TV movies and had a major hit with "Kaante Nahim Katthe Yeh Din Yeh Raat," a duet with actor Kishore Kumar from the film *Mr. India*.

After releasing *Kamasutra* Chinai met with music director Anu Malik, signed with the Magnasound record company, and began to record songs in "Hinglish," a mixture of Hindi and English. The result was *Bombay Girl*, (1993), another huge success that went triple platinum. All of Chinai's previous success was eclipsed with the 1995 release of *Made in India*. A series of up-tempo songs indebted to traditional Indian music but revealing a definite Western influence, the album reached #1 in the Indian charts and stayed there for over a year as it sold over 5 million copies. A special TV program, also called "Made in India," showcased the album. The recording even reached the top spot in charts across Asia as Chinai became the biggest-selling female Indian pop star ever. However, her relationship with Malik turned sour and she filed a lawsuit alleging sexual harassment, and she also fell out with India's most famous producer, Biddu, who had worked on *Made in India*. The success of *Made in India* kept Chinai on stage and TV screens through the mid-1990s, as she appeared in her own TV programs, "Best of Alisha" and "Essential Alisha." Then, in 1998, she released *Antavatma*. The album showed Chinai moving towards a more mature sound, eschewing the poppier leanings of her early work for a more considered style of song focusing on ballads and more orchestrated music. The adverse publicity from the tabloid press on account of her court case and troubles with Biddu apparently affected the public's view of her and the album, which was a relative failure. Following the disappointing sales of the album, Chinai disappeared from the public eye. After settling her differences with Biddu she began work on her ninth album, *Dil Ki Rani*, with Biddu as producer. On the album Chinai sought to return to the pop feel of her previous material but, by now, the Indian market had become saturated by newer, younger artists and her fans changed their allegiances to this new breed. Sales of this album also failed to meet expectations, but Chinai was still in demand on the live circuit and played in sold out theaters across Asia. Recently the "Queen of Indipop" has appeared in commercials for products such as tea.

References

www.mtvindia.com/mtv/music/index909.php3

Clegg, Johnny (South Africa)

Johnny Clegg was born on October 31, 1953, in Rochdale in the north of England, then moved to his mother's native Zimbabwe, and finally settled in South Africa at the age of nine. When he was fourteen he met Charlie Mzila, one of many street musicians who inhabited the area near Clegg's home; the duo improvised songs based on African music but increasingly introduced Western influences. For two years Clegg and Mzila performed at clubs and parties, always in danger of being arrested because they were breaking South Africa's Group Areas Act, an apartheid law that required whites and blacks to stay in their own residential and recreational areas of cities and towns.

Clegg's reputation was growing, however, and soon Sipho Mchunu, a migrant Zulu worker, challenged Clegg to a guitar competition. Afterwards the two became friends. It was a difficult partnership initially because South African law effectively banned them from appearing together, yet in 1976 they won a record deal and released their debut single, "Woza Friday." The song, which was the culmination of Clegg's early experimentation with combining Western rock with African tribal rhythms, became their first hit. Then they formed the band Juluka (a Zulu word meaning "sweat") in direct contravention of the Cultural Segregation laws. As a result their records were censored and then banned, so Juluka undertook a strenuous touring schedule to promote their music. Juluka played a style of music called "mbaqanga" that mixed traditional rhythms from the African countryside with U.S. blues and jazz that was predominantly popular in the cities. Clegg, however, gave Juluka its distinctive style as he introduced minor chords, which were largely unheard of in mbaqanga; after blending it with reggae, soul, and funk, Clegg created what became known as Township Pop. Moreover, Clegg's sociopolitical lyrics made Juluka a truely unique group.

In 1979 Juluka released its first album, *Universal Men*, but the follow-up, *African Litany* (1981), was the breakthrough for the band. Clegg's music and lyrics were now being commented on by the music press around the world, with *African Litany* being his mouthpiece to report to the world on life in Africa and the hardships that the African people faced. It won them a broader audience and led to tours in the United States, Canada, the United Kingdom, Germany, and

Johnny Clegg
Pictorialpress Ltd., London, UK

Scandinavia. The band spent the next years in a constant round of recording and touring and produced seven albums between 1982 and 1987: *Ubuhle Beinvelo* and *Scatterlings* (both 1982), *Work for All* (1983), *Stand Your Ground* and *Musu Ukugilandela* (both 1984), *The Good Hope Concert* (1986), and *Crocodile Love* (1987). All sold well across South Africa. The albums continued to promote the band across Europe as Clegg became determined through his music to focus the world's gaze on South Africa and its politics. Ultimately, however, the heavy touring began to take its toll, and in 1985 Mchunu left to return to his farm in Zululand.

Clegg, who continued to write music, immediately formed Savuka with other South African musicians, blending traditional African music with Celtic folk and a more international rock sound. Following the band's 1987 debut album, *Third World Child*, Savuka began a career that reflected Juluka's in its intensity of recording and touring. *Shadow Man* and *Cruel, Crazy, Beautiful World* were released in 1988 and 1989, respectively, as Savuka consolidated Clegg's growing reputation in Europe—especially in France, where he was the recipient of many awards. In 1988 Clegg found himself at the center of controversy when the British Musicians Union (BMU) forbade him to play at the birthday concert for Nelson Mandela at Wembley Stadium, London. The BMU had voted that no white South Africans could perform in Britain while apartheid was still part of South African government policy; the union saw no reason to alter its rule for a musician who had been persecuted all throughout his career. It was an irony that was not lost on Clegg, who had always fought against censorship, both musical and political.

In 1989 Clegg was presented with the Chevalier des Arts et Lettres by the French government for his contribution to music. At the same time, *Cruel, Crazy, Beautiful World* became the biggest-selling international album in France. The following year Clegg received an award from the French record industry for sales of that record and was named an honorary citizen of the town of Angouleme. Savuka released its final album, *Heat, Dust and Dreams*, in 1993. As Clegg felt the band had achieved all it could with its blend of African rhythms and western/African instrumentation, he had decided to experiment once again.

After the breakup of Savuka, Clegg returned to his old friend Mchunu to re-form Juluka. The resulting album, *Ya Vuka Inkunz* (1996), resembled the group's original releases but added elements of hip-hop and Eurodance as the music settled into a steady 4/4 beat, far more solid than the free flowing rhythms of African music. Clegg continued to perform across South Africa and Europe, both as a solo artist and as part of Juluka, and also visited the United States, where he received the Mayor's Office of Los Angeles Award for the promotion of racial harmony and a humanitarian award from the Secretary of State for Ohio. In 1999 *The Johnny Clegg Anthology* was released; it charted the musician's career since his first album over twenty years earlier. An even more comprehensive compilation, *The Best of Juluka/Savuka Featuring Johnny Clegg*, was released in South Africa in April 2000.

Popularly known throughout the country as the White Zulu, Clegg continues to make music and to influence many young musicians. These newcomers can now flourish in the newly democratic South Africa, due in no small part to the efforts of bands like Juluka and musicians like Johnny Clegg.

References

www.johnnyclegg.com
50 Years of Rock Music by Philippe Paraire (London: Chambers, 1992). ISBN 0550170111

Conway, Deborah (Australia)

Deborah Conway was born on August 8, 1959, in Melbourne, Australia. Her career began in the early 1980s when she recorded an album of dance music that was never released. She then became involved in recording music for the film director Peter Greenaway's *Prospero's Books* (1991) and also joined the band Do-Re-Mi. Although the group won some interest from the music press and public, Conway left to embark on a solo career. When *String of Pearls*, her first solo album, was released in 1991, it won high praise from both the press and the public. Recorded in Melbourne, Australia, and Memphis in the United States, it combined elements of pop, rock, and country and contained the hit singles "It's Only the Beginning," "Under My Skin," and "Release Me." The album won Conway the title of best woman performer at the ARIA awards.

Her follow-up album, *Bitch Epic* (1993) continued in the same vein as her debut release and featured as part of the promotion tubs of chocolate spread with stickers covering the label "Bitch Epic." The album sleeve featured a photo of Conway naked except for a heavy covering of chocolate spread. The tour Conway undertook soon thereafter met packed houses all over the country, and in 1994 Australian magazine *Media Mania* named her singer of the year. *Bitch Epic* was written in collaboration with Willy Zeiger, who later became Conway's musical partner. In 1995 they moved to London to set up a new studio and began to write material for another album. Before the move, however, Conway took part in a recording project with other musicians, including Paul Hester from Crowded House. The resulting album, *Ultrasound*, was recorded in seven days; it was a mixture of instrumentals and experimental songs that reflected Conway's diverse interests.

My Third Husband (1997) contained the material that Conway and Zeiger wrote in London. After its release. The album, according to Conway, was a "dark, throbbing. Hypnotic and dreamy kind of record" based around samples and featuring a more produced sound. Conway returned to Australia for a series of concerts, including a sold-out show at the prestigious Sydney Opera House. Toward the end of 1998 she was invited to compose a song for "Timelines," a project of musical collaborations between young and old for the Year of Older Persons. Her collaborator was George Dreyfuss, one of Australia's most celebrated composers. The song that emerged, "When I Get Younger," was recorded with the Tasmanian Symphony Orchestra and placed Conway high in the charts.

Conway and Zeiger then concentrated on a new album. In 1999, they played a series of anonymous gigs in small venues, testing their new material on unsuspecting members of the Melbourne public under the pseudonym City of Women. The resultant single, "Radio Loves This," won heavy radio promotion. In May 2000 the album *Exquisite Stereo*, containing thoughtful, personal songs, was released; it featured a duet with Neil Finn of Crowded House that put Conway firmly back in the Australian public gaze. As *Exquisite Stereo* began its long run in the local charts, she was offered the lead role in a theater production charting the life and music of U.S. country singer Patsy Cline. "Always . . . Patsy Cline" has been playing to full houses across Australia since September 2001. An album, *The Songs of Patsy Cline*, was released at the end of the year to unanimous critical success. Conway continues to portray the doomed singer, with a view to taking the production on tour outside of Australia in the future. In May 2002 Conway appeared on the album *The Woman At The Well,* a compilation of songs written by fellow Australian singer/songwriter **Paul Kelly**. All the songs were performed by women artists including **Bic Runga**. Conway at present is recording new material for future release.

References

www.deborahconway.com

The Encyclopaedia of Australian Rock and Pop by Ian McFarlane (St. Leonards Allen & Unwin, 1999). ISBN 1865080721

Crash Test Dummies (Canada)

Vocalist/guitarist Brad Roberts (b. January 10, 1964) formed his first band in Winnipeg, Canada, in the mid-1980s with nightclub owner Curtis Ridell. Calling themselves Bad Brad Roberts and the St. James Rhythm Pigs, they played a brand of blues but never took themselves seriously as a group. They were soon joined by Ben Darvill (b. January 4, 1967) on guitar and Ellen Reid (b. July 14, 1966) on keyboards and began to take their music more seriously. Brad's younger brother Dan (b. May 22, 1967) joined on bass at the same time that Michael Dorge (b. September 15, 1960) joined on drums, and the group began to record demos of its own material in 1988 and 1989.

After playing in shows around Canada they signed with Arista Records and produced a promotional album, *Portrait of the Artist As a Young Dummy*, that gained interest among Canadian radio stations. The promise of the young band soon came to fruition in April 1991 when it released *The Ghosts That Haunt Me*; it turned four times platinum, selling 400,000 copies in Canada and another 300,000 worldwide. It brought the Crash Test Dummies the 1991 Juno Award for group of the year. A single from the album, "Superman's Song," reached #1 in Canada and prompted a sold-out tour of the country. Further releases from the album, the title track and "Androgynous," both reached the top ten, confirming the band as a major new force in the Canadian pop world.

After a year touring the United States, Europe, and Australia, the band returned home to begin recording material for the next release. *God Shuffled His Feet*, released in October 1993, continued to feature slow, mournful songs and Roberts's deep bass. The record eventually sold over 6 million copies, including 1 million in the United States, based strongly on the popularity of the single "Mmm Mmm Mmm Mmm" that was released from the album the following February.

"Mmm Mmm Mmm Mmm" won the band a slot on the TV program *Saturday Night Live* and pushed the single to #1. In April 1994 a new radio format was emerging, AAA (Adult Album Alternative) which played the single constantly. It also won extensive airplay across Europe, where the song entered the U.K. chart at #5 and the album at #2. The band toured Europe and North America in a series of sold-out concerts, and by the end of the year it was named MTV's breakthrough artist and was nominated for a Brit Award as best international group. After eighteen months of touring the band took a break while Darvill and Reid began work on solo projects. The Crash Test Dummies returned in 1995 with a single taken from the soundtrack of the movie *Dumb and Dumber*. "The Ballad of Peter Pumpkinhead" reached #1 in Canada.

Roberts was living in London when the band released *A Worm's Life* in October 1996. Although it sold over a million copies, it showed little change from the group's previous style and was inevitably seen as a let-down after the successful sales of the group's previous work. As the band members returned to solo work, Roberts relocated to the Harlem section of New York. Some time later he was invited to a songwriters retreat at the Chateau de Maroutte in

France. While there, he began writing what became *Give Yourself a Hand*, the band's fourth album, released in March 1999. The album featured a newly found falsetto by Roberts, and Reid singing lead vocals for the first time. The change of style unsettled some of the group's fans. The record was only a moderate success, leading the group to be dropped by their record label.

Still popular in Canada, the band toured intermittently as solo projects began to take up more time. In September 2000, while Roberts was on holiday in Nova Scotia, he was involved in a nearly fatal car accident. As he recovered, he began writing new songs and met with local musicians Danny MacKenzie, Dave Morten, and Kent Greene. The group began recording songs under the title *I Don't Care That You Don't Mind*. Although Roberts had envisioned a solo album, as the rest of the Crash Test Dummies heard the new material they began to add their own parts. Ultimately the recording evolved into the Dummies' fifth album, eventually released on Roberts's own label, Cha-Ching Records, in April 2001. The band played a tour of Canada in May 2001 before returning to solo work, as the future of the Crash Test Dummies was put on hold. Towards the end of 2001 both Roberts and Reid released solo material.

Reid's album, *Cinderellen,* was a culmination of work she had begun in 1999 and featured sparse songs sung over a mainly electronic backing. Roberts's album, *Crash Test Dude,* was a live album recorded over a series of concerts he gave across Canada featuring acoustic versions of both Crash Test Dummies songs and cover versions. Both albums fared well in the Canadian charts.

In May 2002 the Crash Test Dummies returned to the studio to record an album due for release at Christmas 2002.

References

www.crashtestdummies.com

Superman's Song: The Story of the Crash Test Dummies by Stephen Ostick (Dallas, TX: Quarry Press, 1995). ISBN 155082130X

Cruz, Donna (Philippines)

Donna Cruz was born on February 14, 1977, in Valenzuela, Bulacan, in the Philippines. In 1988, at age eleven, she entered a TV talent contest and won, becoming the Bulilit Bagong Kampeon as well as reaching the grand final of the Little Miss Philippines competition. The following year she was chosen to represent her country in the Mermaid International Children's Song Festival held in Hiroshima, Japan, where she won the Grand Prix Champion title with the song "Yesterday's Dream."

By the time Cruz was thirteen she had signed a record contract with the local VIVA company, and her eponymous debut album of pop songs went triple platinum. With the success of her album, the movie wing of VIVA decided to try her in a motion picture. She played a small role in the film *Darna*. By the end of the year she had become the best new recording artist at the 1991 Awit Awards. The following year Cruz released her second album, *Kurot Sa Puso'*, and co-starred in her second movie, *Alabang Girls*. It wasn't until Cruz turned seventeen, in 1994, that she released her third album, the gold-selling *Langit Na Naman*. The album was more synth pop and orchestral ballads but her acting career began to take precedence. During the year she appeared in eight movies and won a best supporting actress nomination at the Metro Manila Film Festival for *Pangako Ng Kahapon*. She also appeared in commercials for products such as soap and chocolate as well as becoming a model for a leading Filipino clothes store. Cruz also starred in her own daily soap opera, "Villa Quintana."

When Cruz reached her eighteenth birthday on February 14, 1995, she starred in a TV musical special, "First Blush," that was broadcast across the entire country, the first of its kind in the Philippines. Later that year she released more material, although little of it was original work. *Habang May Buhay* was an album made up mostly of the themes from popular films (such as the Demi Moore and Patrick Swayze movie *Ghost*) and reached four times platinum. Cruz's single from the album, "Only Me and You," won the Awits best ballad and best performer awards. The year 1995 also saw Cruz win a Moreno youth achievement award in Germany as well as being named teenage queen of the movies at home.

Cruz made her stage debut in 1996 playing Belle in "Beauty and the Beast." In December she released *Merry Christmas . . . Donna*, which won her an Awit for best spiritual song for "My Only Christmas Is Jesus." In June of the following year she appeared in the film *Isang Tanong Isang Sagot* with U.S. singer Jason Everly (son of Phil Everly), with whom she had earlier recorded a duet for the singer's *Wish* album. Keeping faith with the style of music that had made her so successful, Cruz released another album, *Pure Donna*, later in the year; it went platinum a week after its release. Cruz also returned to the stage in the role of Lisle in "The Sound of Music" before starring in her own TV special, also called "Pure Donna," and at the end of the year performed in her own Christmas show, "Merry Christmas . . . Donna." In 1998, after releasing *The Best of Donna*, she toured the United States for the first time. By now married, expecting her first child, and choosing to avoid the public eye, she released only one album of sentimental ballads in 1999, the gold-selling *Hulog Ng Langit*.

In 2000 she returned to the university in the city of Cebu to study computer science. She remains semi-retired, although she has recently appeared with her baby daughter in a commercial for baby milk.

References

www.donnacruz.com

Cui Jian (China)

Born in Jilan in the north of China on August 2, 1961, to Korean parents, Cui Jian was taught music at an early age by his family. At age fourteen he was an accomplished trumpet player, and by age twenty he had earned himself a place in the prestigious Beijing Symphony Orchestra (BPO). Cui Jian then began to be influenced by Western pop through tapes that foreign students brought to his college. Although early influences included Simon and Garfunkle and John Denver, by the mid-1980s Western rock bands such as The Beatles, The Rolling Stones, and The Police were beginning to find their way onto the Chinese cultural underground. In 1984, Cui Jian formed a band, Seven Ply Board, with fellow classical musicians and began performing Western pop songs in the hotels and restaurants of Beijing. Although he released an album, *Langzigui* (1984) contained no Cui Jian lyrics and was a recording of old-style Chinese ballads. The influence of rock bands began to exert itself on Cui Jian, however, and he began writing his own songs aiming toward a Western rock sound.

After an appearance at a talent contest in Beijing, he began to attract the attention of the press and public as his songs dealt with subjects such as sexuality and individualism. The topics were deemed overly sensitive by the Chinese government, which still had authority over all state-produced pop music. Cui Jian's rock-oriented songs were unlike anything that other Chinese musicians had attempted before. In 1986, while still a member of the BPO, he took the stage as one of 100 performers at a concert in Beijing commemorating the Year of World Peace wearing peasant clothing and sang one of his own rock songs, "Nothing to My Name." As the performance ended, the audience, until then stunned into silence, gave the singer a standing ovation. Cui Jian's reputation spread among the youth of the country, and immediately he became a figurehead for disenchanted young people.

The following year Cui Jian officially left the BPO and began performing with Ado, a band that included a Hungarian bass player and a guitarist from Madagascar. These foreign musicians introduced Cui Jian to reggae and jazz, genres that Cui Jian later incorporated into his own music. It was the fusion of Western styles with traditional Chinese instruments like the Suona and Gu Zheng, combined with Cui Jian's rock sensibility, that caught the imagination of the students of Beijing. As his star continued to rise at home, he was invited to perform "Nothing to My Name" in a worldwide broadcast to advertise the forthcoming 1988 Olympic Games in Seoul. The exposure from the telecast brought him shows in London and Paris.

After Cui Jian returned home in 1989, an event took place that was to change China forever. Following a student demonstration in Tiananmin Square, Beijing, the government broke up the meeting by deploying tanks. Their action cost many lives, and the political map of China began to change. Students, always the most vocal of the government's detractors, began organizing more demonstrations, and musicians like Cui Jian were at the forefront of the unrest. Despite his outspoken criticism of government policy, it was nevertheless the Chinese government that financed Cui Jian's first tour of the country. Organized to raise funds for the forthcoming Asian Games, Cui Jian began playing to sold-out arenas. During one of the shows he appeared with a piece of red material covering his eyes while singing "A Piece of Red Cloth." The message to the young audience was obvious: that the government of Red China was "blindfolding" the citizens of the country. The rest of the tour was cancelled by the authorities. At the time, all studios in the country were government owned and Cui Jian found that his new releases were being withheld. It was while playing with Ado that Cui Jian released his first album of original material, *Rock n' Roll on the New Long March* (1989), which included a version of "Nothing to My Name."

As the repercussions of the Tiananmin Square incident began to affect Chinese society, the new, relatively more relaxed attitude of the government meant that the recording studios in the country ceased to be state-sponsored and had to make money on their own. As a result more new bands and musicians, inspired by Cui Jian, began to make records. It was with a group of these new musicians that Cui Jian recorded his second album, *Solution*, in 1991. Still rock based, the single "Wild in the Snow" from the album was made into a video for MTV Asia and gave the singer his first Asian hit.

As Cui Jian's influence on the Chinese music scene became ever more encompassing, he diversified into movies and produced a film, *Beijing Bastards*, in which he played an underground rock musician named Cui Jian. Following the inevitable success of the movie, a third album, *Balls under the Red Flag*, was released in 1994. It showed that Cui Jian was still experimenting with his music, as he introduced Chinese percussion instruments and a steel drum. In the same year he played four sold-out shows in Japan and made his U.S. debut in Seattle. A short U.S. tour followed in 1995. One review in the *San Francisco Chronicle* stated, "The major challenge to the [Chinese] government today comes not from democratic activists, but from defiant urban youth and their new hero, a long-haired Chinese rock star." The *Wall Street Journal* simply stated that Cui Jian was "a one-man phenomenon."

The "one-man phenomenon" continued to play all over Asia and was responsible for many new rock bands that were becoming a force on the Chinese music scene. Although a compilation of his early material was released in 1997, it wasn't until the following year that a fourth album appeared. *The Power of the Powerless* showed a marked change from the rock stance of his earlier work, as Cui Jian introduced synthesizers and samplers. A second tour of the United States followed in 1999, and in 2000 he wrote the soundtrack for the controversial movie by Jiang Wen, *Devils at the Doorstep*. He also appeared as a music teacher in *The Feelings of Heaven and Earth*. Later in the year Cui Jian received the Prince Claud award from the Dutch ambassador for "artistic endeavours in the developing world." He also began work on a project with the Hong Kong Dance Company to create a musical, "Show Your Colours," that made its premier in February 2001.

In July he played a series of concerts across Europe before returning to China for more live shows in October and November 2001. The following year Cui Jian continued to perform in China as well as visiting the U.S. in March, although no future releases are as yet planned.

References

www.cuijian.com

D

Daho, Etienne (France)

Etienne Daho was born in Oran, Algeria, on January 4, 1956, but at age six moved to Rennes, France, when his father, a soldier in the army, was posted there. At college in Rennes, Daho learned English and first became involved with music. In 1979 he organized a concert, "Transmusicales," in order to meet his favorite group of the time, punk band The Stinky Toys, who encouraged him to write his own music. Franck Dovcel, guitarist in Marquis de Sade, who also played at the concert, offered to help him with his first demo. The following year, during the second "Transmusicales," Daho appeared on stage with Marquis de Sade and performed five of his own songs. He later recorded his first single, "Cowboy." In 1981, Daho signed with Virgin France and recorded his debut album, *Mythomane*. The album was influenced by the French guitar bands of the time, and Daho used the musicians of Marquis de Sade as his backing band on the recording.

In 1982 he met French singer/songwriter Arnold Turborst, and they began to perform in the clubs and bars of Rennes before moving to Paris. The single "Le Grand Sommeil," written by Daho, began to attract radio play and was put on a compilation album, *Made in France*, showcasing French bands and artists that was released in the United States. By 1984, with the release of his second album, *La Notte, La Notte*, which reached gold status, Daho had become one of France's biggest stars. As his work developed from early punk into a more broadly based rock sound, it was recorded in a simple style that gave the impression that the recordings were little more than basic demos rather than the studio productions they were. The album won him the best newcomer award from the French music industry. Concerts and TV appearances followed, confirming Daho's stature as France's biggest star. *Pop Satori* was recorded in London in early 1986, released in April, and earned Daho another gold disc in September. It soon became the benchmark for avant-grade pop music, as

Daho's melodies and arrangements became more intricate. By now "Dahomania" was taking over the country, and Rennes gave Daho the keys to the city for raising the profile of his adopted town. He then moved into films, appearing in the drama *D'esorare*, which became a multiple award winner at the Venice film festival.

In 1987 Daho began producing other artists and launched his own label. As this left little time to record new material, he next released an album of b-sides and re-mixes. The following year Daho again traveled to London to record new material. Released as *Pour Nos Vies Martiennes*, it was still based very much on traditional instruments and it went gold on the first day of its release. Meanwhile the burgeoning dance scene was providing Daho with new ideas. He continued writing for other artists and preparing for a tour in 1989 that played to over 200,000 people in less than four months, including a run of six sell-out shows at the Zenith in Paris. A double live album of the Zenith shows was released in 1990 and went double gold.

Ten years after its release in 1981 *Mythomane* received a gold disc, but this was surpassed in December by *Paris Ailleurs*, which went double platinum. The album showed Daho becoming more influenced by dance music. The single "Saudade" stayed at #1 for several weeks and was re-mixed by deejay Dimitri From Paris and the U.S. band PM Dawn. The album was illustrated with photographs by Darg Nichol, who had taken the photographs for the book *In Bed with Madonna*.

In 1992 Daho used his influence to bring together twenty-seven French artists to contribute to the album *L'Urgence*, which raised 13 million francs for AIDS research. The following year, *Paris Ailleurs* was named album of the year and won a worldwide release. The tour that accompanied the album took in fourteen countries, with a percentage of the profits going toward AIDS charities. While promoting his own records, Daho continued to write and produce for many other French artists, including Sylvie Varton, Brigitte Fontaines, and Guesh Patti (who appeared as the singer in Peter Greenaway's movie *The Pillow Book*).

Daho returned to London in 1995 to write more material and met the British electronic band St. Etienne, with whom he recorded an EP. The recording became a single of the week in the music paper *NME*, reached #11 on the British chart, and earned the band an appearance on the country's biggest music show, *Top of the Pops*, alongside David Bowie and Oasis. Daho's time in London also led to the recording of *Eden*, which was released in November 1996. It received a gold disc in the first week of its release and was named album of the year in France, as Daho once again subtly altered his style and offered a more downbeat electronic mood. Daho commenced the "Kaleidoscope" tour of France in 1997 to promote the album. The public response was overwhelming, and "Kaleidoscope Part 2" began in March 1998 as demand grew to see Daho perform live. In 1999 he continued to show his support for AIDS charities when he appeared on the album *Sa Raisin d'être*, organized by French AIDS charities with all profits going to support research on the disease. In 2000, Daho again returned to London and began recording his seventh album as he continued to work with many different artists throughout France.

In April 2000 the material he had been working on was released as *Corps et Armes*. The album again showed Daho in reflective mood and the music was quiet and sombre in tone. Daho spent the rest of the year touring through France.

At the beginning of 2002 Daho was awarded the Chevalier de l'Ordre National du Mérite by his country for his outstanding contribution to French music. In April he appeared on French TV presenting a program focusing on the French entrant for the 2002 Eurovision Song Contest, which took place in May.

References

www.etiennedaho.com

Deacon Blue (Scotland)

Vocalist Ricky Ross (b. November 22, 1957) began a solo career before forming Deacon Blue (named after a Steely Dan song) in 1985 in Glasgow, Scotland. Recruiting guitarist Graeme Kelling (b. April 4, 1967), bass player Ewen Vernal (b. February 27, 1964), keyboard player James Prime (b. November 3, 1960), drummer Dougie Vipond (b. October 15, 1966), and Lorraine McIntosh (b. May 13, 1964), who shared the vocals with Ross, the band began to refine its sound around the clubs of Scotland. In 1986 the band signed with CBS on the strength of its live shows and one song in particular, "Dignity," which became the band's first single in 1987. "Dignity" was taken from the group's debut album, *Raintown*. Released in May 1987, the album was a collection of Ross songs detailing the loves, lives, and losses of ordinary people.

Although the releases did not make the charts, the band began to attract public attention, and both the single "Dignity" and album *Raintown* were re-released in 1988. "Dignity" was completely re-recorded with a bigger budget affording a lush production, and *Raintown* was released as a special double album. The re-packaging was a success, as the records rose to the top twenty. A succession of singles taken from the album, including a top ten U.K. hit, "Chocolate Girl," increased the band's tenure on the charts as the group toured Europe and made initial inroads in Australia. By the end of the year the single "Real Gone Kid" received a nomination in the annual Brit Awards for best single.

The follow-up album, *When the World Knows Your Name* (1989), continued to highlight Ross's lyrics reflecting the hopes and despairs of the British working class. The album reached #1 on the U.K. charts, spawning another trio of top ten hits in "Fergus Sings the Blues," "Love and Regret," and "Queen of the New Year." In 1990, the band released a collection of cover versions called "Four Bacharach and David Songs." The single "I'll Never Fall in Love Again" reached #2 in the singles chart. To keep up the band's momentum, a collection of rare b-sides was released under the title *Ooh Las Vegas* (1990). Though available only on limited release, it managed to reach #3. Meanwhile the group continued touring arenas in the United Kingdom, Holland, Germany, and Spain.

In 1991, BBC TV commissioned and broadcast a play that was based on the adventures of a young Deacon Blue fan in Glasgow. As Ross continued to write gritty songs about "real" people, the material was released as *Fellow Hoodlums* and the album reached #3 toward the end of the year. The band's New Year's Eve concert from the Royal Concert Hall in Glasgow was broadcast live on BBC Radio 1, the country's most listened-to pop radio station. The band spent the next year mainly in the studio recording its fifth album, *Whatever You Say, Say Nothing*. Although the record broke no new ground lyrically or musically, it satisfied the group's huge fan base; the single "Your Town" was another top twenty hit as the album peaked at #4 in 1993 and the band embarked on a tour of Europe.

By 1994 Ross was eager to continue the solo career he had postponed when he formed the band in 1985. As a result Deacon Blue released a greatest hits album, *Our Town*, which entered the chart at #2 and soon thereafter became the band's second #1 album. Three more albums—*Riches and More, Walking Back Home*, and *Homesick*—were released in the intervening years but failed to match the success of their predecessors, as they contained no dramatically different material. Deacon Blue played two concerts in its home city of Glasgow at the Barrowlands as Ross continued his successful series of one-man concerts. The band re-formed to play another series of shows around the United Kingdom in the summer of 2001, mostly highlighting their early material. The concerts were so successful that the band toured again in November, with Ross opening with a version of his solo show. Another compilation album, *The Very Best of Deacon Blue*, was released in November 2001. In April 2002 Ross released a solo album, *This Is The Life,* that continued to show him as an empathetic songwriter. Deacon Blue toured the U.K. in November 2002.

References

www.deaconblue.com
Deacon Blue: Just What I Feel by Dave Bowler & Bryan Drag (London: Sidgwick & Jackson, 1995). ISBN 0283062479

Delirious? (England)

Originally from the town of Littlehampton on the southern coast of England, in 1992 singer Martin Smith (b. July 6, 1970) and drummer Stew Smith (b. January 27, 1967) began a Christian church meeting for young people in London, concentrating on songs rather than the traditional sermons that they considered off-putting to many teenagers. As the monthly event began to grow, Smith and Smith recorded a tape of the songs they had been writing and sold the tapes at the meetings. Although the band was still a relatively informal group, more musicians joined, with Stu Garrad (b. July 6, 1963) on guitar, Tim Jupp (b. January

5, 1966) on keyboards, and Jon Thatcher (b. July 1, 1976) on bass. Ultimately the band settled as a five-piece. As it performed up and down the country, the members were still holding day jobs. In the summer of 1993 they released an album of devotional songs, *Cutting Edge*.

A turning point occurred in 1995 when Martin Smith was driving back from a church meeting with his wife, Anna, and fellow band member Jon Thatcher. Smith fell asleep at the wheel and, though his passengers were unhurt, he ended up in the hospital. During this period he "felt that God was telling me to get out there and raise the flag." Thus on April 1, 1996, the friends decided to leave their jobs, and Delirious? was formed. Later that year the first Delirious? album, *Live and In the Can*, was released on the group's own Furious? label. In 1997 the band released its first studio album, *King of Fools*; this was preceded by the single "White Ribbon Day," which almost made the national top forty. Although the songs were based on traditional instrumentation, they had yet to acquire the more secular rock-oriented direction of the group's later releases. The songs were more pop, focusing on melody and devotional lyrics. The band's next single, "Deeper," reached #20 on the strength of the group's dedicated following, despite a lack of radio play. It did, however, win the band some press attention—though this was primarily because it was a Christian rock band—and as a result the album reached #13.

Although rock music has long been a genre explored by religious bands and songwriters, Delirious? now became the subject of debate. The Church claimed the band was "selling out" in an attempt to win fame and fortune, and the music industry was wary of the band trying to preach through its songs. In 1997 the band traveled to the United States, where it signed both with the Christian record label Sparrow Records and with Virgin, the former handling the Christian market and the latter the more mainstream market. Then the band decided to re-release "Deeper" in Britain, but radio was still not interested and the single failed to make any impression. Delirious? was touring heavily at the time, however, and playing to sold-out audiences across the country. At the end of the year the group released another live album, *d:tour*. In 1998 the band toured America and re-released its previous three albums. In an effort to not be away from their families for too long, the band toured the United States in two-week segments; this left time to complete work on the fourth album (the group's second studio album) in England.

By now the band members were beginning to be frustrated that they were pigeonholed as a Christian act rather than seen as a band in their own right. In February 1999, Delirious? released a single, "See the Star," which was followed by an album, *Mezzamorphis*, in April. The single gained the group its highest chart placing, peaking at #12, but the band was still ignored by radio despite the fact that the music had evolved into the anthemic rock sound that bands such as U2 had popularized. The single fell from the charts as quickly as it had climbed. The album was released in America in a more secular form, with Virgin Records removing the worshipful songs such as "Kiss Your Feet" and "Jesus' Blood." Another album, *Glo*, was released early in 2000 as the band took on another tour and again played to sold-out crowds.

Summer 2000 saw the band touring the United States again. This time they were playing in front of huge audiences at festivals across the country, including 55,000 at the Creation festival in Shirleysburg, Pennsylvania, as American fans embraced the group's big rock sound. After the band supported Bon Jovi on a U.K. tour during the summer, it released a fifth studio album, *Audio Lessonover*, in August 2001. Although the album was still essentially the Delirious? rock sound, the band was introducing more intricate melodies and song arrangements. Another album was released in the United States in the fall of 2001: *Deeper: The D:finitive Worship Experience* was a collection of songs from the band's U.K. releases and included a new song, "Not Forgotten." In November the band undertook a U.K. tour before releasing a new single, "I Could Sing of Your Love Forever," in December. The song showed Delirious? continuing to progress with its brand of stadium rock. However, mainstream radio was still reluctant to play "I Could Sing of Your Love Forever," and it received only sporadic airplay, leading numerous fans to write, phone, and e-mail radio stations in the United Kingdom accusing them of anti-Christian bias. Although the stations denied the claim, Delirious? still gained little airplay. In January 2002 the band visited Australia and New Zealand and then toured Europe and the United States. *Audio Lessonover* was due for release in the United States in April 2002.

References

www.delirious.co.uk

Purepop? The Delirious? Journey So Far by Craig Borlase (Arundel, England: Furious? Records, 1998). ISBN 0953464709

Die Prinzen (Germany)

In the early 1980s Tobias Künzel (b. May 26, 1964), Sebastian Krunbeigal (b. June 5, 1966), and Wolfgang Steer (b. September 4, 1966), all graduates of the St. Thomas Choir of the Leipzig Kantorei, an institution that teaches choral music, were performing in various bands in Leipzig, Germany. By 1989 they had been joined by two more St. Thomas members, Jens Sembdner (b. January 20, 1967) and Henri Schmidt (b. August 17, 1966) and became Die Prinzen. The group won immediate interest as they performed their own 20th-influenced compositions a cappella (not using any instruments) during their concerts. In September 1990, music publisher George Luck and producer Annette Humpe heard demos by Die Prinzen and took the group into the studio.

The band released its debut single, "Gabi and Klaus," in May 1991. Although it had little publicity, the song found an underground following that convinced Luck and Humpe they should invest more time and money in the band. The album that followed, *Das Leben ist grausam* (1991), became an immediate hit in Germany, reached #5 on the charts, and went on to sell in excess of a million copies. After a second album, *Küssen Verboten*, was released in 1992, the band began its first tour with drummer Ali Zieme, the only instrument used during the concerts. The album and subsequent single, "Bombe," both reached the top ten, with *Küssen Verboten* earning a triple gold disc. At the beginning of 1993 the group was named best act at the ECHO awards, while the single "Alles nur geklaut," released in August, became the group's biggest hit to date, entering the chart at #3. The band was still basing its recordings around the voice rather than instruments and an album, also called *Alles nur geklaut*, entered the chart in November at #4. As the band continued to play live it added a bass player, Mathias Dietrich, as its sound began to evolve. At the end of the tour Die Prinzen played to 50,000 fans in Leipzig. The show was filmed and later released on video, which went on to win an Echo award for best video.

Die Prinzen was now beginning to experiment with its music, and in 1995 the group's album *Schweine* introduced elements of techno. This was a radical departure, but *Schweine* earned the band another platinum record as it reached #4 in the German charts. To date all the band's albums had been produced by Annette Humpe; but, still looking for new ways of presenting their music, the band decided to record its next album, *Alles mit'm Mund*, with Stefan Raab. The result, an eclectic mix of guitar-driven rock songs that took the emphasis away from the band's vocals, was not received with the kind of enthusiasm that Die Prinzen was accustomed to; in fact, it was the group's first album not to make the top ten. Following the disappointment of *Alles mit'm Mund*, the band released a "best of" compilation called *Ganz Oben* in 1997.

During 1998 the band members relocated to Sicily and began writing new material. After returning home early in the following year, Die Prinzen was presented with one of Germany's most prestigious awards, the Fred Jay prize for lyricists. (Fred Jay was an Austrian songwriter who, after moving to New York in 1939, wrote for Ray Charles and Perry Como.) In the following month the band released a single, "So viel Spaß für wenig Geld," that took the group back to the top of the country's charts as it opted to return to the a cappella style of its early material. An album of the same name followed and reached #9. Early in 2000 Die Prinzen released another album, *Festplatte*, which once again placed the band in the top ten as it toured Germany. With the group still concentrating on the unique mix of Steer and Krumbeigal's tenor voices, the baritones of Künzel and Schmidt, and sparse musical backing, in 2001 Die Prinzen released its seventh original album, *D*. It is another example of the unique goth take on pop music that has helped Die Prinzen sell over 5 million albums, including fourteen gold and six platinum releases.

References

www.dieprinzen.de

Dobbyn, Dave (New Zealand)

Dave Dobbyn was born in 1957 in Auckland, New Zealand. His career in music began at the very top when his first band, Th' Dudes, won the best band award from the New Zealand record industry in 1979 and his song "Be Mine

Tonight" won best single, reaching #1 in the local chart. They began to act like superstars and began drinking and taking drugs. The band's arrogant behaviors began to lose it fans both in the music industry and from the public and, as numbers at its concerts began to dwindle, the group decided to split in 1980. Because of the band's initial success Dobbyn then embarked on a career that helped him become one of the most influential artists in New Zealand.

Dobbyn subsequently released two solo singles, neither of which made the charts, before he formed a new band, DD Smash, with guitarist Rob Guy, bass player Lisle Kimey, and drummer Peter Warren, and began a heavy touring schedule around the country. The results made history. *Cool Bananas* (1982) immediately went to the top of the charts with its mix of folk and rock songs. It was the first time a debut album had gone straight to #1 in the country. The record spent twenty-four weeks in the charts and earned a double platinum disc. It also won Dobbyn the title of male vocalist of the year; the band, group of the year; the record, album of the year; The album also won producer, engineer and album sleeve of the year from the New Zealand record industry.

During the summer of 1982 the band toured Australia but failed to make any impact on the local music scene. DD Smash then returned to New Zealand and in the following year released the single "Outlook for Thursday," which spent twenty-three weeks on the charts, the band's sound was augmented with the introduction of a brass section. During the year the group toured again and a recording of one of the shows, later broadcast on TV, was also made into an album, *Live: Deep in the Heart of Texas*. By the end of the year the New Zealand music industry once again rewarded the band as Dobbyn won his second successive vocalist of the year award, DD Smash won its second group of the year award. "Outlook for Thursday" won in the single and video categories, and *Live* won album of the year.

Early in 1984 the band released another studio album, *The Optimist*. At a gig in early summer the crowd got out of control, and a few unwise words from the stage by Dobbyn aimed at the authorities led to him being arrested and charged with incitement to riot. The band did not tour at all during the remainder of the year. If any blame was attached to Dobbyn for the problems at the concert, the public did not hold it against him. In 1985 he was invited to write the music for a motion picture, *Footrot Flats*. One of the songs he wrote for the film, "Slice of Heaven," sold double platinum and topped the charts for eight weeks in New Zealand and four in Australia, where more fans were beginning to warm to Dobbyn's music.

Eighteen month later, a new album was released. Although *Loyal* did not match the success of his earlier work, Dobbyn had now become accepted as a national treasure. His song "Whaling" was an unofficial national anthem, encapsulating a uniquely New Zealand way of life based on the island culture. The entire album tapped into the national consciousness as it dealt with life in the towns and countryside of the nation. Encouraged by the sales of "Slice of Heaven," Dobbyn returned to Australia but made little impact on the music scene there. Still involved with soundtracks, he wrote the music to a puppet-based TV series, *Space Knights*; but the series had little success and the record flopped. It took him five more years to release another album, *Lament for the Numb* (1993). Recorded the previous year in Los Angeles, the album was a pared-down, somber affair that reintroduced Dobbyn to the people of New Zealand. His rehabilitation was completed in 1994 when he released *Twist*.

Although the biggest sales were behind him, the work that followed—including *The Islander* (1998)—won Dobbyn great critical acclaim and marked him as one of New Zealand's foremost pop/folk/rock artists as his new material began to reflect a darker, more isolated nature. A retrospective, *Overnight Success*, was released in 1999 and a new album, *Hopetown*, in 2000. In *Hopetown* Dobbyn introduced a new array of instruments, including flugelhorn, sitar, and the hurdy-gurdy. The album also steered away from the folk-rock style as he began to explore Latin and African rhythms as well as the blues. In August Dobbyn joined Tim Finn and **Bic Runga** on a sold-out tour of New Zealand. After the highly successful tour, an album of the concerts was released in November. In 2001 a list of the top thirty most popular songs ever in New Zealand musical history included five of Dobbyn's: "Loyal" (#3), "Slice of Heaven" (#7), "Whaling" (#12), "Be Mine Tonight" (#27), and "Beside You" (#29). At the beginning of 2002 Dobbyn performed at a sold-out concert in London with Runga and Finn.

References

www.davedobbyn.co.nz

Doe Maar (Holland)

In 1978 Ernst Jansz (b. May 24, 1948), Piet Dekker, and Jan Van Pijnenburg (b. December 29, 1955) began playing songs that Jansz had written as a teenager. Pijnenburg soon left the fledgling group, and Jan Hendriks (b. September 20, 1949) and Carel Copier joined Jansz and Dekker. The same year, 1978, an Amsterdam nightclub called the Paradiso organized the "Festival of Fools" and asked the four musicians to form the Foolsband, to write music for the project. After the festival closed, the four decided to stay together under the name Doe Maar.

The band then undertook a hard schedule of gigging, playing five shows a week with Jansz organizing all the concerts as well as sending out demos to record companies, producers, and venues. Soon the pressure began to take its toll on Jansz, and he asked Frank van der Meyden to be the group's manager. Van der Meyden accepted with the unusual proviso that the band "don't become too big," as he was unwilling to spend a lot of time working for the band. The band, in turn, asked only that it get a record deal. Van der Meyden sent a tape to Telstar, which immediately signed the group. In the summer of 1979, Doe Maar released an eponymous debut album of piano and guitar based pop songs but took the option of not promoting it with any live shows, still with the idea that they should not become too popular. Six months after the release of their debut album, its traditional rock stance had failed to impress the Dutch people and it had only sold 2,000 copies.

In February 1980 Dekker left the band after falling out with Jansz over the group's musical direction, and the three remaining members decided to disband Doe Maar. Before they could, however, they had to fulfill some contractual obligations, so they found a new bass player in long term friend Joost Belinfante (even though Belinfante had never played bass before). Soon thereafter the band had a change of heart and decided that there was a future for Doe Maar after all, so the group asked a friend, Henny Vrienten (b. July 27, 1948), to join. Vrienten had already declined a previous offer but this time accepted and began writing for the band's second album, *Skunk*, which introduced ska and reggae influences. Although the band was optimistic about the chances for success of the new album, the record company thought it was too near Christmas to properly promote and so held it back. It was due for release in mid-1981, but some tracks were picked up earlier by deejays who began playing them. The songs were an immediate hit. Listeners inundated radio stations with requests for more material. One song in particular, "Sinds een dag of twee," was gaining a lot of attention, but the public found it difficult to remember the title. So the record company decided to change it to "32 jaar," much to the band's dislike. The public, however, was delighted, and the single went on to sell more than 20,000 copies. (In Holland, sales of 10,000 is seen as a great success.)

At this time Copier left the band and was replaced by Rene van Collum. When the band's next album, *Doris Day En Andere Stukken* (1982), was released, Doe Maar fever hit Holland. The band's playful, upbeat, ska-influenced songs caught the imagination of the Dutch people, and sold-out concerts followed. By 1983 van Collum had been replaced by original band member van Pijnenburg. The group's following album, *4US Virus*, went platinum on pre-orders before it even reached the shops. At the same time the band began merchandising T-shirts, button badges, posters, and headbands that took off on a scale never before seen in Holland.

The group's continually changing membership did not disturb its continuity, and by the end of 1983 it had sold over a million records. The pressures of fame were hanging heavily on the shoulders of the band members, though, and they decided to keep a low profile in the hope that they could return to their original plan of just "being in a band and making records." But the plan backfired, as their lack of concerts and public appearances attracted even more attention from the media. While the band was preparing to record its next album, the members finally decided to split up. A double live album, *Lijf Aan Lijf*, was released shortly thereafter, as well as numerous compilations, but Doe Maar had become a victim of its own success. Always more interested in playing music than being stars, the band members found it difficult to cope with their status as Holland's premier group.

Although little was heard of the various band members over the following years, they re-formed in 2000 and released a new album, *Klaar*, to great acclaim, as the Doe Maar sound remained virtually intact. Another new album, *Hees Van Ahoy* (2001), once again saw the band at the top of the Dutch charts, a place it has been accustomed to for nearly twenty years. Since re-forming, Doe Maar has become more popular than in its original heyday and continues to perform to huge crowds all over Holland.

References

www.doemaardichtmaar.nl

Dragon Ash (Japan)

Dragon Ash was formed in Kawasaki, Japan, early in 1996. Drummer Makoto Sakuri (b. February 7, 1979) and guitarist/vocalist Kenji Furuya (b. February 9, 1979), both only sixteen years old, met at college, where their mutual love of U.S. grunge and rock brought them together. Their youthful enthusiasm was tempered with the addition of older bass player Ikuzo Baba (b. November 1, 1965). A veteran of several previous bands, the thirty-one-year-old brought a musical focus to the group. On August 5, 1996, Dragon Ash performed its first gig at Club Citta in Kawasaki.

Furuya, son of the Japanese actor Ikko Furuya, had appeared in the movie *Gerende ga Tokeru Hodo Koi Shitai* (1995), and the confidence he gained from that experience made him the perfect theatrical front man. Within four months of the band's debut concert a mini-album of grunge-inspired songs, *The Day Dragged On*, was released. Immediately successful among the growing alternative and punk following in Japan that was quickly discovering Western guitar music and eager to find new music different from the record company manufactured boy/girl bands that were appearing daily on TV and in the charts, the band released a second mini-album in April. *Public Garden*, an extension of the group's first release, won few new fans but established the group among their faithful followers.

With demands on their time increasing, the band members next released a single, "Rainy Day and Day," in October 1997. The band's first full album, was released in November. Then Dragon Ash found a fourth member: the deejay Bots. A friend of Sakuri and Furuya at high school, he had become a deejay playing mainly U.S. hip-hop. It was Bots's style that began to influence the band's music and set the group apart from its contemporaries in the rock genre. The album, *A New Mustang* (1997), became a huge seller, the band played to growing audiences. Meanwhile, TV had not been ignorant of the new band, and Dragon Ash was invited to play in the MTV Japan tour in the summer of 1998. Heavily promoted by the station, the tour was a great success and the group was projected to idol status. Eager to compound its success, the band released *Buzz Songs* in September before MTV invited the group to perform at the second MTV Japan tour in December.

Confident of its position, the band embarked on its first headline tour in March 1999 topping the bill at venues across Japan, the same month as "Let Yourself Go, Let Myself Go," the group's third single, was released. Although it was now one of the biggest bands in the country among "alternative music" fans, Dragon Ash publicly stated it had little interest in trying to "break other territories" and insisted it was happy to continue building support in Japan. Such support was forthcoming, as the band headlined festivals throughout the summer while recording its third album, *Viva La Revolution* (1999).

The album was the first to feature some lyrics in English, and it swiftly became the most successful Dragon Ash album to date as it combined the group's early grunge sound with Bots's mixing and scratching. In September the band embarked on its "Freedom of Expression" tour. A fifth single was released soon thereafter: "I Love Hip-Hop" firmly stated the musical direction the band was taking. For the next few months the group took a break from the constant round of concerts and recording, waiting until May 2000 to release any new material. *Deep Impact*, the group's next release, continued their rap/rock hybrid and confirmed Dragon Ash as Japan's most popular band outside the mainstream. They played at more summer festivals before releasing "Lily's EP" in November.

At the beginning of 2001 the band released *Lily of Da Valley*, a blend of rap, rock and hip-hop that sold especially well in Japan but was also successful in other parts of Asia, eventually selling in excess of 1 million copies. Another round of promotional concerts followed, establishing a work routine that continues to the present as the band remains at the top of the "alternative" charts in Japan. A new single released in October, "Shunkashuto," returned them to the top of the national chart as well. Dragon Ash still shows no inclination to expand into other countries, happy to be Japan's #1 rock band.

References

www.dragonash.co.jp/english

Dreams Come True (Japan)

Miwa Yoshida (b. May 6, 1965) always dreamed of becoming a singer. In 1988, when she met Masato Makamura (b. October 1, 1958), they formed Dreams Come True with Takahiro Nishikawa (b. May 26, 1964). The band achieved overnight success with the release of its eponymously named debut album in March 1989, with their brand of electronica highlighted by Yoshida's singular style. In November they released their second album, *Love Goes On*; this album was driven by Makamura, who was producer, composer, arranger, and engineer as well as bass player for the group. It was Yoshida, however, who was rapidly becoming an idol to teenage Japanese girls as she wrote the lyrics for Makamura's music. Her unique mix of Western jazz and the traditional, improvised vibrato style of Japanese singing that often had Yoshida wailing across Makamura's music set the band apart from its contemporaries.

As Dreams Come True played concerts across the country, it became involved in writing soundtracks for TV programs, movies, and video games, as well as Makamura producing other artists. These extra activities did not stop Dreams Come True from releasing an album a year between November 1990 and December 1993: *Wonder 3, A Million Kisses, The Swinging Star*, and *Magic*, respectively. Although the recordings showed little expansion on the basic formula the band blueprinted with *Love Goes On*, each album became multi-platinum as sales topped 1 million for each record. The band was now working on a Web site, and within the first month of being online it received over 10 million hits. The band's popularity was well established, and *Delicious* (1995), its seventh album, reached #1 in the chart as it continued the run of million-sellers.

Yoshida's position of influence among Japanese women was confirmed in 1996 when she appeared on the front of *Time Magazine Asia* as an example of the "Divas of Pop." Although the band was now among the biggest artists in the country and the success of another #1 album, *Love Unlimited* (1996), confirmed this, the group was eager to try other markets. The result was *Sing or Die* (1997), the group's first album to be available in the United States. The album easily made million-plus sales in Japan and Asia, but Yoshida's vocal delivery may have been too colloquial for the album to be noticed in America. The band then returned to the studio and began recording new material that appeared in 1999 on *Wonderland*. To promote the album the band toured Asia: The Winter Wonderland tour even took the group to Taiwan for the first time, where it played a concert in the capital, Taipei, to over 20,000 people. Later in the year Yoshida formed another band, Funk the Peanuts, in which she sang in a more straight pop style. The group released a Japanese #1 single, "You Go Girl," in the winter of 1999.

As the band prepared to release a greatest hits album, it asked fans to pick the tracks by voting over the Internet. The result was *The Soul*, released on St. Valentines Day 2000, and it became another #1. Although the group's last attempt at breaking into the English-speaking market did not yield any success, in May 2001 the band began to re-record their twelfth album, *The Monster*, in English.

References

www.dreamscometrue-virginrecords.com

E

Ella Baila Sola (Spain)

Marta Botia (b. September 15, 1974) and Marilia A. Casares (b. December 15, 1974) met while they were studying at San Agustín school in Madrid, Spain. Before long they joined a local rock band as singers. As they began to write their own material, however, they felt stifled by the rigid formula of the band they were in and left to form their own group, The Just. As leaders of The Just, Botia and Casares explored a pop style and wrote all their material in English. After a series of small gigs, they met record producer Gonzalo Benavides through a mutual friend who convinced them their future lay with the Spanish language.

Having changed their group's name to Ella Baila Sola (She Dances Alone), they spent the next three years recording demos with various profession musicians, through Botia and Casares were the group's focus; although still influenced by rock and pop, the demos introduced a Spanish style that had already been successfully employed by fellow Spaniards in the group **Mecano**. Ella Baila Sola began to play at small venues around Madrid as the group continued to gather material for future release. The result was the eponymous debut album released in 1996. It sold over a million copies and produced two hit singles, "Lo Echamos a suertes" and "Cuando los Sapos Bailen Flamenco." The former went straight to #1, the latter made the top five.

Over the next twelve months Ella Baila Sola played a string of concerts around Spain and Spanish speaking-countries and released the singles "Amores de Barra," "No lo vuelvas a hacer," and "Por Ti." All became top five hits in Spain, making the band one of the best loved in the country and winning it the 1997 Premios Amigos award for best Spanish group. Following the grueling tour schedule, Ella Baila Sola took a year off to concentrate on writing material for its next album, *E.B.S.* (1998). Reflecting the same musical style as the group's debut album, *E.B.S.* won critical acclaim and dominated the Spanish music charts, as did the single "Y Quisiera," which reached #1. The album earned the band a Premios Ondas award for best Spanish group, as it sold almost half a million copies in Spain and 400,000 in South America. The band continued to perform live and made many TV appearances to promote the record before taking a year off to prepare new material.

When the group's third album, *Marta y Marilia*, was released in November 2000, the single "Como Repartimos los Amigos" took the band to the top of the charts again. In March of the following year the band toured Latin America and planned dates for the United States, where *Marta y Marilia* was the group's first American release. Later that year, Ella Baila Sola headlined a major outdoor festival in Barcelona as the group promoted its latest single, "Sin Confesarlo Todo"; a tour of Spain followed. By September the band was in the United States for the nomination ceremony for the Latin Grammy awards. The actual awards were postponed, however, following the events of September 11, 2001.

Ella Baila Sola then released a single, "Mujer," for a breast cancer charity. Meanwhile, rumors of a possible split began circulating in the Spanish music press. The rumors were confirmed when the band broke up on October 23. Both Botia and Casares have begun work on solo careers, although no new material has been released.

References

www.ciudadfutura.com/ellabailasola

Enya (Republic of Ireland)

Born Eithne Ni Bhraonain in the Republic of Ireland on May 17, 1961, Enya (her name was a familiar one used by family and friends) had her first taste of success when she joined the group Clannad. Formed in 1972, it won popular acclaim in Ireland with its haunting, etheral music combined with lyrics sung in Gaelic, the ancient language of Ireland. Enya's association with Clannad lasted only two years, 1980–1982; although mainly participating as a live musician, she appeared as a vocalist on the band's album *Fuaim* (1982).

Although Enya was soon in demand to write music for a succession of film and TV projects, it wasn't until 1987 that her work caught the ear of Rob Dickens, head of Warner Music UK. He immediately offered her a contract, and later that year the album *Enya* was released. Although it sold well in Ireland, where she was already an established name, Enya became known outside of Ireland only following the release of the album *Watermark* (1988) and the single "Orinoco Flow." The single featured all the trademarks of Enya's and, indeed, Clannad's music: haunting, whispered melodies and unintelligible lyrics. As Enya made appearances on TV, sitting at a piano wreathed in flowers, the single reached #1 in seventeen countries across Europe.

Three years later Enya released a third album, *Shepherd Moons* (which won a Grammy for best New Age album). In the intervening years Enya had contributed to more film soundtracks, including those of *Green Card* (with Andie

Enya
Pictorialpress Ltd., London, UK

McDowell and Gerard Depardieu) and *L.A. Story* (with Steve Martin). In 1992 Enya released *The Celts*. Used as the soundtrack for a BBC TV documentary about the history of Ireland, it was a re-mastered version of Enya's debut album, but it served to reintroduce her early music to an audience that mistakenly assumed "Orinoco Flow" was her first release.

In 1993 she released an album of new material, *The Memory of Trees*. Reflecting the style that had become synonymous with Enya, the album won her another New Age album Grammy. Although she never reached the top of the charts after "Orinoco Flow," her relative inactivity helped make each of her album releases an "event," as have been her concerts, which are few and sporadic. In 1997 a compilation of her material was released, *Paint the Sky with Stars*, and the following year saw the re-release of "Orinoco Flow" on its tenth anniversary.

After a five-year hiatus Enya released her seventh album, *A Day without Rain*, in November 2000. It continued to show her love of Celtic themes and her distinctive sound made the album another multi-platinum disc. The single "Only Time," although achieving a relatively poor showing in the charts, followed the path of her earlier work by appearing as part of the soundtrack to a movie, *Sweet November* (with Keanu Reeves). In November 2001 Enya once more contributed to the soundtrack of a movie, *The Lord of the Rings*. The film was an adaptation of J.R.R. Tolkein's famous trilogy, and Enya's atmospheric music fit perfectly into the fantasy world that Tolkein had imagined. "The Council of Elrond" and "May It Be" displayed all the hallmarks that Enya has become known for over the course of a twelve-year career that has seen her sell in excess of 33 million albums.

References

www.enya.com

Enya—A Day without Rain, (London, England: International Music Publications, 2000). ISBN 1903692369

F

Falco (Austria)

Johann Holzel was born in Vienna, Austria in 1957. After leaving school at age sixteen, he enrolled at the Music Conservatory in his hometown and joined a succession of guitar-based glam rock bands in both Vienna and West Berlin. In 1977 he changed his name to Falco, after the East German skier Falco Weis-spflog. As a bass player, Falco became increasingly frustrated at the lack of attention he received at gigs; so, when offered a solo contract by the local Gig record label, he readily accepted.

His first release, *Einzelhaft* (1982), was a fairly traditional rock album that included a song that had long been a stage favorite when played by Drahdi-waberl, Falco's previous band. The song, "Ganz Wien," was about the drug scene in Vienna and was banned by local radio stations. The notoriety that the song brought to Falco helped his debut single, another standard rock song called "Der Kommissar," become a bestseller. It took Falco two years to produce a follow-up album, *Junge Romer*; although it was a hit with critics, it flopped in the charts. A year later the album *Falco 3* was released, and it proved to be a major breakthrough. The album employed heavy keyboard riffs behind Falco's mock operatic vocals. One of the songs from the album, "Rock Me Amadeus," was released as a single and reached the top of the charts across the world, becoming the first single by an Austrian artist to reach the top of the charts in Britain and enjoying a four-week stay at #1 in the United States. However, Falco's next single, "Jeanny," shared the same fate as "Ganz Wien"; the lyrics were interpreted to include references to rape and murder, and subsequently the song was banned by radio across the world.

Although Falco was happy with the exposure that such actions brought to his career, his private life was becoming complicated with marital problems and an increasing dependency on alcohol. He released three more albums—*Emotional* (1986), *Wiener Blut* (1988), and *Data de Groove* (1991)—but they showed little sign of musical development and were largely ignored by the public. In 1992

Falco
Pictorialpress Ltd., London, UK

Falco made a comeback in his native country as *Nachtflug* went to #1. The single "Titanic" stayed in the charts for eighteen weeks, and the album of the same name (released at the same time) charted for seventeen weeks, as Falco went on tour again for the first time in six years presenting his mix of heavy guitars and drums and weavier keyboard riffs.

In 1996 Falco decided to leave Austria, as the media and public were becoming more interested in his private life than in his music, and settled in the Dominican Republic, where he began work on a new album in which he explored computerized dance music. Provisionally entitled *Egoist*, the album was never completed because Falco was involved in a car crash and died on February 6, 1998. The material he had been recording was released posthumously as *Out of the Dark* (1998). Various "best of" albums have since been released, as well as books, videos, and some previously unreleased material. A biographical film is planned for future release as fans and musicians across Europe stage conventions and tribute concerts to keep the music of Falco alive.

References
www.falco-calling.com

Farmer, Mylene (France)

Mylene Farmer was born Marie Hélèn Gauthier in Montreal, Canada, on September 12, 1961. After moving to Paris at age seventeen she began to take acting classes. In 1984, when she met songwriter Laurant Boutonnat, she first took singing seriously and changed her name to Farmer (after the American actress Frances Farmer, an alcoholic who had spent much of her life in a mental institution and who later died of cancer). Together with Boutonnat she released a single, "Mamon a Tort," but it failed to chart. It was successful enough for the industry to notice her, however, and within two years she had signed a contract with Polydor. The resultant album, *Cendres de Lune* (1986), was a collection of highly polished, orchestrated pop songs that sold 700,000 copies.

It was as much Farmer's videos as her music that caught the public's eye. Farmer began to introduce her love of acting into her pop career and made videos that became "mini movies" in which she courted notoriety by appearing nude. The overly dramatic videos captured the drama of her songs, which owed much to the French *chanson* style. Popularized by Edith Piaf in the 1930s, *chanson* was a dramatic style of vocal delivery, almost spoken at times, with the singer displaying a theatrical emotion. Farmer's follow-up album, *Ainsi soit-je . . .* (1988), continued her growing popularity as it sold over one and a half million copies, mainly in France but also across mainland Europe. A live album, *En Concert* (1989), followed before she released her biggest-selling album to date *L'autre* (1991). This release sold 1,800,000 copies across Europe and in the French-speaking parts of Canada.

However, by this time Farmer, always wary of the press, found the intrusion on her privacy too much and stayed away from the public eye. The record company released a dance re-mix album of her material in 1992, but she remained silent for the next three years. Her 1995 single, "XXL," barely sold one-tenth as many copies as her previous single (1,360,000 copies for "Désenchantée" in 1991). The album that "XXL" was taken from, *Anamorphosee* (1995) fared better, however, as it broke the million mark and reached the top of the charts in France. Farmer then embarked on a major tour of the country. One of the taped concerts, in the town of Bercy, was released in 1997 as *Live à Bercy*. Also during this period Farmer fulfilled a lifetime ambition and appeared in a feature film, *Giorgino*; but the film had no commercial success and disappeared quickly.

In 1999 Farmer released her first new material in four years with the album *Innamoramento*, which became another top ten hit for her. The record was another hugely theatrical affair using classical string arrangements. As Farmer began another wide-ranging tour of Europe in the following year, the shows were recorded and later released as *Mylènium Tour* (2000). Farmer was then invited to record a song for the movie *Rugrats 2*, set in the French capital, Paris. The single "L'histoire d'une fée c'est . . . " was released in February and reached the French top five. During the summer of 2001 a compilation album, *The Best of Mylene Farmer*, was released and took her again to the top of the French pop charts. New material was released in October when she recorded a duet with English artist Seal. The duet, "Les Mots," was a simple love song and became another top ten hit. Another album, *E*, released in November, was another collection of classy ballads and saw Farmer remain one of the country's most popular women artists.

References

Members.aol.com/arnomf.

Fernandez, Pops (Philippines)

Born Maria Celito Lukban Fernandez on December 12, 1964, in the Philippines, Fernandez began her career in 1981 as a sixteen-year-old. After leaving the International School in Makati as an honor student, she signed with the Octo Arts label and soon released the album *Colours*, which took her into the top ten of the country's charts. Further up-tempo, synthesizer-based pop albums influenced by Western artists such as Madonna and Cyndi Lauper followed, with *Pops* and *Pops Fernandez Live* helping her earn a place among the elite of the Filipino music industry.

In 1986 she married **Martin Nievera**, already a superstar in the country, and the duo embarked on a series of concert tours throughout the country that earned her the title "Concert Queen of the Philippines"; her husband became the "Concert King." The couple also made successful trips to the United States and Canada and were especially successful in Hawaii. As Fernandez continued to release albums throughout the 1980s that heavily featured ballads, among them *Heading for the Top* and *Awesome*, she became a presenter on the TV variety program "Penthouse Live" with her husband. (The position proved useful as she was able to give her friend **Regine Velasquez** valuable exposure that helped her become a star, later dubbed "Asia's Songbird.") Fernandez also became involved in movies, both as actress and producer, but her role as wife and, later, mother of two children began to take precedence. As she retired from the public eye, Nievera's career continued to rise. An album, *The Best of Pops*, was released in the early 1990s and reached the top of the charts as the Filipino public continued to regard Fernandez as one of the biggest stars of the country.

In 1994 she presented her own music program on TV, "Pops on High," while visiting the United States with her husband to play a series of concerts. In 1997 she released the album *Timeless Collection*. Although her career was taking a back seat to that of Nievera, in 1998 a TV show was broadcast of a concert she had performed in Manila under the title "Shine." The following year, after weeks of press speculation, it was announced that Fernandez was divorcing Nievera. Within weeks she began a tour of shopping malls that the public flocked to, sparking a resurgence in her career. In November her tenth album, *Moments*, went gold as it again focused on the lush orchustrated ballads her fans had come to expect. It also re-launched her film career as she appeared in the movie *Linlang*. Although (or because) the film was at the center of controversy in the press owing to its nude scenes, it became one of the highest-grossing films in the history of the Philippines.

In December 1999 Fernandez became spokesperson for a Filipino children's charity and began preparations for a comeback concert. The result was "Shindig" on July 6, 2000. It was Fernandez's first show in over three years and was later broadcast as a TV special. The concert was such a success that "Shindig 2" took place on December 2 and "Shindig 3" on December 22. The taped Christmas concert was released as a live album at the beginning of the new year. Fernandez then appeared in the launch of MTV Philippines and was featured on the station's "Fabulous Divas" show. In February 2001 she appeared with fellow Filipino artists in the group A-Side at a show in Manila that was the biggest concert ever in the Philippines. A month later she appeared to have settled her differences with her former husband, as she appeared on stage during one of Nievera's concerts. Another "Shindig" concert took place in May 2001 in New York, as Fernandez continued to re-establish herself as a major artist in the Philippines. In January 2002, Fernandez began a series of concerts called "Weekend With Pops." These concerts showed her maturing as an artist as she incorporated her quieter songs into the program, leaving aside her more powerful, up-tempo numbers in favor of intimacy. A new album, *The Way I Feel Inside,* was released in June 2002, and made the top ten of the Filipino charts.

References

http://members.tripod.com/pinoyboy 7/

Fin.K.L (South Korea)

Ok Juhyun (b. March 20, 1980), Lee Hyolee (b. May 10, 1979), Sung Yuri (b. March 3, 1981), and Lee Jin (b. March 21, 1980) were a group of teenage girls in South Korea that had no band name and no recorded material. Discovered individually, they were four singers waiting for songs to be written. From the "girl power" origins of the U.K.'s Spice Girls, to the R&B of America's Destiny's Child, Fin.K.L borrowed from other successful groups and forced its own Asian style onto its original songs. The group was first established after Juhyun entered a radio competition for amateur singers in 1998. After hearing her perform cover versions of local pop songs, the organizers decided that she should form the basis of a new band they were creating. The other members were found through auditions. This newly manufactured band needed a name, so a request was posted on music Web sites by the radio competitions organizers, now their managers, for fans to offer ideas. The acronym Fin.K.L came about with the joining of "fine" and "killing liberty," which were offered by fans but had no meaning. The band was now ready to perform, and its debut on May 2, 1998, as part of the MBC music competition, was eagerly awaited by their fans—who knew nothing about them other than the photographs they had seen on the fan club sites. When the band finally released a single, "Blue Rain," it was an upbeat, synthesizer-driven pop number that followed the style of most "girl groups" around the world. "Blue Rain" (also the name of the group's debut album) shot to #1 on the Korean charts and stayed there until it was dislodged by the band's second single, "To My Boyfriend." "Ruby," a third single from the album, also reached #1. Each release sold a million copies.

To take advantage of the massive popularity of Fin.K.L, a second album was produced early in 1999. *White* reproduced the sound and success of the group's previous record, and the singles "Everlasting Love," "Self Esteem," and "Waiting for You" all reached #1. This success set a new chart record for a Korean act. Then, in order to give fans more input into the band, the group members were christened with "colors" (in much the same way that The Spice Girls had nicknames). Juhyun became "black," Hyolee was "red," Yuri was "white," and Jin became "blue." The new names gave rise to a new marketing ploy: Commercials showed the band as "manga"-style cartoon characters, with each member dying her hair her given color. (Manga cartoons, both in comic books and in animated films, are stylized figures that, although identified as Asian, are usually drawn with westernized facial features.) It gave the record company another angle with which to promote the band apart from its music on the growing number of Web sites dedicated to Fin.K.L. In mid-1999 a live album, recorded during a stage show in Seoul, South Korea, was released. Fin.K.L now enjoyed all the trappings of success and appeared on the front covers of magazines across Asia. The group's members also became TV stars not only on pop and "youth" programs but also on commercials.

Still attending university, and with a huge new demand on their time due to their publicity schedule and the demand for them on TV, radio, and for personal appearances, the band members had little time to record new material, so they released a re-mix album, *2.5 Special* (2000). The public showed little sign of tiring of the group, and the record reached the top of the charts. Unwilling to let too much time pass between releases to maintain their fan base, the group released a new album in October 2000. *Now:Fin.K.L volume 3* followed the formula of the group's previous successes and again put the band at the top of the charts. As the band undertook the promotional duties necessary to keep Fin.K.L on the TV screens and in the magazines of Asia, its members continued to combine their education with the commercial promotion of the group. At the beginning of 2002 the band released a video containing some of its biggest chart hits to date including "Blue Rain" and "Waiting For You." In April it was announced that each band member was going to spend time on solo careers. Sung Yuri and Lee Jin are to make their debuts as movie actresses, Lee Hyolee as a TV presenter, and Ok Juhyun is to become a deejay. With the band members insisting that they need time for their own projects, the future of Fin.K.L is in doubt.

References

www.surf.to/finkl

Front 242 (Belgium)

In Brussels, Belgium, in 1980 Daniel Bressanutti was working in a record shop when he released two songs under the name Prothese for a series of compilation albums. Patrick Codenys and Jean-Luc De Meyer were playing small, underground clubs as the band Under Viewer, and Richard Jonckheere was playing with the group Tranik Ind. Although all the musicians knew of each other (inevitable given the size of Belgium's musical underground), it wasn't until the following year that they began to make music together.

In 1981 Bressanutti formed Front 242 with Dirk Bergen. Ostensibly a keyboard/guitar duo, they released an album, *Principles*, that spawned a minor hit in "Body to Body." In the following year Codenys and De Meyer joined the band, and "U Men," a single, was released. (Jonckheere, now calling himself R23, appeared on the record but did not become a full-time member until 1983.) The band's fist gig was at the first Belgian Rhythm 'n' Box Festival in the town of Beursschouwburg in 1982, but within twelve months Bergen left to become a graphic artist and Front 242 settled as a four-piece. By now the band's music had condensed into uncompromising electronic beats that won them admirers in the United States, where they signed with the Wax Trax label in 1984. Back home, in August, the band played its biggest show to date as part of the Seaside Festival in La Panne to 16,000 somewhat dazed Belgians: The band's dress of black leather and cropped hair alongside their habit of performing wearing paramilitary goggles while surrounded by slogans stating "determination," "persistence," "assimilation," and "infiltration" left local audiences stunned and disturbed. The band's severe style was sometimes read as championing a sinister ideology, much the same as Slovenian industrial band **Laibach**. In September the group was back in the United States supporting the hard rock band Ministry and performing to an American audience. With the release of the album *No Comment* in 1985, Front 242 introduced a new musical style that resonated across Europe. At a loss to compare it to anything that had gone before, critics christened Front 242's music Electric Body Music (EBM). The new concept spawned numerous other bands in its wake. EBM was an uncompromising array of fast, hard beats, deep bass, and stabbing keyboards, with little room for lyrics that were used sparingly.

In 1986 the group released *Official Version* and won unanimous praise in the music press; this led to a tour with another band that created dark, electronic music: Depeche Mode. As touring was now beginning to take a vast amount of the band's time, in lieu of new material an album of b-sides, rarities, and hits was released. *Back Catalogue* introduced the band to a wider audience and won front-page coverage on influential music papers around Europe. To build on this new interest, the band spent the first six months of 1989 touring Europe, Japan, and North America. Its growing reputation did not go unnoticed, and in September 1990 the group signed a major label deal with Epic. With a clause in their contract retaining for the band "absolute artistic independence," the album

Tyranny for You found a wider distribution thanks to the influence of the group's new company. Released in over thirty-five countries, the album and its promotion obliged the group to embark on another world tour from March to October 1991. Early in 1992 Bressanutti and Codenys created a multimedia company, Art and Strategy, and released an exhibition of computer-generated graphic art that was shown in New York, Chicago, and Los Angeles.

Front 242 was the only electronic band to play in the 1993 Lollapalooza tour of the United States. Covering thirty-six dates in thirty-one cities, the tour exposed the band to a bigger U.S. audience than the group could have imagined, but its relationship with Epic was deteriorating. With the band unwilling to compromise its music, and Epic requiring more commerciality, a split between the two was inevitable. It finally occurred in 1994 after the release of a live album, *Live Code*. The breakup did nothing to dishearten the band, however, and it released a new album in the same year. *Animals vs. Angels* (1994) showed the band taking an even harder direction with industrial vocals and rhythms. By now the individual members were developing ideas that took them in different directions from the restrictions of the band. R23, always a more peripheral member than the rest, had already performed with the group Revolting Cocks in 1986 and now formed Holigang. In 1995 DeMeyer formed the group Cyber Tec and in the following year released material under the name Cobalt 60. Not to be outdone, Bressanutti and Codenys became the group Grisha Zeme.

The solo projects meant that it was difficult to produce new Front 242 material, so in 1997 an album of old material, re-worked and re-recorded, was released. The album, *Re: Boot*, introduced the band to a new generation of electronic artists, and in the following year a number of bands—including Frontline Assembly, Leather Strip, and Noisex—recorded a tribute album to Front 242. As the group played dates in the United States and Europe, it released a new album, *Sacrilege*. In the same year the band produced a limited-release album, *Modern Angels*, as it took EBM to more extremes.

The band members are still involved with individual projects—R23 playing with the group Latchak; DeMeyer releasing an album, *Cut*, under the name C-Tec; and Bressanutti and Codenys becoming the group MorF. Meanwhile, Front 242 toured and appeared at festivals across Europe during the fall of 2001. Although it is not the biggest-selling group in Belgium, the band created a musical genre that continues to influence new, young bands as well as push back the boundaries of industrial music.

References

www.front242.com
Blissed Out: The Rapture of Rock by Simon Reynolds (London: Serpents Tail, 1990). ISBN 1852421991

G

Garbi, Keti (Greece)

Born in Athens, Greece, on June 8, 1963, Keti Garbi began her singing career at age thirteen. Performing in nightclubs around the city, she and her sister Liana appeared as the Garbi Sisters. They continued to appear together performing traditional Greek songs for the next ten years, until Liana decided to start a family and Keti embarked on a solo career.

Keti's breakthrough took place in 1987 when she was invited to record a song for a compilation album, *Ta Io Dekaria*. Her track, "Saint Tropez," was a lushly produced ballad that gained immediate recognition, and Garbi eventually landed a record contract. Her first album, *Prova* (1989), was an instant success, and Garbi soon became one of the most recognized singers in the country as she toured the nightclub scene. *Prova* was the first of a string of successful releases that included *Gyalia Karfia* (1990), *Entalma Syllhpseos* (1991), and *Toy Feggapioy Anapnoes* (1992). The albums predominantly featured the kind of ballad that she first introduced with "Saint Tropez," backed with simple yet catchy orchestral arrangements. In 1993 Garbi was the Greek entry in the Eurovision Song Contest; her song "Ellada, hora tou fotos" finished in ninth position, the highest placement for a Greek entry in the thirty-year history of the competition.

Also in 1993 she began a fruitful partnership with the Greek songwriter Fivos, the most successful composer in the country for many years. The result was another string of highly successful albums of ballads and more up-tempo pop numbers, *Atofio Xpysafi* (1994), *Apxizo Polemo* (1996), and *Evesthisies* (1997) earned gold and platinum discs as Garbi became a regular on TV, radio, and magazines in Greece and found similar popularity in neighboring Cyprus. She also performed small yet sold-out shows to Greek expatriates in Europe and North America, taking part in in-store record signings for enthusiastic fans.

In between touring and recording, Garbi married fellow singer Dyonisis Schinas in May 1996 and gave birth to Dmitri in November 1999. While she was away from the public eye during her pregnancy, Fivos wrote the songs for a double album, *For Kati*, which Garbi recorded soon thereafter. The album, released in 2000, became her biggest hit to date, going quadruple platinum in both Greece and Cyprus and later named as the best-selling album of the year in Greece. In the same year Garbi appeared on two albums of music by various Greek artists that were made available in North America, *Thalassa Club 2000* and *Oti Kalitero 2000*. Both albums were produced not only for the expatriate audience but also in an attempt to introduce Greek music to the United States and Canada.

Early in 2001 Garbi appeared with another popular Greek singer, **Anna Vissi**, from Cyprus, in a nightclub act, "Fever," that from the first has enjoyed a sell-out run in Athens. Her 2001 album, *Apla ta pragmata,* had a more modern feel through its production, though Garbi still used Greek rhythms to give the album its distinct "Garbi" sound. After promoting the record at home she travelled to the United States and Canada in May 2002 and performed in relatively small clubs for an enthusiastic, mainly ex-patriot audience. The following month Garbi continued with the modernization of her songs with the release of a new single, "Remix 1." The songs were old hits that had been given a modern twist with the introduction of dance beats through samplers and keyboards, and they continued her success in the Greek charts.

References

www.geocities.com/keti_garbi

Glay (Japan)

Future vocalist Teruhiko Kobashi (b. June 8, 1971) first met future guitar player Takuro Kubo (b. May 26, 1971) at elementary school in their hometown of Hakodate, on the southern tip of Japan's northern island, in 1983. By 1987 the friends had formed the basis of what later became the rock band Glay. The fledgling group had its first performance in the winter of 1987 when it played on the same bill as the band Ari. Ari featured a guitarist, Hisashi Tonomura, (b. February 2, 1972) who by the summer of 1989 joined Teru and Takuro. Glay had by now become a popular band in the area but was still looking for more permanent members. In 1990, after the trio graduated from high school, they moved to Tokyo to begin a career in music. Although they played in clubs around the city and its suburbs, there was little sign of success as Glay's brand of Western rock left the Tokyo public singularly unmoved.

A year later the band was still without a permanent drummer or bass player, and the trio was finding it increasingly difficult to play shows. After a concert at The Loft nightclub in Tokyo, they began talking to an old acquaintance from Hakodate, Yoshihito Wagama (b. October 17, 1972), who had long been a fan of the band. In October 1992 he joined as bass player, and the band continued to play in the clubs of Tokyo. A year later, in October 1993, after a show at the Ichikawa Club, the group signed a contract with Extasy Records. In December the band began recording its debut album, *Hai to Daiyamondo*. At the beginning of 1994 the group traveled to Los Angeles and recorded its first single, "Rain," for Platinum Records.

In May 1994 both "Rain" and *Hai to Daiyamondo* were released, followed by another single, "Manatsuno Tobira," in June. The releases had little success as far as the charts were concerned, as the group's brand of Western rock and Japanese lyrics confused the pop fans of the country. The band's reputation was growing among Japan's alternative music fans, however, and in July the group played a show in Shibuya that sold out within two hours of tickets going on sale. By the end of the year the band had secured its own weekly radio show, "FM Rock Kids," on Hokkaido's Air-G station. A single, "Freeze My Love," released in January 1995, gave the band its first chart placing at #19. The album that followed in March, *Speed Pop*, displayed the band's love of fast rock and entered the national charts at #8. During concerts to promote the album, a keyboard player, D.I.E., and a drummer, Toshi Nagai, became semi-permanent members of the band for live shows.

In January 1996, seven years after the formation of the band, the single "Glorious" debuted at #4; *Beat Out!*, released in the following month, entered the Japanese charts at #1. Later in the year the group played its first shows outside Japan—in Iceland, where the band also made a video for the single "Beloved," which reached #3 in August—while still playing sold-out events at home. "Beloved" later won the 29th Gold Request award presented by the Japanese music industry for best single. In November Glay released a new album, *Beloved*, which followed its predecessor in style and success. It reached #1 and also became the group's first million-seller.

After taking their first vacation in over three years, in May 1997 the band released its eleventh single, "Kuchibiru." Used as the theme song to the TV program "Hey! Hey! Hey!—Music Champ," the single entered the chart at #1. Another sold-out tour of Japan followed, and then the new release "However" became the group's third #1 single. In November, 27,000 people attended an open-air concert in a sports stadium that was filmed for use as a video. Meanwhile, the album *Beloved* and the single "However" won best album and best single at the Nippon Record Taishou awards as the band's songwriting matured without losing its raw feel. The group's prolific output continued: In April 1998 Glay released two singles, "Yuuwaku" and "Soul Love," which entered the charts at #1 and #2, respectively. Later in the year the band's fourth major-label album, *Pure Soul*, still unashamedly rock despite the title, also reached the top of the chart, while a videorecording of the arena tour undertaken as the band were now too successful to play club ventures "Pure Soul Tour '98," entered its respective chart at #1.

The band was invited to present more radio shows for stations across the country, enabling the group to remain at the forefront of the nation's music scene. Glay's fifteenth single, released in November 1998, was another #1 for the group, as was its next release, "Winter Again," in February 1999. Still featuring a traditional rock line-up of guitar, bass, and drums, the band released another album, *Heavy Gauge*, in October 1999. In November the band won the Grand Prix at the Yuusen Taishou Awards. The majority of 2000 was taken up with another tour of Japan and the release of three singles, "Happiness," "Mermaid," and "Tomadoi." The band continued its hectic schedule through 2001, releasing "Global Communication" in April, "Stay Tuned" in July, "Hitohira No Jiyuu" in September, and a new album, *One Love*, in November. The album was a collection of Western rock songs that showed little development from the band's earlier records but satisfied the fans. Although the group's most recent releases have struggled to match the success the band enjoyed in the mid and late 1990s, Glay remains one of the most popular bands that Japan has ever produced. The group continues to write and record after eighteen years in the music industry.

References

www.glay.musicpage.com

Go-Betweens, The (Australia)

Robert Forster and Grant McLennan were students at Queensland University, Australia, in 1978 when they discovered a shared passion for films and the New York punk scene. Within a few months the pair recorded two Forster songs, "Karen" and "Lee Remick," printed 500 copies with their own money, and began to distribute them. At this time the U.S. indie label Beserkley was ready to offer the duo a deal, but then it encountered financial difficulties and was unable to sign them. Forster and McLennan then recruited Lindy Morrison on drums, Robert Vickers on bass and later, Amanda Brown on violin/oboe. The group subsequently traveled to London, where it signed with Rough Trade, which released the band's debut album, *Send Me a Lullaby*, in February 1982. The band's gentle, poignant music immediately received positive attention in the music press and began to find a small but highly dedicated following in both Britain and Australia.

The band's second album, *Before Hollywood* (1983), recorded in the small British seaside town of Eastbourne, reflected the whimsical nature of the group's two songwriters. Four more albums followed: *Springhill Fair* (1984), *Liberty Belle and the Black Diamond Express* (1986), *Tallulah* (1987), and *16 Lovers Lane* (1988), all focusing on the trials and tribulations of small-town life. Forster's yearning, cracked vocals conveyed a genuine angst and world-weariness that struck a chord with many young fans. Despite overwhelming critical praise and tours with bands such as REM, the group's singles struggled to find a hold at the top of the charts. The band continued to be seen as an underground phenomenon, as mainstream success eluded it. Ultimately the strain began to show. After twelve years of working together Forster and McLennan decided to explore other musical ventures, and the band split up in 1990.

Forster and McLennan continued to have very successful solo careers that helped the legacy of The Go-Betweens, which as a name began to achieve more success than the group had had while still performing. In fact, the group's former record label, Beggars Banquet, released all The Go-Betweens' previous recordings in 1996 on the growing reputation of a group that had broken up some six years earlier. Although Forster and McLennan continued to perform solo concerts, they performed together on several occasions. In 1999 they decided to tour together. While on the road they made plans to record once more as The Go-Betweens. In 2000 they released *The Friends of Rachel Worth*, and the band toured to promote the new record. The concerts' success showed that The Go-Betweens were still able to write delicate songs that tugged at the heartstrings. In the summer of 2001 both McLennan and Forster toured with their own bands. McLennan was in Australia, and Forster performed in Germany with The Rockin' Boys. The future of the Go-Betweens is unclear, but the group has forged a career of public and critical respect, leaving a legacy of memorable songs that will continue to find new admirers.

References

www.go-betweens.net

The Encyclopaedia of Australian Rock and Pop by Ian McFarlane (St. Leonards: Allen & Unwin, 1999). ISBN 1865080721.

Gray, David (England)

Although David Gray was born in Manchester, England, in 1970 and grew up in Wales, his career owes more to the public of Ireland who first championed the singer/songwriter. After Gray moved to Liverpool to study, he joined his first band; but upon finishing his education, he moved to London and began to concentrate on writing. After securing a record deal in both Europe and America, he released the single "Birds without Wings" in late 1992 and followed it with his debut album, *A Century Ends*, in 1993. The album showed hints of Bob Dylan with Gray's acoustic guitar playing to the forefront but whereas Dylan was more politically motivated Gray's songs were less confrontational and more emotional. A single, "Shine," released from the album, was taken up by Irish deejay Donal Dineen and given heavy radio play on his show; this earned Gray a TV appearance on the music show "No Disco." The acoustic-based, personal nature of his songs touched Irish music fans, and a sold-out show at Whelan's Pub in Dublin helped cement his reputation in Ireland as he embarked on a tour of Europe.

After Gray's second album, *Flesh*, was released in 1994, Gray toured America supporting the British avant-garde rockers Radiohead. The new album carried on in the vein of *A Century Ends,* mixing acoustic numbers with a full band sound. Although it was received favorably by critics, it failed to make the charts. The lack of commercial success led to Gray being dropped by his label, but he soon found a home at EMI. Playing a constant series of gigs, Gray was beginning to find a growing audience—especially in Ireland, where Dineen continued to play his records at every opportunity.

In 1996, Gray released a third album, *Sell, Sell, Sell*, but the content was similar to that of his other albums and was released only in Ireland and the United Kingdom. Shortly thereafter, Gray found himself without a record label for the second time after disappointing sales. Chastened by his experience, he returned to London and began recording a fourth, self-financed album in his apartment. The result was *White Ladder* (1998), a less-produced effort than his previous releases, with the sound of traffic audible in the background as the noise drifted in through Gray's window. Aided by a sell-out tour, the album went straight into the Irish charts, where it remained for over a year. The first single from the album, "This Year's Love," was released at the beginning of 1999. One of five songs that Gray wrote for a British film of the same name, "This Year's Love" refused to leave the Irish singles chart. Gray's next release, "Babylon," was featured at a headline concert at the Galway Big Beat Festival in front of 4,500 fans. The single was a gentle, acoustic guitar based number that relied on a simple guitar riff that underpinned Gray's aching, melancholic vocal performance. As Gray's career appeared to reach a pinnacle in Ireland (*Hot Press* magazine voted him best non-Irish act of 1999), the British public suddenly became aware of him. "Babylon," although similar to Gray's earlier material, entered the British charts in the top five. A tour of America followed, where Gray appeared on the popular TV program "Saturday Night Live."

Gray's apparent appearance from nowhere lead to his receiving best kept secret and best act in cable channel VH1's 1999 poll. As he continued to appear on stages and TV in Europe the *White Ladder* album reached sales of 90,000 in Ireland with its collection of personal, warm songs delivered in Gray's gruff, emotional voice and featuring his unaggressive guitar playing. By January 2000 the album had reached #1 in Ireland but a sold-out tour of the U.K., originally planned for the fall, had to be cancelled when the strain of Gray's increasing work schedule saw him suffer a throat problem.

A year later, in November 2001, a video of an earlier concert was released in the US and the following month another single from the album was released. "Say Hello, Wave Goodbye" was originally a hit in the 1980s for U.K. synth band Soft Cell but Gray's yearning vocal gave the song a new poignancy and depth. As Gray begins preparations for a tour late in 2002, *White Ladder* has spent over eighty weeks on the UK chart and has reached sales of over seven times platinum.

References

www.davidgray.com
David Gray: A Biography by Michael Heatley (London: Omnibus, 2002). ISBN 0711988676

Guano Apes (Germany)

Stefan Ude, a cabinet maker, Dennis Poschwatta, a bank clerk, and Henning Rumenapp, who held various jobs, had been friends since childhood in the German town of Goettingen. Always interested in music, they formed a band to find relief from their daytime occupations. When they decided their band needed a singer, they were introduced to budding artist Sandra Nasic through a friend of Ude's. Thus, the band Guano Apes was born in 1994.

Initially rehearsing in a converted barn owned by Ude's parents, in 1996 the band was one of 1,016 entries in a competition called Local Heroes organized by VIVA TV (a German version of MTV). The band won the competition and, as part of the prize, filmed a video of one of its songs. Then the group entered the studio to record what became its debut single, "Open Your Eyes," with the they had won in competition prize money. The song was a heavy, grunge-like recording, and the subsequent video was played heavily on VIVA TV; as a result, the band won a recording contract with Gun Records. The band then re-entered the studio to record tracks for the album *Proud Like A God*, which sold over 650,000 copies and won the band a German music award for best video.

The band's success was remarkable because the group gained little radio play. The band's melding of rock, rap, scratching, and programming—combined with Nasic's vocals, which veered from quiet, almost spoken delivery to full-on screaming, often within the same song—was wildly different from the pop that most German radio stations were playing. As a result, mainstream radio were reluctant to play the Guano Apes' music, concentrating instead on local pop acts and foreign artists. The fact that Nasic wrote and sang only in English also alienated the band from the music establishment, but Guano Apes was still named as newcomer of the year in 1997 by music magazines *Visions* and *Intro*. The group also won an international contract with BMG.

In November 1997 the band was invited to write a song for the forthcoming European Snowboarding Championships in Fiberbrunn, Austria, which were to take place in September 1998. The song, "Lords of the Boards," became another huge hit in Germany. (By now the media had come to love Guano Apes for its down-to-earth attitude and high-energy live shows, and the group was regularly interviewed in music and lifestyle magazines.) The song also won the band the unwanted reputation of being a snowboarder's "cult" band, which the band members tried to dismiss with the help of a video showing their own ineptitude on snowboards. In the following year the band released "Don't Turn Your Back on Me," from the film *Meschugge*, and with the song's distorted guitars and heavy backbeat the Guano Apes once again topped the charts. During 1999 the group played shows outside continental Europe and released "Proud Like a God" in the United States.

As more singles ("Big in Japan" and "No Speech") followed in 2000, the band continued to play their brand of hard rock to new territories, including Russia and Scandinavia. In October 2000 the band released a DVD of a concert it had played at the Paradiso club in Amsterdam, and the record company began plans to release it as an album in the United States. In January the group released a new single, "Dodel Up!"; in March it released the album *Don't Give Me Names*. Both releases were promoted with a small series of shows in Europe. The album showed little in the way of musical development, but it cemented the band's reputation with its growing number of fans. The band played a small number of concerts across Europe in May 2002, and in June, entered the studio to begin work on a third album due for release later in the year.

References

www.guanoapes.com

Gyllene Tider (Sweden)

In 1977 two eighteen-year-old school friends from Sweden, Per Gessle and Mats Persson, took the stage as a folk style duo calling themselves Grape Rock. Later the same year, brothers Micke and Janne Carlsson joined them, and the newly formed four piece became Gyllene Tider. The group spent the year 1978 sending demos to record companies but was continually rejected until EMI Sweden signed them to a distribution deal. They had yet to play a gig but were the subject of a magazine article in the publication *Expressen*; a staff member who had heard a demo praised this up-and-coming new rock band. In May, Gyllene Tider played its first show in front of fifty friends in the town of Getinge. By the end of the year, however, due to musical and personal differences Gessle decided he wanted Janne Carlsson out of the band, so he himself left to form a new band, Hjartekrossaren. Gessle then invited the other members of Gyllene Tider (except Carlsson) to join his new band. After they did, they changed the name back to Gyllene Tider. Anders Herrlin replaced Carlsson.

Because the band's contract was only for distribution of material, its first recordings had to be self-financed. The single "Billy" was picked up by radio stations, which played the track heavily. EMI liked the song and in August 1979 decided to send the band into the studio in Stockholm to record its debut album.

In January 1980 "Flickorna pa TV 2" was released as a single, and the band took Sweden by storm with its over the top brand of glam rock. In the following month *Gyllene Tider* was released, and the band promoted the album by undertaking a tour that lasted for 111 dates and took all year. By July 1980 the album had sold 50,000 copies, with the single selling 25,000. While the band was on tour, a second single was released: "Nar vi tva blir en" sold 100,000 copies and stayed at #1 for sixteen weeks. On the strength of the single, the band's eponymous debut album returned to the top of the chart for the second time in a year.

Moderna Tider, the band's second album, showed the band taking a harder rock direction, it was released in March 1981 and sold 390,000 copies. Once again, Gyllene Tider took to the road and completed ninety-four dates. By now the band had settled into a routine and headed to London in April 1982 to record its third album at the famous Abbey Road studios. More touring of Sweden began in July before the album *Puls* was released in August. Although each member of the band entered the army in January 1983 as part of their compulsory national service, it did not curtail their music. In February, Gyllene Tider won a Swedish Rockbjornen award for best artist of 1982. In March, Gessle, who was writing continuously, released his eponymous debut solo album in much the same style as Gyllene Tider. The album reached #5 in the chart. In June the band went into the studio to begin work on its next album, *The Heartland Café*.

The Heartland Café differed little musically from the group's previous releases, except that it was the band's first English-language album. After its release in February 1984, it was considered a flop despite selling 45,000 copies. The band then undertook more performance dates and was joined by Marie Fredriksson on backing vocals. (Fredriksson, already known on the Swedish music scene after releasing a number of records, went on to join Gessle in a new band, **Roxette**.) In the latter part of the year Gyllene Tider took a break, allowing Gessle to record his second solo album, *Scener*. Gessle released the record in June 1985, and Gyllene Tider split up soon thereafter.

As Gessle and Fredriksson's group Roxette began to win world acclaim, Gyllene Tider once again came to public notice with a re-released single, "Sommartider," which sold 25,000 copies in Sweden in 1989, followed by a five-CD box set of all Gyllene Tider's material in June 1990. As Roxette continued to conquer the world, a Gyllene Tider greatest hits album, *Halmstads Parlor*, was released in May 1995; it spent twelve weeks at #1 before dropping down a place and spending more than a year on the chart. The following month Gyllene Tider reformed and played a single concert to 15,000 people in Halmstad.

The success of the show persuaded Gessle to take some time off from Roxette. Consequently Gyllene Tider toured again in July and August 1996, including a record-breaking show in Stockholm to over 32,000 people. In 1997 the group released an authorized biography and a live CD of the previous year's concerts. Gyllene Tider appears to have once again split up, and no material is due for release.

References

http://bobylon.caltech.edu/gyllene

H

Hanoi Rocks (Finland)

Formed in the spring of 1980 in Helsinki, Finland, the original line-up of Hanoi Rocks included Michael Monroe, Nasty Suicide, Stefan Piesnack, and Nedo and Peki Sirola. Although the band debuted at the Tavastia Club during the summer of 1980, the group split up soon thereafter. During its brief early career, however, Andy McCoy (b. October 11, 1962), a veteran of Finland's first punk band, Briard, had seen Hanoi Rocks perform and became convinced that it was the group he could take to international stardom, having become frustrated with the small scale of the music scene in Finland. McCoy moved to Stockholm, Sweden, with bass player Sam Yaffa (b. August 4, 1963) and joined Monroe (b. June 17, 1962) and Nasty (b. February 27, 1963 as Jan Stenfors) to re-form Hanoi Rocks. In Stockholm they found drummer Gyp Casino (b. 1961) and began writing material while taking various low-wage jobs to pay for their rehearsal time.

In January 1981 the band began its first tour of Finland and found itself in numerous fistfights, as many Finns were offended by the group's stage outfits of make-up, outrageous haircuts, and colorful leather clothes. Although the band's brand of glam rock found some popularity with the youth of Finland, it wasn't until Seppo Vesterinen became the group's manager that it secured a record deal. Immediately thereafter the band entered a recording studio in Sweden to work on its first album, *Bangkok Shocks, Saigon Shakes, Hanoi Rocks* (1981). Although the record was released only in Finland and Sweden, the band became the subject of intense press interest because it was the first glam-rock band in Finnish music. At the same time, Japanese music fans who had heard the band on the radio took Hanoi Rocks to their hearts and propelled the group to superstar status in Japan.

Then it was decided that the group's second album should be recorded in London in an attempt to broaden the band's appeal in Europe. *Oriental Beat*

Hanoi Rocks
Pictorialpress Ltd., London, UK

(1982) won plaudits from the British rock press, although the respected music magazine *NME* was less than impressed and was offended by the album's cover, which depicted women's breasts covered in paint. As the band's profile grew in England, it undertook a tour. After a show at the Marquee in London, an Englishman called Razzle (Nicholas Dingley) declared he wanted to join the group as drummer. In a curious twist of fate, Casino had already decided to leave the group (he cited his dislike of touring as the reason, although it was widely reported that he did not get along with McCoy). Razzle, however, fit in with the Hanoi Rocks image of "sex, drugs, and rock and roll."

After short tours around Europe, the band traveled east to build on its success in Japan and played to thousands in India. While the group was on tour, an album of b-sides and unreleased material was compiled as *Self-Destruction Blues* (1983). In 1984 the group released another studio album, *Back to Mystery City*, which won the band new fans in Europe and in many parts of Asia. As a result of this new success, a live album was recorded at the Marquee Club in London: *All Those Wasted Years* (1984) was warmly received by the music press. By now the band was beginning to attract the interest of many major companies, and by the summer Hanoi Rocks had signed with CBS.

The band's next album, *Two Steps from the Move* (1984), was recorded in Toronto, Canada. The album's promotional tour in the United States proved a defining period in the band's career. At the beginning of the tour in Syracuse, New York, Monroe broke his ankle and the performances had to be cancelled. To help the band get over the disappointment, former Mötley Crüe vocalist

Vince Neil arranged a party for the group in Los Angeles. While the band was there, Neil took Razzle for a drive in his sports car and lost control, hitting two other cars. Although Razzle was rushed to the hospital, he died on December 6, 1984, taking the heart of the band with him.

The rest of the U.S. tour was immediately cancelled, and the group returned to Finland to play a concert as part of the Europe-A-Go-Go television program. Two concerts in January 1985 were dedicated to the memory of Razzle. Although both events were received with great enthusiasm, Yaffa had already decided to leave the band and was replaced by Rene Berg. The decision to hire Berg proved a disaster, as he tried to impose his will on the resentful group. During a tour of Poland, Berg was forced to keep to the back of the stage, dressed in black with little stage lighting, but the situation was untenable. Monroe left soon thereafter, and then Hanoi Rocks broke up. A live album of the shows in Poland was released with the apt title *Rock and Roll Divorce* in the summer of 1985, followed by a greatest hits compilation, *Decadent, Dangerous, Delicious* (1986). The various members of the band went on to take part in other musical projects with varying degrees of success. Although Hanoi Rocks never reached the heights of stardom envisioned by McCoy, the band broke the mold for Finnish music.

During the summer of 2001 Monroe and McCoy toured together as Hanoi Rocks Revisited. The shows were such a success that in March the following year Hanoi Rocks reformed, although only Monroe and McCoy remained from the original line. A new single, "People Like Me," continued the original Hanoi Rocks sound, albeit with a less glam and more modern rock feel. The single reached #1 in Finland as the band prepared to record a new album.

References

www.hanoi-rocks.net
The Rough Guide to Rock, edited by Jonathan Buckley and Mark Ellingham (London: Rough Guides Ltd., 1996). ISBN 1858282012

Hassan, Nazia (Pakistan)

The career of Nazia Hassan, in partnership with her brother Zoheb, encompassed only three albums between 1980 and 1994, but her impact on Pakistani pop music remains strong today. Born in Pakistan in 1965 and raised in England, Hassan was influenced by the disco scene of the mid-1970s, and she took the influence of the Bee Gees and Abba with her to India. She soon became the first British-Asian girl to make an impact on the Indian film industry, known as "Bollywood."

Hassan was just thirteen years old when she sang "Aap Jaisa Koi Mere Zindagi Mein Aye," taken from a popular Indian film, *Qurbani*. The song blended Western ideas with traditional music and became an anthem for both Pakistani and Indian youth alike. Recorded with India's most successful producer, Biddu, it was billed as the first-ever Asian pop song and stayed at the top of the charts for over a year, a record that still stands. In 1981 the siblings released *Disco Deewane*, which quickly became the biggest-selling album Pakistan had ever experienced. What made the duo so unique in Pakistan was the influence of their English upbringing on their music: A blend of Western disco rhythms and traditional instrumentation was unique in Pakistan at the time.

The fame that Hassan enjoyed also marked a turning point in Pakistani pop history. Until then, stars had been made on TV before turning to a recording career; but Hassan reversed the trend. Although TV was soon to recognize her, her performances were censored due to what was seen as over-sexual movements. She was shown only above the waist, the same censorship that Elvis Presley had experienced almost thirty years earlier in the United States. There were even protests from the press stating that a sister and brother appearing together was immoral, but the public ignored such complaints and the duo's popularity soared.

A second album, *Boom Boom* (1984), continued to promote the duo's East-meets-West blend of music and enjoyed the same success as the duo's previous album. Eight years later a third album, *Camera Camera*, was released; but the record displayed little development beyond the sound that had proved so popular almost a decade earlier, and it enjoyed only modest success. At the same time as the release of the album, it became known that Hassan was ill. In 1995 she underwent an operation for stage one ovarian carcinoma. Although she subsequently appeared to be returning to health, in 1998 she was diagnosed with lung cancer. Although she initially declined chemotherapy, she relented after suffering a relapse but remained ill.

Nazia Hassan died of lung cancer in London on August 13, 2000, at age thirty-five.

References

www.naziahassan.com

Haza, Ofra (Israel)

Born in the slum housing of the Hatikva quarter of Tel Aviv, Israel, on November 19, 1957, Ofra Haza became a national and international star singing the songs of the "Diwan" (a collection of devotional poetry covering religious and secular subjects and performed on festive occasions), loved by the Israeli people as she remained true to her Yemenite roots despite her global fame.

In 1969 actor and director Bezalel Aloni (who would later become Haza's manager) formed the Hatikva theater group in an attempt to give the depressed area an artistic outlet. The twelve-year-old Haza became one of the group's leading singers and remained with it for over seven years. After Haza had spent two years in the Israeli army as part of national service, Aloni, by now her manager, encouraged her to take on stronger roles. In 1979 Haza appeared in the

Ofra Haza
Pictorialpress Ltd., London, UK

movie *Shlagger* singing "Shir Hafrecha," which rose to the top of the national chart. Although at the time many Israeli songwriters refused to work with Haza on account of her "slum" background, Aloni continued to promote her. After the release of *Shlagger*, in 1980 Haza became the Israeli singer of the year. She held the title for the next four years. By then her solo career was gaining momentum. Featuring a unique blend of traditional Yemenite songs with Euro disco beats, *Temptations* (1982), *Songs for Children*, (1982), and *Earth* (1985) all became platinum albums.

In 1983 Haza represented Israel in the Eurovision Song Contest and came in second with the disco-influenced "Hai." It proved to be valuable exposure to a wider audience, but as Haza traveled throughout the country performing for ever-increasing audiences, she was involved in a plane crash from which she escaped unscathed. This period marked the beginning of a new phase in Haza's career, as she released her first international record. A single, "Im Nin Alu," had a more international disco sound and went to #1 in Germany and remained there for nine weeks in 1988. In the same year *Shaday* (1988) sold a million copies. In 1989 Haza won two German Tigra awards for best singer and best song, as well as the New Music Award for best album, presented in New York.

Having already appeared on the soundtrack to the Isabelle Adjani movie *Queen Margot*, she then recorded for the movie *Colors*, starring Sean Penn and Robert Duvall. Other soundtrack appearances followed, with Mickey Rourke's

Wild Orchid and *The Governess* with Minnie Driver. Haza also contributed to Steven Speilberg's *Prince of Egypt*, for which she recorded one song in seventeen different languages. Invited to perform at the Montreux Jazz Festival in 1990, she followed the appearance by accepting a World Music Award in Monte Carlo for bestselling Israeli artist. *Kirya* featured songs in both Hebrew and English and employed both percussion and saxophones to give it a more western focus. The album, featuring Iggy Pop, rose to #1 in the Billboard World Music chart and the album's subtle blend of flowing Israeli rhythms, western drum patterns and Haza's bright vocals won it a Grammy nomination for best album in the World Beat category.

Haza's apparently charmed life took another dramatic turn when in April 1994, during a flight from London to Israel, her plane was hit by lightning but the aircraft landed safely. Later that year she released her first Israeli album in eight years. The album, *My Soul*, continued to feature traditional music with Western sensibilities. Received enthusiastically, it reached #1 and went platinum. In December 1994 Haza was invited by the then Israeli prime minister Yitzhak Rabin to perform at the Nobel Peace Prize ceremony in Oslo, Norway.

In 1997 Haza recorded an eponymous album that became her last original release. After completing numerous concerts around the world and working on movie soundtracks, she returned to Israel. Unknown to the general public, Haza had become ill and was diagnosed as being HIV-positive. Although she had been taking medication at home, she refused to enter a hospital until, in February 2000, she was admitted to the Sheba hospital in Tel Hashomer. TV reporters and fans descended on the hospital with rumors as to the true cause of her illness.

On February 23, 2000, the hospital staff read a statement saying that Haza had died. The nation was plunged into a state of shock. As she lay in state in the Hatikva quarter, thousands of fans filed past her coffin. Haza left a career output of sixteen original albums, all of which became either gold or platinum, and made her Israel's best musical export.

References
http://home.global.co.za/;jvd/ofra.htm

Heroes Del Silencio (Spain)

In 1985 vocalist Enrique Bunbury (b. August 11, 1967) formed a band in the Spanish town of Zaragosa with guitar player Juan Valdivia (b. December 5, 1965) bass player Joaquin Cardiel (b. June 2, 1965) and drummer Pedro Andreu (b. April 5, 1966). The group soon became the best-known band in the area and eventually secured a record deal with EMI. Eighteen months later the group, Heroes Del Silencio, released a mini-album, *Heroe de Leyenda*, it was enough for press and public alike to recognize the talent of the new rock group. An appearance at Madrid's San Isidro festival confirmed the popularity of the group. Although the year 1988 was mostly taken up with a tour of Spain, the band found enough time to record the hard-rocking *El Mar No Cesa*, which achieved platinum status within a few weeks of its release.

A second, full-length album was recorded in 1990, produced by Roxy Music's Phil Manzenera: *Senderos de Traicias* raced up the Spanish charts to #1 and sold over 400,000 copies. Thereafter the band undertook a promotional tour around the country, playing its brand of stadium rock to sold-out shows of ecstatic fans while still remaining unknown outside Spain. In the following year, however, a German promoter organizing a music festival in Berlin, Rock Against Racism, was persuaded to listen to the band and immediately booked it to play alongside Crowded House and English stars Paul Young and Alison Moyet. This was the beginning of massive popularity in Germany for Heroes Del Silencio, which undertook a full German tour that resulted in album sales in excess of 100,000 copies.

As the band booked more tours and festivals throughout Europe in 1991 and 1992, including sharing the bill with Elton John and Bryan Adams in Germany, its success grew and album sales reflected its newfound popularity. By the end of 1992 *Sendros de Traicias* had sold over 800,000 copies in Europe, reaching gold status in Germany and Switzerland. This success continued into Latin America when the group toured Mexico at the end of 1992 and sold 150,000 copies of the album.

At the start of 1993 the band visited England, recording material for its third album, *El Espirito del Vino* (1993). The first single, "Nuestros Nombres," was shown repeatedly on MTV Europe, as was "La Herida" (released in September of the same year), showcasing the band as one of the most popular rock acts in mainland Europe. The group spent the summer playing at festivals around the continent, including appearances with Aerosmith in Finland, which helped the album to reach gold status in Spain, Germany, and Switzerland. The band then undertook a six-week tour to Mexico, Argentina, and Chile. The last months of 1994 were spent in the French Pyrenees, preparing material for a fourth album. Then the group moved to London in January 1995 and began recording under the production eye of Bob Erzin, who was well known for his work with Alice Cooper, Pink Floyd, and Kiss. The resulting album, *Avalancha* (1995), built on the epic rock sound of the band's early recordings. Following its release the band undertook another world tour, and sales of the album were as successful as the group's previous efforts had been.

By the end of 1995 Heroes Del Silencio was becoming increasingly tired with the recording and touring schedule, and the band began to fracture. A fifth album, *Para Siempre* (1996), featured live material with some new songs; but it was the swan song for the band, which split up shortly after the album's release. Another album, *Rarezas*, containing unreleased and hard-to-find material, was released in 1998 by the record company.

References

www.ap-asesores.com/heroes

Hikaru, Utada (Japan)

Born in New York on January 19, 1983, Utada Hikaru is the daughter of a music producer father and a mother, Feiko Fuji, who was a popular singer in Japan but retired owing to a throat injury. As the child of a pop singer and a producer, Hikaru spent most of her childhood in studios watching her parents work. In 1990 her family formed a group, U3, that the seven-year-old Hikaru joined to sing backing vocals while her father sang lead. In 1993 the group released a single, "Star," in the U.S. Soon thereafter, Hikaru took over on lead vocals as the family band changed its name to Cubic U.

Although Hikaru's early releases were all in America, it wasn't until she moved to her parents' native Japan that the public began to notice her. A single, "Close to You," and the album *Precious* were both released under the name Cubic U in 1997. The group's music was based on synthesizer programming and upbeat pop songs. Although these releases garnered interest, Hikaru did not really became an artist of importance until she began to release records under her own name. Although the single "Automatic" was released under her own name, the sound was very much like the music of Cubic U. "Automatic," released in December 1998, broke all Japanese airplay chart records, with the song being played over two hundred times a week. A second single, "Movin' On without You," released in February 1999, confirmed her popularity.

The album that followed in March 1999, *First Love*, displayed a strong grasp of soul and R&B rather than the pop that her family group recorded. The album sold out before it was released on pre-orders from the Japanese public. When reprints were ordered it broke yet more records, selling nearly 5.5 million copies within the first three months of its release. The album also set records for debut album and original album sales. In April, she released a single, "First Love," a slow, dreamy number that focused on Hikaru's childlike vocals. The song later became the theme to weekly TV drama "Majo no Joken." Also in April she had her live concert debut performing in Osaka, Japan and later had her first appearance on TV on the program "Music Station."

Hikaru was fast becoming a major artist in Japan, and by August 1995, *First Love* had sold over 8 million copies. Another single, "Addicted To You," was released in November and it followed the musical direction of her earlier work. Focusing on modern R&B, the song was written by Hikki (as she had become known to her fans) and was given an air of authenticity by the U.S. production team of Jimmy Jam and Terry Lewis. The single sold over a million copies on the day of its release. By the end of the year the singer had sold over 13 million records. In March 2000 Hikaru was named singer of the year at the Golden Disc Awards, as *First Love* and "Automatic" again picked up best album and best single awards.

By the year 2000 Hikaru was attending an American school in Tokyo but was still releasing her brand of R&B/soul-influenced pop. By now she was writing all her own material, and in April the single "Wait And See" reached the top of the Japanese charts. As Hikaru's popularity continued to grow, she announced she was about to embark on an 18-date tour named "Bohemian Summer." Tickets for the shows sold out in 30 minutes. In June, another R&B ballad, "For You," reached the top of the national charts, but as Hikaru continued to write her own material, she retired from the public eye to work on a new album. In October 2001 she was invited to perform on "MTV Unplugged," only the second Japanese artist to do so, after **Chage & Aska**. Hikaru's tenth single, "Travelling," was released in November and once again reached the top of the Japanese charts.

It wasn't until February 2001 that she re appeared in the charts. The single "Can You Keep A Secret?" showed that Hikaru's writing was still maturing and the smooth, keyboard-led song saw her once again in the charts, and won her an MTV video award. The chance to introduce herself to a more international audience offered itself when she appeared on the soundtrack to the Chris Tucker and Jackie Chan movie *Rush Hour 2*. Although it failed to gain her a wider audience, in July she released her second album, *Distance*. The songs on the album were more polished R&B and soul and were again penned by Hikaru.

References

www.toshiba-emi.co.jp/hikki

HIM (Finland)

His Infernal Majesty (HIM) was formed in 1995 when vocalist Ville Valo (b. November 22, 1976) and bass player Mikko Paananem (b. December 19, 1974), already best friends, joined up with guitarist Mikko Lindström (b. August 12, 1976). Influenced by the British heavy metal and goth scene, the band released its debut single in 1996. The single, "666 Ways to Love," caused an immediate stir in the local music scene. HIM's habit of dressing in black leather, sporting tattoos and heavy make-up, had been pioneered in Finland in the 1980s by fellow countrymen in the group **Hanoi Rocks**, but HIM brought a new satanic image to the music. Although satanic imagery had long been used in the British metal scene with bands such as Iron Maiden and Black Sabbath, it was something new among Finnish bands. In fact, it gave HIM a notoriety that won the group valuable publicity in the country's music magazines. Before long, Paananem and Lindström adopted the pseudonyms Migé Amour and Lily Lazer to add extra glamour, while Valo dropped the use of his Christian name and soon became the image of the band, emphasizing his androgynous looks (similar to those of Marc Bolan and David Bowie).

In October 1996 the band released a cover version of Chris Isaac's "Wicked Game" that earned them a record contract with BMG. By now the drummer Juhana Rantala had joined the group, though he did not become a permanent member. Twelve months later the band released its first single for BMG: "When Love and Death Embrace" (1997), a dark, guitar-laden song about the similarities between love and death, entered the top ten and prepared the Finnish public for the release of the band's debut album, *Greatest Lovesongs Vol. 666* (1997).

The record was a collection of traditional heavy rock songs with a slight tongue-in-cheek feel that was reflected in the album's title. The record went gold across Scandinavia and was named best debut album in end-of-year magazine polls. In January 1998 the band was presented an Emma award as newcomer of the year.

In February 1998 HIM released a second single for BMG, "Sweet Six Six Six," which also reached the top ten. The band then toured Scandinavia and Europe, securing a huge fan base in Germany, where the group began to become even more popular than it was at home. Feeling that its live set was missing some musical "color," the group recruited Jussi Salminen (b. September 26, 1972) from the rock band Mary Ann to play keyboards and promptly renamed him Zoltan Pluto. In July 1999 the band released a new single, "Poison Girl," that reached the top end of the charts. But in November the group released a song that, although a typically hard rock number, took them further into the mainstream of Scandinavian music: Asked to provide a song for the soundtrack to the film *The 13th Floor*, directed by Roland Emmerich (*Independence Day; Godzilla*), the group released "Join Me." The song won a limited release in Scandinavia but nonetheless reached #1 in Finland and Germany.

As the band began to record its second album, Rantala left the group and HIM began writing songs backed by a drum machine. After the album was recorded in this manner and was ready for release, a new drummer joined the ranks: Mikko Karppinen (b. February 8, 1971), who was well known on the Finnish music scene as drummer with the metal band Kyyria. After he joined HIM and was given the name Gas Lipstick, the band decided to re-record the album with Karppinen playing the drums. The result was *Razorblade Romance* (2000). The album soon reached #1 not only in Finland but also in Germany, where the group was due to tour. On learning that all the German venues had sold out, the promoters moved the shows to bigger arenas, which similarly all sold out.

A single, "Right Here in My Arms" (2000), continued HIM's chart success as the group began to appear on TV programs across Europe. Another single, "Pretending," was released in July, and then a third album, *Deep Shadows and Brilliant Highlights*, released in August, reached the top of the charts. The album featured more hard rock and the band's satanic imagery. As the band toured Scandinavia in October another single, "Gone with the Sin," also reached the top ten in Scandinavia and Germany. Although HIM has conquered the Scandinavian and German markets, the band has struggled to achieve major success elsewhere. Nonetheless, the record company BMG continues to promote the band across Europe and in the United States.

In January 2002, HIM was nominated for best international alternative rock band at the German Echo awards, alongside Linkin Park and Limp Bizkit. Although they failed to win, the following month the band released its first UK album, *Deep Shadows and Brilliant Highlights*. The record reflected the band's heavy guitar play and Valo's emotionally charged vocals, and made the top fifty in the UK charts. During the summer and fall of 2002 the band played a number of festivals across Europe.

References

www.heartagram.com

"Market Focus in Finland," *Audience* (February 2001), p. 22. London: Miracle Publishing Ltd.

Hintjens, Arno (Belgium)

Born on May 21, 1949 in Ostend, Belgium, Arno Hintjens was raised by his grandmother and two aunts, who exposed the future singer to artists such as Jean Cocteau and Juliette Greco. The smoky, chanson style of such singers later influenced much of the music Hintjens made during his career. At age eighteen Hintjens was working as a chef in his hometown but had begun to write music on his acoustic guitar, and in 1970 he placed second in a folk contest. Three years later he formed a band, Freckle Face, and released a self-produced album. Two more albums of pop folk and blues–influenced rock followed, *Who Cares* (1975) and *Plat du Jour* (1978), before Freckle Face broke up. Soon thereafter the band changed its name to TC Matic and released four albums between 1981 and 1985 (*T.C. Matic, l'Apache, Choco*, and *Ye Ye*). Although the band's albums displayed the same style of pop-rock backed by a traditional instrumentation, the group found a growing fan base throughout the Low Countries and in Germany. During this time the band appeared on the most popular music shows in Holland ("Top Pop") and Germany ("Rockpalast").

In 1980 Hintjens wrote the music for the film *Le Concert d'Un Homme Seul*, and by 1982 the band was headlining Belgium's biggest rock festival. Although the group toured with British rock act Simple Minds in 1985, Hintjens soon was invited to play Faust on stage at the Opera de Paris. In fact, his solo projects were beginning to intrude on the band's schedule. The group was also feeling frustrated by the fact that despite being the most popular group in Belgium it was unable to generate interest in a wider circle. In 1986 Hintjens left TC Matic and released his first solo album, *Arno*, which was based more on folk than on rock and showed a maturing songwriter. More film work followed, delaying the release of his second album, *Charlatan*, until 1988. On this album Hintjens sang in English for the first time.

After the release of *Ratata* in 1990, Hintjens won the first of five consecutive awards for singer of the year presented by the Belgian Humo Pop poll. He then went to Nashville, Tennessee, in a bid to introduce an authentic country feel to his fourth album, *Idiots Savants* (1993). This album went gold in his home country, and subsequently both Belgian and French TV devoted programs to his career. In 1994 Hintjens embarked on an 82-date tour of Europe, including many festivals, and also wrote the music for eight films.

Hintjens then retreated to rural France to work on his next album, *Water* (1994), which was recorded in a mobile studio. The experience of living in France influenced his next work, *Arno à la Français* (1995), which was sung in the chanson style. The album reflected his earliest influences in Ostend listening to chanson while growing up in the care of his aunts, and it propelled

Hintjens to major artist status in France, where he undertook a sell-out tour to promote the record. In 1996 Hintjens was awarded the Prix de la Press d'Ostende for services to his hometown and was asked to write the Flemish translation of the songs to Walt Disney's *Toy Story*. As a result of this collaboration, Hintjens released his first album in the United States. The outcome, *Give Me the Gift* (1997), was a compilation of his earlier successful songs. In 1998 Hintjens formed a band for the third time in his career: Charles and the White Trash European Blues Connection. This group released an eponymous album of traditional blues in the same year. After releasing *Le European Cowboy* (1999), the band spent the next twelve months touring Europe. Hintjens appeared solo at a concert in support of Amnesty International in November 2000, before preparing new projects for future release. In November 2000 Hintjens released *The Best Of,* which charted the singer's career from the inception of TC Matic. By February 2002 an album of new material, *Charles Ernest,* had reached the French top ten as Hintjens continued with his blend of folk, blues and rock.

References

www.arno.be

Arno: White Ass European Cowboy by Arno Hintjens (Ghent: Imschoot Vitgevers, 1999). ISBN

I

I Mother Earth (Canada)

Brothers Jagori and Christian Tanna had been playing guitar and drums, respectively, for many years when, in 1990, a mutual friend introduced them to singer Edwin Gordon. As a result, the prototype I Mother Earth began jamming in various rehearsal rooms and studios in Toronto, Canada. After finding a temporary bass player, the group began to play small club dates in the Toronto area; the band's progressive-rock, slightly psychedelic style soon earned it a small but dedicated following, which caught the attention of many record labels. After signing with EMI in Canada and Capitol in the United States, the band began to look for a new permanent bassist and chose Bruce Gordon (b. August 8, 1968), no relation to Edwin. Although the band had a record deal, it was another two years before the group felt they had enough quality material and entered the studio to record its debut album. After *Dig* was released in the summer of 1993, the band embarked on a tour that took up the better part of the next three years with engagements all over North America and Europe. As a result of the group's heavy touring schedule, *Dig* sold in excess of 100,000 copies, brought the band a platinum record, and won the Canadian Juno award for best hard rock album.

During a break in its hectic touring schedule, the band entered the studio to begin work on its second album, *Scenery and Fish* (1996). Although by now the band was playing arena-sized venues in its home country, problems were beginning to show. Edwin had never contributed material to I Mother Earth and in January 1997 was reported as saying, "If my creative input isn't . . . harnessed, then I have no reason to be here." Meanwhile the album continued to sell well, eventually reaching 200,000 copies and earning the band a double platinum award, as well as two CASBY awards for favorite new release and favorite new song (for the sprawling guitar heavy "One More Astronaut"). The band also continued to tour sold-out arenas.

Just as the group was reaching its commercial peak, however, Edwin announced he was leaving to begin a solo career. But the band was under contract to play a tour, so Edwin honored the shows amid speculation that they might be the last I Mother Earth gigs. Now thousands of prospective singers sent demo tapes to the band, which had announced it was looking for a new singer. In November 1997 the group found a replacement for the popular Edwin: Brian Byrne, a native of Newfoundland, who had been playing in various rock bands for years around the clubs of Canada. At twenty-four years of age he was ten years younger than the other members of I Mother Earth, but the band was certain he was the right man for the job. During this period, despite becoming one of the biggest acts in Canada, the group had no record contract. The band soon signed with Universal, after which it prepared to make its debut with the new singer. Byrne, to date, had played only club gigs; now he learned that his first show with the new band was to be in front of 25,000 people at the Summersault Festival in Toronto in 1998. He was accepted from the beginning by the band's fans, and the group soon found itself once again in the studio recording what became its third album, *Blue Green Orange* (1999).

The record followed the progressive style of the band's earlier releases but failed to match the previous albums' sales (although it still managed a more-than-respectable gold disc). I Mother Earth then began a lengthy promotional tour, during which, in the summer of 2000, it was booked on the same Calgary Stampede festival bill as its former singer, Edwin Gordon. Although a series of less-than-complimentary interviews from both sides found their way into the music press, in the end both artists were equally well received and the feud appeared to be settled. Both I Mother Earth and Edwin Gordon continue to record new material in Canada. In March 2001 EMI released a compilation album charting the band's career with Edwin as singer. *Earth, Sky & Everything Between* was a mix of studio tracks that featured lengthy improvised jamming and acoustic unplugged numbers, and sold only to dedicated I Mother Earth fans.

References

www.imotherearth.com

J

Jam, The (England)

By the time The Jam split up in 1982, it was arguably the biggest band in Britain. The group helped re-introduce the Mod fashion (three-button suits, ties, and short hair; riding Lambretta and Vesper scooters), which had been massively popular in Britain in the mid-1960s, to the nation's youth. The group's popularity spawned numerous bands such as Secret Affair, Purple Hearts, and The Chords. Many of these bands followed The Jam's lead in writing songs concerned with social commentary and dressing in Mod fashions. Although many of these bands split up as the fashion faded, The Jam became increasingly popular with each subsequent release.

Guitar player **Paul Weller** (b. May 25, 1958) had known bassist Bruce Foxton (b. September 1, 1955) and drummer Rick Buckler (b. December 6, 1955) at school in Woking, a town on the outskirts of London, England. Although Weller named his fledgling group The Jam in 1973, it went through several line-ups before settling as a trio. The group performed regularly in the pubs and clubs of Woking and the surrounding areas, playing a mix of Weller originals and 1960s soul/R&B covers. With the punk explosion in London in 1976, the band began to get more shows in the capital and Weller began to write songs with more youthful themes, keeping with the punk ideal. The group became firmly established as a new band in the punk/new wave scene.

In 1977 the band signed with Polydor Records, and its first single, "In the City," released in April, reached #40 on the charts. In the following month the group's debut album, also called *In the City*, reached #20 with a collection of fast, guitar-driven, three-minute songs focusing on Weller's bitter, spiteful lyrics. As the band began to tour the country, Weller continued to write; by November of the same year the band's second album, *This Is the Modern World*, had reached #22. The critics, however, argued that the band had lost its creative edge as the album's melodies and arrangements showed no progression from its

The Jam
Pictorialpress Ltd., London, UK

debut. Slightly chastened by the reviews, and following an ill-advised tour of the United States supporting rock band Blue Öyster Cult in which the young British Mods found little empathy from the U.S. group's fans, the band returned to the studio to work on a third album. Although the group had already recorded a number of songs, the band was not happy with the results and decided to start again. The result was *All Mod Cons* (1978). The first single off the album, a double a-side of "A Bomb in Wardour Street" and "David Watts" (a cover of a song by U.K. band The Kinks), reached #25. The album was a pared-down affair focusing on the three instrumentalists. In the following month a second single from the album, "Down in the Tubestation at Midnight," became the group's highest ranking release to date at #15, and the album reached #6.

The band now established a routine of touring, TV and press promotion, and recording. Although the group toured Europe and briefly visited the United States, the critics' and public's perception of its "Englishness" made it difficult for audiences to find empathy with The Jam. Indeed, the group's Mod clothing and Weller's lyrics dealing with the problems of being young in Britain under the newly elected, right-wing Conservative government of Margaret Thatcher were hard for foreign audiences to relate to.

After two more singles, "Strange Town" and "When You're Young," reached #15 and #17, respectively, the band's fourth album, *Setting Sons* (1979), reached #4. The release was initially meant to be a "concept" album concerning the adventures of a group of friends, but when the songs displayed little the-matic continuity, Weller dropped the idea. Ultimately the songs on *Setting Sons* were very different from the group's early work, containing many guitar over-dubs and a string section to create a dense-sounding work. The release also gave The Jam its first U.S. chart placing when the album entered at #137.

At the time, the U.K. youth scene was going through a revival of the Mod movement, spurred by the release of The Who's movie *Quadrophenia* (based on the band's album of the same name) about The Who's early years as leaders of the London Mod movement. As a result, The Jam suddenly found that its image was fashionable, and a single from *Setting Sons*, "The Eton Rifles," reached #3.

In February 1980 "Going Underground" entered the chart at #1, as did the follow-up, "Start!" The band, still touring heavily, now had a large following in Japan, but audiences in the United States and most of Europe remained unin-terested. Two singles released in 1981, "Funeral Pyre" and "Absolute Begin-ners," both reached #4 in the UK; the latter employed a horn section as Weller tried to expand beyond The Jam's rigid three-piece formula. At the end of the year, in November, the group released *Sound Affects*, which went to # 2 in the United Kingdom and #72 in the United States. The album's sparse sound showed a marked difference musically from *Setting Sons*, although the brief ad-dition of a horn section and keyboards provided a hint of what was to come. In February 1982 another double a-side was released; from this album the singles "Town Called Malice" and "Precious" featured the horn section and keyboards that had briefly appeared on *Setting Sons* in a more prominent role entered the chart at #1. The band was invited to perform both songs on the same edition of the music show "Top of the Pops," the first time this had ever happened on the show. The next month *The Gift* was released and became The Jam's first #1 album.

Although the band was routinely hailed as the best in Britain by the music press, in the summer of 1982 Weller told Foxton and Buckler that he was leav-ing, effectively splitting the group up. The decision was meant to be secret, but the press caught wind of it and began to release articles to that effect. In the end, the band issued a statement confirming its fans' worst fears. A single, "Beat Surrender," was released in November and entered the charts at the top. A live compilation album released in the following month, *Dig the New Breed*, reached #2 as the band played its last tour, ending with a show in Brighton (the Mods' spiritual home) just before Christmas 1982. An album covering the best of the band's material, *Snap!*, was released in September 1983, as were the band's previous fifteen singles, all of which reached the top forty.

Thereafter Weller formed a new group, The Style Council, and had a number of hit singles and albums before embarking on a successful solo career in the early 1990s. Foxton released a single, "Freak," that was a minor hit. He cur-rently plays with the Irish punk group Stiff Little Fingers. Buckler formed the group Time UK, but the band never had any success.

In 1998 a boxed set, *Direction, Reaction, Creation*, was released containing all the band's albums and many tracks that had never been released. In the fol-lowing year *Fire and Skill*, an album of songs by The Jam recorded by artists such as Oasis, Garbage, and The Beastie Boys, reached the top ten. On April 29, 2002 the band's first single "In The City" was re-released to celebrate 25 years since the inception of The Jam, and it climbed into the UK's top thirty.

References

www.thejam.org
The Jam: A Beat Concerto by Paolo Hewitt (Omnibus Press). ISBN 071190393X

Jassi (India)

Jasbir "Jassi" Gurdaspuria was born in the small village of Dalia Mirjanpur in the Gurdaspur region of India on February 7, 1970. Although Jassi was exposed to Punjabi classical music via the radio during his youth, he began his adult life as an engineer. However, after he came under the tutelage of the well-known folk singer Puran Shah Koti a career for him in music seemed possible, and he began training in the theater, where he remained for two years. He eventually gained a master's degree in classical vocal music from the Apeejay College of Fine Arts. The performances Jassi gave while in the theater won him notices from critics; but he had a desire to promote the language and art of the Punjab, and a commercial record was the best way to do so. After a short stint in the Punjabi police department, Jassi was chosen to contribute to a 1993 compilation album featuring some of the most popular performers of the day. His song "Channa ve teri Channani" became the most popular one on the album and captured the attention of both the press and the radio. As a result he recorded an album that made him one of India's biggest stars.

The album, *Dil Le Gayee* (1994), a collection of songs that mainly featured traditional arrangements and instrumentation, was released to unanimous praise. The album won Jassi three Zee Sangeet awards for best album, best track, and best lyrics (the latter two for the single "Dil Le Gayee Kuri Gujrat Di," a paean to a Gujrati girl.) Jassi's career continued to grow as his live performances generated headlines in the regional newspapers such as "mind-boggling" and "spirit-soaring" due to his energetic and singular dance routines. With his newfound fame Jassi, always capable of giving his own forthright views (he has called Pakistan a "terrorist state"), began to criticize other singers for putting style before content. Shortly thereafter he played to 12,000 fans at the Gymkhana Club in Jalandhar.

In the years following his initial success, Jassi was invited on several occasions to star in "Bollywood" movies (the melodramatic musicals that the Indian film industry releases in vast numbers). Although a career in Bollywood would have cemented Jassi's fame across the country, he acted only sporadically, preferring to concentrate on his ambition to expose the Indian public to the traditions of the Punjab through his modern interpretation of the music. It wasn't until 1999 that Jassi released a second album, *Kudi Kudi*. Although still reflecting the Punjabi musical style, the album introduced sampled and synthesized bass and drum sounds that gave the tracks a heavy downbeat while also featuring Jassi's traditional Punjabi vocal delivery. Although a studio recording, the album caught the energy of his live performances. The Indian public, having been denied any new material from Jassi for nearly six years, bought millions of copies as he remained one of the biggest attractions in the country. Later in the year he appeared at the New Moon celebrations in Gautuma before performing outside of India for the first time with shows in England and Dubai and, in April 2000, the United States. In 2001 a new album, *Nishani Pyar Di,* featured songs that were more classically Punjabi based, as he moved away from his more pop-oriented sound. More recently, in 2002, an album titled *Greatest Hits—Jassi* was released that gave an overview of his career to date.

References

www.jasbirjassi.com

Junoon (Pakistan)

Salman Ahmad was a veteran of Pakistan's first pop rock band, Vital Signs, when he began looking for other musicians to collaborate with. At the same time Ali Azmat, a vocalist in the local band Jupitor, was beginning to feel frustrated at what he perceived as a lack of ambition on the part of his group. After the two musicians met, it seemed inevitable that they would begin working together. Inviting musician Nusrat Hussain to complete the line-up, the group, named Junoon, blended guitars with traditional instruments on its debut, self-titled album, released in 1991.

The band struggled to gain recognition with their Western take on Pakistani pop music, but then the group had a stroke of luck when Ahmad began acting in a TV drama, *Aahat*. Junoon provided the soundtrack for the series, and a single, "Chori, Chori," began to be shown on the Music Channel TV show. Meanwhile the band played shows in Pakistan and India but still had no breakthrough. In 1992 Ahmad visited New York, where he had spent some time in college, and met up with an old friend, Brian O'Connel. Soon O'Connel was invited to join the band as bassist and he moved to Pakistan to take the place of Hussain, who moved on to solo projects.

After the release of its second album, *Talaash* (1993), the band released a video for the single "Ne Heeray" but still found it difficult to establish itself. After two years of playing low-key shows in small venues, the group issued the album *Inquilaab* in 1995. Now the band began to gain recognition from the Pakistani public owing to the growing number of live performances the group undertook. In December 1996 Junoon released the single "Ehtesaab," a song that was heavily critical of the politics of the country. The subsequent video was banned by Pakistan's state TV on the grounds that it would destabilize the country on the eve of national elections. The single was a major hit. In the following year the Cricket World Cup visited Pakistan, and the country was united in support of the national team, which was the cup holder. Junoon capitalized on the mood of the country and released the top five record *Jazba Junoon*, an album of uplifting pop/rock songs that honored the national cricket team. Later in 1997 the "best of" album *KashmaKash* was released; it quickly hit the top spot in Pakistan's charts.

By the end of 1997 the band's mix of Western instrumentation (guitars, bass, drums) and the rhythms and instrumentation of their native East had won them enough admirers to convince EMI to sign the group. The band's debut album for its new company, *Azadi*, confirmed it as one of the most popular rock bands not only in Pakistan but in neighboring India as well. It was the first of the group's albums to be released in India. The single "Sayonee" reached #1 in all the charts in Asia and the Middle East and stayed there for two months. During a tour of India in 1998 the band played to audiences of 50,000 at each show. However, the huge success Junoon was experiencing did not mellow the band's political views: After the nuclear testing of 1998 by the Pakistani government, the band criticized the arms race between Pakistan and India. The Pakistani government continued to ban the group's music, although Junoon was allowed to play "private" shows in schools and colleges (a loophole that members of the public were happy to take advantage of). The ban followed a controversial recording the band had made of Pakistan's national anthem. Pakistan's minister of culture later charged the group with making comments amounting to sedition and treason.

In November 1999 the band performed a concert with Sting and Def Leppard as it won the award for best international group at India's Channel V Music Awards in New Delhi following the release of the album *Parvaaz* (1999). In the United Kingdom, Junoon was the closing act at each of the three nights of the BBC's Mega Mela festival in London, celebrating the music of Asia. In the same month the band won a UNESCO award for outstanding achievements in music and in promoting peace. In May 2001 Junoon took part in a benefit concert, United for Gujarat, in New Delhi to raise money for the victims of an earthquake that had devastated that part of the country earlier in the year. As the group's profile in the United States continued to grow, it became the subject of a VH1 documentary, "Islamabad Rock City." In October 2001 the band organized a benefit concert for Afghan refugees before launching the United for Peace initiative. Junoon then played shows in the United States in November as it continued to promote charitable causes. In 2002 the band released a new album, *Daur–e–Junoon,* that contained live material as well as new songs. The band continued to champion its causes when, in May 2002, it played the "Fight for Literacy" concert in Pakistan.

References

www.junoon.com

K

Kelly, Paul (Australia)

Paul Kelly was born in Adelaide on the southern coast of Australia on January 13, 1955. Initially a trumpet player, after leaving school he learned guitar and made his debut at age nineteen in the town of Hobart, Tasmania. After two years he returned to the mainland and lived in Melbourne, where he formed his first band, The Dots. This group was part of the growing Australian punk scene, and in 1979 it released its first single, "Recognition." A series of singles followed, as did two albums, *Talk* (1981) and *Manila* (1982), both of which were guitar-led and contained fast, three minute punk explosions before the band split up.

Kelly remained silent as a recording artist for the next three years. Then, in 1985, he released "From St. Kilda to King's Cross." The single, from the album *Post*, 1998, introduced a more personal songwriting style that lead to Kelly, in 1993, being described as "[Australia's] best songwriter and one of our finest poets." In 1998 Kelly released a double album, *Gossip*, that was named Australian record of the year by the music press. The album became his first release in the United States in 1987; it was warmly received by critics but was largely ignored by the public.

His third solo album, *Under the Sun*, was released in 1987 as Kelly toured the country performing to increasingly appreciative audiences. In 1988 he released three singles: "Forty Miles to Saturday Night," "Don't Stand So Close to the Window," and "Dumb Things." Kelly continued to write about life in the small towns and big cities of Australia, displaying empathetic feelings for his subjects that his fans could identify with. Now his popularity rose. Each release became more successful than the previous one as his music settled comfortably in the higher reaches of the charts of Australia and New Zealand. Kelly then toured Europe, Asia, and the United States, but his songs, heavily indebted to Australian culture, found few fans abroad.

In 1989 he released *So Much Water, So Close to Home*. The album was produced by Scott Litt, who had worked extensively with REM, but if the collaboration was meant to improve Kelly's chances of mainstream success in the United States, it did little to that effect (although the album was an expected hit in his home country). Kelly released two more albums in 1991 and 1992, *Comedy* and *Hidden Things*, respectively. Also in 1992 he was invited to act in and write songs for a play, "Funerals and Services," about racial tensions between Aborigines and whites in small-town Australia. The production opened at the Adelaide Festival to warm reviews and played the following year at the Melbourne Festival.

In 1993 Kelly began to feel a need to experience a different way of life. He moved to Los Angeles for nine months, writing new material and performing as a solo artist in the clubs of the city. Toward the end of the year he was invited to record the soundtrack to a TV series that was being planned by the Australian Broadcasting Company (ABC). The music to *Seven Deadly Sins* became a collaboration with fellow Australian singer **Deborah Conway**. In 1996 he began work on the soundtrack for the film *Everynight . . . Everynight*. It left him little time to write new songs for himself, and *Live at the Continental and the Esplanade,* was released. As Kelly completed the soundtrack, a live album, a retrospective of his work, *Songs from the South* (1997), containing highlights from his fifteen-year solo career, entered the national charts. An album of new material followed, but the songs on *Words and Music* (1998) continued Kelly's folk leanings. It was *Smoke*, released the following year, that saw a more dramatic change in style. He recorded the album with fellow Australians Uncle Bill, and featured bluegrass, made popular in the American South. *Professor Ratbaggy*, the album, was an eclectic mix of dub reggae, funk, and R&B that confused some fans but displayed Kelly's ease with different musical styles. In October 2000 he released the single "Roll over Summer," where he returned to his usual style of storytelling over a guitar lead.

After touring with Bob Dylan in Australia in March 2001, and as a prelude to the release of a new album, Kelly released "Somewhere in the City" in July 2001. The single hit the top ten of the Australian chart, and the album, *Nothing But a Dream*, returned him to the top ten of the album charts. Another single taken from the album *Love Is the Law* was released at the same time as the movie *Lantana*, for which Kelly wrote the soundtrack. In November he undertook a European tour.

In May 2002 an album of Kelly material, *The Woman at the Well*, was released. The songs on the album were all performed by women artists from Australia and New Zealand, and included contributions from Deborah Conway and **Bic Runga**.

References

www.paulkelly.com.au
The Encyclopaedia of Australian Rock and Pop 1999 by Ian McFarlane (St. Leonards: Allen & Unwin, 1999). ISBN 1865080721

Kirkorov, Philip (Russia)

Born to a Bulgarian father and Russian mother in 1970, Philip Kirkorov followed his father, a singer, on tour from the age of five. Initially turned down by a theatrical institute for "a lack of ability," Kirkorov first took to the stage in 1985 at the Gnesins Music School in Moscow. Later that year he made his TV debut. He continued to study at the music school until 1987, when he went with the Leningrad Music Hall to perform in East Berlin, at the time still part of Communist Europe. In 1988 he visited Mongolia, performing for the Soviet army, where he received an invitation from the poet Ilya Reznik to take part in the "Christmas Meetings," a series of concerts that took Kirkorov away from the theater and into show business. During these shows he met the late Leonid Derbenev, who wrote Kirkorov's breakthrough material: "You, You, You," "Sky and Earth," "Atlantis," and "At Night and in Daytime." These works were almost operatic. During 1989 Kirkorov toured Australia and Germany as part of the Alla Pugacheva Theatre, but subsequently he left the troupe, promising to return after he had become "a better performer."

As his career as a solo performer began in 1990, Kirkorov won the Hit '90 competition in St. Petersburg with "Sky and Earth," which quickly made him a star in Russia. The video that accompanied "Atlantis" was voted the best in 1992, and the album *You, You, You* (1992) sold millions of copies. By now Kirkorov had introduced a highly theatrical style into his work, combining outrageous stage outfits with orchestral backing for his ballads and up-tempo numbers based on traditional Russian folk themes. By 1992 he had toured the United States, Canada, and Israel but was beginning to be the target of press campaigns questioning his sexuality, fueled by stories from people involved in Kirkorov's past. If the stories were meant to jeopardize his career, they failed: Kirkorov won the Ovatsiya prize as singer of the year in 1993. In the following year he married **Alla Pugacheva** in an attempt (according to the press) to deflect attention from the stories of his past.

In 1995 Kirkorov received two more Ovatsiya prizes, best program (tour) and best singer. At the end of the year he played nine sold-out shows at Moscow's Variety House promoting the album *The Best Favorites Only for You* (1995). In 1996 the album won him a golden statuette at the World Music Awards in Monte Carlo for best circulation of any album.

Indisputably the major star of Russian pop music, Kirkorov had a penchant for flamboyant stage outfits that was becoming as famous as his music. In 1997 he played at Madison Square Garden, a show that sold out three weeks in advance and for which tickets were exchanged for $200 on the black market. He entered the arena that night in a replica of the Trojan horse; his stage outfit consisted of purple high-heel boots, a leather corset trimmed in green rhinestones and silver fringe, a yellow silk cape, and long feathers as he flew over the audience on cables. In 1998, Russian TV broadcast three hours of Kirkorov's concerts from the same year to an audience of 50 million. In 2000, Kirkorov released the first Spanish-language album ever recorded by a Russian, *Sueño de*

Amor, which he debuted at the FAMA awards in New York in January. The album was such a hit that he was invited to perform on the popular Latin American TV show "Sábado Gigante" in March. Another album, *Oh Mama, Shika dam!* (2001), included cover versions of songs by the Turkish singer Tarkan. Kirkorov ended the year with shows in Mongolia after four months of negotiations with the government. He released another massively successful single in December 2001, "I Will Die for You."

References

www.kirkorov.ru

Kwok, Aaron (Hong Kong)

Kwok Fu Shing was born in the former British dependency of Hong Kong on October 26, 1965. After completing his education at St. Joseph's High School, he joined the ranks of dancers employed by TV station TVB in 1984. For the next five years the newly named Aaron Kwok (the use of an English name is expected from artists in Hong Kong, China and the surrounding areas) appeared in TV shows such as "The Rise of Ghengis Kahn" and "Twilight of a Nation" and had bit parts in movies such as *Close Escape* (1989) and *Story of Kennedy Town* (1990). In 1992 he won his first lead role, in *Relation of the Last Hero*. Despite his many film appearances, it was while appearing in a commercial for motorbikes in 1990 that Kwok was first noticed by Capitol Records, which signed him to a recording contract. The first albums released by Kwok were available only in Taiwan. The songs on the albums *Love You Forever* (1990), *Aaron Kwok 2*, (1991), and *Who Could Please Tell Me* (1991) consisted of up-tempo love songs with a synthesizer backing track. All three records sold reasonably well.

In February 1992 the album *Endless Dancing, Endless Loving, Endless Singing* won Kwok success in Hong Kong. A compilation of his three earlier albums, *Endless Dancing . . .* became a springboard for Kwok. His success led to the media calling him one of Hong Kong's "Four Music Kings" (also known as the "Four Heavenly Kings") with **Andy Lau, Leon Lai**, and **Jacky Cheung**. As with the other "Kings," Kwok was also developing a highly successful career as a movie star while remaining at the top of the pop charts. Between 1991 and 1993 he starred in fifteen major films. The movies were all based around the same formula of romance, action and comedy, with Kwok invariably playing the romantic lead, all of which played to full theaters. By 1994 Kwok had decided to attempt to break into the Japanese market and released *Desire*. Even though he sang in Japanese, the album failed to make much impact in the crowded Japanese pop market. However, Kwok's other nine releases of that year all charted in the top ten of Taiwan, China, and Hong Kong, making Kwok one of the biggest earners in the country. By now Kwok was in demand to endorse various products and appeared in commercials for hot chocolate, jewelery, jeans, tea, coffee, cell phones, credit cards and Nintendo. (He also become the "face" of Pepsi in Asia in 1997.)

In 1996 Kwok released another typical, for him, pop album, *The Most Exciting Empire*, which broke all Hong Kong records, remaining at #1 for several weeks. During the summer he played a string of fifteen sold-out shows at the Hong Kong Coliseum. The album and concerts led to him winning the first of many awards, including best dance song ("Emperor's New Song"), best pop song ("Love's Calling"), and best rock song ("Expiration Date"), as well as being named most improved male artist. Taking up the charity mantle expected of pop stars in Hong Kong, Kwok visited a number of homes for the elderly in 1998 before recording a promotional film for the Hong Kong Board of Education, *Saying Thanks—The Spring Wind*. On June 5, 2000, the Aaron Kwok International Charity Fund was established.

Although no new material was released in 1998 or 1999 (he released four compilations, two re-mix albums, and a live album), Kwok visited the United States and performed in Atlantic City, Los Angeles, and Las Vegas, largely to the Chinese community. At the end of 1999 he returned home to find he had been voted Asia's most popular singer in press polls. During 2000 Kwok released three movies, *2000 AD, And I Hate You So*, and *China Strike Force*. The latter two were also accompanied by a soundtrack album recorded by Kwok. Over the Christmas period he played twenty shows around Hong Kong. More albums and movies are planned, as he played his first dates in Singapore in April 2001.

References

www.aaronkwok.net

L

Lai, Leon (China)

Leon Lai Ming was born into a wealthy family on December 11, 1966, in the Chinese capital, Beijing. After his family moved to Hong Kong in 1970, Lai was sent to England at age sixteen to attend Christ's College and, later, Princeton College, also in England. Following the path of other successful Hong Kong and Chinese stars, he began appearing in movies and playing minor roles in various TV series. In the late 1980s he placed third in an amateur singing contest. Finding encouragement in this near miss, he entered another contest in 1989 and won. Subsequently Polygram signed him and released an album, *Leon*, in July 1990. Although the album broke no new ground in its content of straight pop tunes, with the backing of his major record label, which promoted the record on TV and in the press, it was an immediate success, reaching #1 in the pop charts, and selling more than 6 million copies. By the end of the year Lai had won the first of many awards in Hong Kong, being named most welcome new singer.

In 1991 the album *It's Love, It's Destiny*, released in June, continued in the same vein as his previous release and was named album of the year. In the following year Lai traveled to Taiwan to appear in the TV drama *Legendary Ranger*, a series that won the highest TV audience ever in the country. The show's success boosted Lai's singing career; in fact, his 1992 albums, *Hope We'll Not Just Be Friends* and *Accumulating All My Love*, reached the top of the charts in both Taiwan and Hong Kong. As a result of the success of these albums, Lai was named one of the "Four Music Kings" of Hong Kong (with **Andy Lau, Jacky Cheung**, and **Aaron Kwok**).

In 1993 Lai continued his remarkable career trajectory, as he released five albums and was named singer of the year in local polls. In 1994 he won the first of his four song-of-the-year titles with "There's Not a Day I Don't Think of You" (along with "Love Words Not Yet Spoken," 1996; "Just Love Me for One

Day," 1997; and "I Love You Like This," 1998). Also in 1994 Lai played his first concerts outside Asia when he visited Canada to play some low-key dates, mainly in front of the Chinese community there. This visit to North America influenced his future videos, as he introduced plot lines that involved the mountains of Canada and the beaches of Florida. Lai used his acting experience to create three-minute movies while his actual acting career was still winning critical and commercial success as he won the 1997 Golden Statue Award for best actor for the movie *Comrades: Almost a Love Story*. In March 1998 Lai signed with Sony and released *Longing March*. In an attempt to continue to make money from its former artist, Polygram released two compilation albums, *Collections* and *Collections II*, which sold more than his new release. At the end of the year Lai won three categories in the Commercial Radio 2 awards. Lai's fans wrote thousands of letters of complaint to newspapers arguing that Lai had been overlooked in favor of other, lesser talents and should have been nominated in many other categories as well.

Ultimately Lai's heavy recording and filming schedule began to take a toll on his health, and in 1999 rumors circulated that he had attempted suicide after a bout of heavy drinking. Lai denied this, stating that he had been recording late into the night and was simply exhausted. Nevertheless Lai released his thirty-fourth album, *Leon Now*, in June. The style and content of Lai's songs had changed little despite his substantial output, yet once again the album reached the top of the pop charts. After more concert dates around Southeast Asia, Lai appeared in the movie *Skyline Cruisers* in 2000; not only did this place Lai at the top of the Hong Kong box office, but the film won distribution among small art theaters in the United States. His next film in March 2001, *Dream of Warrior*, again saw Lai playing the all-action, romantic hero and was also released in the United States, as the soundtrack stood at #1 in the local charts. Meanwhile Lai's heavy workload continued as he released a Mandarin-language album, *The Red Shoes*, in June and appeared at many charity events. In August 2001 he performed at the opening of the China University Sports Championships in Beijing, then he organized his own Christmas concerts in Hong Kong for December. A new DVD album, *Leon: Live is Live,* featuring a live concert of Lai performing his hits was released early in 2002.

References

www.leonlai.com

Laibach (Slovenia)

Two former members of the Yugoslav army, Thomaz Hostnik (b. 1961) and Miran Mohar, (b. 1958), formed Laibach in 1980 in Trbovlje, Slovenia. Laibach's dark lyrics, militia-style clothing and hard, uncompromising music have brought controversy over the artists' career. The band expanded into a five-piece group with Ivan Novak as vocalist and their first project, "Red Districts," was a multimedia effort that challenged the political structure of the town. The piece, a collaboration with other artists, became known as the NSK (Neue Slowenische Kunst, or "New Slovenian Art"). The NSK were a triumvirate: Laibach, who furnished the music; Irwin, a group of painters; and the Scipion Nasice, group of actors. "Red Districts" was banned before it had the chance to open, delaying the band's first public appearance.

It was two years before Laibach made its first performance, in Ljubljana at the Malic Belic Hall. (Laibach's insistence on wearing military uniforms on stage while playing in front of a backdrop of images from past wars, particularly World War II, made both audiences and authorities uncomfortable, often leading the latter to ban the group's performances.) The band followed the concert with a small tour around Yugoslavia, which led to their first TV appearance—not on a pop program, but on a political news program. The interview provoked the authorities, once again, into banning public appearances by the group and banning the name "Laibach" itself. ("Laibach" is the ancient name for Ljubljana, the capital of Slovenia. The name "Laibach" was banned in Yugoslavia after World War II because it had been used by the Nazis.)

In November 1982 the band played in Zagreb, a performance that was later investigated by the police. The following month, on December 11, Hostnik was found dead in his home. Whether it was suicide or foul play was never clearly established. He was twenty years old. Ivan Novak now found himself as the mouthpiece for Laibach. Although the line-up of the band has undergone numerous changes throughout the years, Novak has remained as the single voice of the group.

As a way around the constant bans, the group toured Western and Eastern Europe at the end of 1983. This was followed a year later by an anonymous appearance at a festival in Ljubljana, which would have led to the band's arrest had the authorities been aware of its identity. In 1985 the band released its first album. A collection of hard electronic rhythms behind a harsh, barked vocal, it became the trademark of Laibach releases, as did the symbol the group employed as an identification mark, still unable to use the name "Laibach." Later the same year, a second album, *Rekapitulacija 1980–1984*, was given an international release by a German label. More releases followed in 1986 (*Nova Akropola*) and 1987 (*Opus Dei*). In February 1987 the band made its first appearance in Slovenia since the anonymous show of 1984 and its first official concert since 1983. Also in 1987 the group had two songs banned in the United States, "Geburt Einer Nation" and "Life Is Life," because of the provocative videos that accompanied them. By the end of the decade Laibach had undertaken more shows in Europe and had performed at small clubs all over North America. By now the band had declared its own autonomous state within its home country and issued "passports" to those fans who wished to join. During a European tour the band declared each venue a colony of its state for the night.

Laibach celebrated its tenth anniversary in 1990 by performing in its home town for the first time since its planned debut show had been banned a decade earlier. The following years saw collaborations with members of the NSK and Western artists. For example, Laibach contributed the music to dancer Michael

Clark's "No Fire Escape in Hell." The band also provided music for several documentaries and movies as well as fifteen theater projects.

In 1996 the band appeared on a compilation album, *Industrial Revolution*, that was released in the United States, as well as issuing its own album, *Jesus Christ Superstars*. In the following year the group released *MB December 1984*, a live recording of the first gig the band performed at the Malic Belic some thirteen years earlier. Later in the year the group played the opening event of the European cultural month that aimed to bring together artists from across the continent in Ljubljana in front of the leaders of several Baltic states and was backed by the Slovenian Philharmonic Orchestra. Laibach's set included "dark" versions of such well-known songs as Edwin Starr's "War," to which the lyrics were partly altered to include the initials of the global corporations IBM and CNN. The show caused upset, and the Slovenian Philharmonic cancelled all further collaborations.

During 1996 a documentary was released detailing the history of the NSK. The film, *Predictions of Fire*, premiered at the Sundance Film Festival and later played at the new York Film Forum as the group prepared for its "Occupied Europe NATO Tour." A recording of the tour was released under the same name that October. As 1998 began, Laibach performed with artists from the East and West at a crosscultural festival in Sarajevo, the capital of the newly formed Bosnia-Herzegovina (which, until a few years earlier, had been at war with the band's home country). In February 2000 an Italian label, Radio Luxor, released a tribute album to the band, following it in May 2001 with a second, similar release. To commemorate twenty years together, the group played an unannounced concert in Slovenia during June 2000. In the same month Laibach received an award from the town of Trbovlje recognizing the group's achievements. Most recently the band played shows in Prague and at the Wave-Gotik-Treffen festival in Leipzig, in June 2001, alongside other luminaries of Techno and industrial music such as **Front 242**. Although Laibach's recorded output is irregular, the group continues to be involved in the cultural scene of Slovenia as writers and musicians.

References

www.laibach.nsk.si

MTV-Cyclopedia by Nick Duerden, Ian Gittens, and Shaun Phillips (London: Carlton, 1997). ISBN 185868336x

Lau, Andy (Hong Kong)

Lau Fook-Wing was born on September 27, 1961 in the rural town of Taipo in the New Territories, Hong Kong. After he finished his education, in 1980 he joined the 10th Acting Academy sponsored by Hong Kong's main TV station, TVB. Andy Lau, as he was now known, appeared in minor roles in TV series before winning his first role in a motion picture, *Boat People* (1982). In the following year he performed his first lead role, in *On the Wrong Track*. Lau continued to play lead roles that usually saw him cast as the romantic/action figure until, in 1985, TVB decided he should embark on a singing career to complement his growing popularity in the movies.

When Lau's first album of typical Hong Kong pop, the keyboard-driven love songs on *Only Know That I Still Love You*, won few admirers, it seemed that his singing career would be over before it had started. Although his single release, "Love's Forbidden Area" (1987), entered the top ten, Lau was heavily involved in film and appeared in ten movies in 1988 and fourteen in 1989, winning the Taiwan Golden Dragon best actor award in 1988 for *As Tears Go By*. Lau was still releasing records during this period; but with little time to promote them, they never made the upper reaches of the chart.

In 1990 Lau finally reached #1 with the album *Would It Be Possible?*, which became a triple platinum disc. Although the album showed little difference or development from his debut, it caught the imagination of the public and turned platinum seven times over in Taiwan and caused Lau to be named most popular male singer at the Jade Solid Gold Awards of 1990. It was a trophy that Lau won again in 1991 and 1992. Over the next few years, Lau was the recipient of a string of awards, including being named Asia's most popular singer in 1995 and 1997, Asia's outstanding all-around actor by MTV, and a Billboard award for Asia's most popular singer. Lau was still being cast as the romantic lead in movies on an almost monthly basis (thirty-five between 1990 and 1992), but in 1993 the demand for him as a singer became so great that he played his first-ever concerts at the Hong Kong Coliseum. A run of twenty sold-out shows confirmed him as a major star. He then found himself named by the media as one of the "Four Music Kings" (with **Aaron Kwok, Leon Lai**, and **Jacky Cheung**.)

In 1995 Lau opened his own museum, Andy Lau's Showcase, exhibiting his awards, platinum discs, and movie and stage costumes. After he performed across Asia in 1996, a live album of the event was released and joined his other albums at #1. Singing in both Cantonese and Mandarin for the Taiwanese and Chinese markets, respectively, Lau, who features songs of unrequited and requited love, has become one of the wealthiest artists in Asia. Although his schedule kept him either in the recording studio or on a movie set for the majority of the year, and his own production company had him working with other artists as well as looking after his own interests, he was still finding time for charitable works. In July 1998 he traveled to the Guangdong district to open a primary school, and in the following year he won a Hong Kong top ten youth award for his efforts.

In 2000 he appeared in TV advertisements for a Special Athletes Marathon, an event he also produced a song for. He even ran in the race, giving the event a higher profile than it would otherwise have received. The same year saw the release of Lau's 100th movie, *A Fighter's Blues*, which again reached the top of the box office charts. By March 2001 Lau was filming with Japanese actor Sorimachi Takashi on the movie *Professional Killer*. He followed this with an appearance at a charity concert at the Hong Kong Coliseum where he sang a duet with follow Hong Kong singing star **Coco Lee**, "I Don't Love You Enough." After visiting Australia in September 2001, Lau returned to Asia for a series of concerts in Singapore and Malaysia. He continues to be a major star in Asia.

References

www.andylau.net

Lee, Coco (Hong Kong)

Mayling Lee was born in Hong Kong on January 17, 1975, shortly after the death of her father. At the age of eight she moved to San Francisco with her mother and two sisters, as her mother had decided the girls should learn English. After Lee graduated from high school she contemplated a career in medicine and enrolled at the University of California in Irvine. Before beginning her studies, however, she returned to Hong Kong and began singing in karaoke bars. Within weeks she had entered a talent contest and placed second, being the only entrant to sing in English. As a result of the competition she signed with a small record label in neighboring Taiwan. After quickly learning Mandarin she released two albums in 1995, *Brave Enough to Love* (in English) and *Woman in Love* (in Mandarin). Both records had a modern U.S. R&B feel, but Lee combined it with the pop music style of Taiwan to create a sound that was extremely popular in Asia (and less so in the English-speaking market). As a result, the latter record earned her huge success in Taiwan. Within a year she signed with the Sony label.

A single, "Former Love," won the Golden Dragon Award for best single in 1996. When two more albums were released, *Coco Lee* (in Mandarin) reached the top of the charts while *Coco's Party* (in English) also sold well. Lee's success continued into 1997 when her Mandarin album *Each Time I Think of You* earned her the title of best female artist at a local awards ceremony.

In 1998 Lee released what became her biggest hit: "DiDaDi." It won her the MTV International award for best music video on its way to selling over a million copies. The album, *Sunny Day: Feeling Good*, followed Lee's formula of Western R&B and Asian pop and went on to win MTV Asia's best album award in the same year. In August she performed in front of 30,000 people in Taiwan and was chosen to voice the role of Mulan in the Mandarin version of the Disney film of the same name. In the following year she released her first album in the United States, *Just No Other Way*, but it failed to receive any attention. However, Lee won another award from MTV International as best female artist for her efforts in Asia.

In the summer of 2000 Lee sang to an audience of millions at the opening ceremony of the soccer World Cup in France. As Lee, and her record company, continued to look for success in the United States, she sang on the soundtrack to the Julia Roberts/Richard Gere movie *The Runaway Bride* late in 2000. She also worked on another English-language album aimed at the U.S. market, *You and Me* (2001) which again failed to sell in any great numbers.

In the following year Lee returned to Asia to record the music for director Ang Lee's *Crouching Tiger, Hidden Dragon*, which included the ballad "A Love before Time." She was then invited to perform the title song at the Oscar ceremony in Los Angeles in April. In October Lee released another Mandarin album, *Promise*, that once again reached the top of the local charts with its "easy listening" sound, as did her singles "So Crazy" and "Easy Come, Easy Go." Lee then embarked on a series of concerts in Hong Kong and China. Although she was still struggling for recognition in the United States, her popularity in Asia remained constant as she appeared on the front of *GQ Taiwan* magazine; performed a duet, "I Don't Love You Enough," with one of the Four Singing Kings, **Andy Lau**; and sang at the Miss Hong Kong 2001 pageant. A collection of old songs re-mixed over a disco beat, *D.IS.CO CO*, was released in June 2002. Lee is currently recording a new English-language album for release in the United States by the end of the year.

References

www.cocolee.org

Leningrad Cowboys, The (Finland)

The history of The Leningrad Cowboys is shrouded in mystery. No one outside the band's circle knows exactly when the group first performed as a band, and the band members themselves are reticent about their past. Comprised of Sakke Jarvenpaa, Veeti Kallio, Mato Valtonen, Vesa Kaapa, Silu Seppala, Mauri Sumen, Pemo Ojala, and Ega Niiva, the group is joined on stage by the "Leningrad Ladies," Pink Isohanni and Mari Hatakka. The Leningrad Cowboys play an eclectic mix of cover versions, interspersed with their own material, that has made them household names in their native Finland.

The band first won notice in Finland in 1989 when it released *Leningrad Cowboys Go America*. The album was the soundtrack to a film of the same name that documented the hapless band, self-named "the worst rock and roll band in the world," traveling throughout the United States in a Cadillac. Strapped to the roof of the car was a coffin containing the frozen dead body of a former band member. The surreal humor of the film set the benchmark for The Leningrad Cowboys. With their bizarre stage outfits of foot-long Elvis Presley Style hair quiffs and two-foot-long pointy shoes, the band members caused a sensation whenever they performed in Finland as they cranked out their heavy guitar tunes. After the success of their debut, more albums followed as their popularity increased in Europe. *We Cum from Brooklyn* (1992), *Live in Prowinzz* (1993), and *Happy Together* (1993) all featured the same formula of cover versions and original material that owed more to U.S. rock and roll than any traditional music from Finland. Although never setting the charts alight, the records continued to promote the band well enough that its touring schedule was beginning to take in the major festivals of Europe.

In 1993 the band was invited to play with the choir of the Russian Red Army. The "Total Balalaika Show" took place in Helsinki before an audience of thousands of people. As a result of the show, every restaurant in Helsinki was fully booked for the entire day as most of Finland congregated in the capital. This success lead to Nokia sponsoring the band and producing a Leningrad Cowboys cell phone. The Leningrad Cowboys also produce their own brand of beer and vodka. In the following year the group was invited to perform at the MTV Europe Awards; and although the group was not nominated to receive an award, it became the star of the show. The band also played a concert in Berlin in 1991 championing its motto of "Make Tractors, Not War." This was also the year of the Cowboys' second movie, *Leningrad Cowboys Meet Moses*, another slice of surreal and irreverent humor.

The fame of the Cowboys had now reached Australia, where the band was invited to perform at the Womadelaide festival for the Year of Tolerance. After another album, *Go Space*, was released in 1995, the band began to play shows in the United States while continuing its success at home. The climax of its U.S. shows was at the Nokia-sponsored Summer Meltdown festival in Dallas in 1997. A "best of" album was released in the same year; called *Thank You Very Many*, it was named after the catchphrase that the band used after every song.

In 1998 the band opened a museum in Helsinki and organized a charity ice hockey match that involved stars of the sport from around the world as well as pigs, chainsaws, firecrackers, and a car. The match sold out in hours and raised DKK 175,00 ($27,000) in ticket sales for a children's cancer department in a Copenhagen hospital. Two years later the band released the film *LA Without a Map*, but the group's profile was beginning to wane everywhere except in Finland. The band released another album of crashing rock guitars, *Terzo Mondo*, in 2000; but with the band seldom playing any shows, the album was only a minor hit. The band played a concert in Germany in May 2002 but there are no plans for future releases.

References

www.leningradcowboys.fi

Ligabue, Luciano (Italy)

Luciano Ligabue was born on March 13, 1960, in Correggio, Italy. He initially held a series of jobs, including mechanic and deejay; only when he was twenty-seven years old did he first perform in public, with the band Orazero (in 1987). The group won an amateur band contest and the chance to record some songs, two of which, "Anime in Plexiglass" and "Bar Mario," were released as a single. An album, *Tra me e me*, followed in 1988, but Orazero's brand of traditional rock won little notice. In the same year Ligabue had something of a breakthrough when one of his songs was included on the album *Sogni di Rock and Roll* released by a well-known Italian singer, Pierangelo Bertoli. The exposure lead Ligabue into a record deal.

His first album, *Ligabue* (1990) was a collection of polished adult-oriented rock (AOR) music. After its release Ligabue (or Liga, as his fans came to know him) embarked on a comprehensive tour of the country that set the agenda for the artist for the next four years. As he released a series of albums that did little to excite the Italian public, *Lambrusco Coltelli Rose e Popcorn* (1991), *Sopravvissuti e Sopravviventi* (1993), and *A che ora è le fine del mondo* (1994), he toured constantly. In 1995 he had a breakthrough with *Buon compleanno Elvis*. The recording, a collection of mid-tempo rock songs, followed the style of his previous releases; but this time the album reached #1 in Italy selling enough copies to become a platinum album five times over and stay in the chart for over seventy weeks in the meantime. Once again Ligabue toured the country, this time filling stadiums; the tour was recorded and later released as a live album, *Su e Giù da un Palco* (1997).

During his lengthy tours Ligabue found time to write a book of short stories, *Fuori e dentro il borgo*. Two of the stories, "Il girotondo di Freccia" and "Radio fu," formed the basis of a motion picture that Ligabue was invited to direct by the film's producers. He accepted, and *Radiofreccia* was released in 1998, along with an album of the same name. The film was shown at the Venice Film Festival. Although it did not win any prizes, it was warmly received. In the same year Ligabue began another lengthy series of concerts, the "Never-Ending Tour"; He performed over 250 shows across Italy as a single, "La musica è salita alle stelle," remained in the chart for forty weeks.

In September 1999 Ligabue released his eighth album, *Miss Mondo*, which once again settled in the upper reaches of the Italian chart. Exactly one year later he appeared in Bologna at a free concert celebrating the third birthday of MTV Italy. By the end of 2000 he had been named singer of the year and won an award for best tour. He was also presented with the IFPI Platinum Europe Award in Brussels, Belgium, for *Miss Mondo*. A single he released with artist Francisco Guccini, "Ho ancora la forza," won the duo the Tenco 2000 prize. As Ligabue's straight rock style was continuing to win fans, *Bambokina and Barracuda*, released in November 2000, was another enormous success. While recording his last album, Ligabue continued to be involved in movies and spent the next year directing *Da Zero a dieci*, which was released in August 2001. In May 2002 Ligabue released a new album, *Fuori come va*. The album was less a heavy-rock album and had a somber mood. In the summer he played some concerts in Italy, including two in Milan, where he performed in front of over 30,000 fans each night.

References

www.ligabue.com

Lind, Espen (Norway)

Espen Lind was born in the Norwegian capital, Oslo, on May 13, 1971. The oldest of five children, Lind would sing and dance on store counters in the city's malls as his mother did her shopping. As the store assistants and customers applauded his talents, the young Lind was encouraged to sing more until his mother returned to collect him. When he was five years old the family moved to Tromso, a fishing town on the northern coast of Norway, and Lind began his musical career by learning to play the recorder. Within two years he was playing the piano, violin, and guitar and dreaming of becoming a pop star after hearing the Bee Gees' "Too Much Heaven" on the radio. By the time he was eleven he had written his first song and had joined the first of many bands he formed during his teenage years. At age sixteen he landed a job in a recording studio. Although he received no wages for his efforts, he often stayed in the studio after it closed for the day, recording his own songs and learning the intricacies of the recording process.

Frustrated by the music scene in his own country, in 1993 Lind moved to Los Angeles armed with his demos and attempted to find a record deal. For over a year he presented his pop rock songs to music executives, but, as Lind himself noted, "unfortunately, I couldn't get arrested." Running out of money, Lind took the word of one A&R man ("Artists & Repertoire," record-company employees who discover new talent) who advised him to return to Norway and start his career at home before trying to "break" America. Back in Norway, Lind borrowed money from his grandparents and set about recording songs in his own home studio. Using the experience he had gained from his earlier job and playing all the instruments himself, he released the single "Yum Yum Gimme Some" in May 1995 under the name Sway. Distributing the single himself to the nation's radio stations, he found that his uptempo, guitar pop tune had become one of the country's most requested songs. This led Universal's Norwegian label to offer him a recording contract. The album that followed, *Mmm. . . . Prepare to Be Swayed*, was voted album of the year by the Norwegian press for 1995 as its collection of smooth, melody-driven guitar pop songs struck a chord in Lind's home country.

Anxious to pursue his career, Lind had already begun recording songs for a second album while his debut was still receiving attention from the media. In 1996, after being invited to perform for the head of Universal Music in New York, he was immediately signed to a worldwide deal. This ensured that Lind's music would receive the wider stage that he had always dreamed of achieving. *Red*, the album that Lind had begun recording at home in 1995, was finally released two years later and became another huge success in Norway and other parts of Scandinavia. It showed Lind to be maturing in his writing and subject material. A single, "When Susannah Cries," held the #1 chart position in Norway for six weeks while the album turned double platinum.

In the intervening years Lind's career did not progress at the rate he hoped for, but in 2000 he traveled to South Africa with fellow Norwegian singer **Sissel** to record a video for a single, "Where the Lost Ones Go." Sissel had already won international recognition for vocals on the *Titanic* movie soundtrack. Working with Sissel and her neoclassical music appeared to influence Lind's third album, *This Is Pop Music*, released in November 2000. The record, a very mellow affair, reached #3 on the chart. Two singles released from the album, "Life Is Good" and "Black Sunday," both reached the top twenty. Although no new material was released in 2001, Lind found himself on the album charts as "Where the Lost Ones Go" found its way onto Sissel's album, *In Symphony*, that was released in November.

References

www.espenlind.com

M

Madness (England)

Between 1979 and 1989 Madness released fourteen singles in the United Kingdom and became the country's most loved "Nutty Boys." Originally called the North London Invaders, the seven members of Madness brought together their love of ska and reggae, added an edge that the recently defunct punk scene had brought to British music, and created what became known as the "Nutty" sound. Madness sang about playground fights ("Baggy Trousers"), buying your first condom ("House of Fun"), falling out with girlfriends ("My Girl"), and other youthful scenarios that struck a note of recognition in millions of schoolchildren in general, and schoolboys in particular. Complementing the songs were a series of videos, innovative and good humored but always, like the songs, reflecting working-class life in Britain.

After many changes in line-up, Madness finally settled as a band with keyboard player Mike Barson (b. May 21, 1958), drummer Dan Woodgate (b. October 19, 1960), guitarist Chris Foreman (b. August 8, 1958), bass player Mark Bedford (b. August 24, 1961), saxophonist Lee Thompson (b. October 5, 1957), and vocalist Graham "Suggs" McPherson (b. January 13, 1961). The first Madness single, "The Prince," was released on Two Tone, a record label created by the British group The Specials to promote a new brand of ska music that multiracial bands across the United Kingdom had begun to perform. Madness appeared on the music show *Top of the Pops* and was joined on stage by "nutty dancer" Chas Smash (b. January 14, 1959), who later became a full-time member of the band as an extra vocalist and occasional trumpet player. The group's debut album, *One Step Beyond*, reached the top five in 1979 and preceded a three-week tour of the United States that took in New York, California, and Texas. In May of the following year *One Step Beyond* reached #128 on the U.S. chart after the band signed with Sire records. In the years that followed, Madness became regarded as the United Kingdom's most-loved singles band through songs like "Embarrassment," "It Must Be Love," and "The Return of the Los Palmas 7."

In 1985 the band had its only U.K. #1 with "Baggy Trousers," which stayed on the chart for twenty weeks. Madness was now at the peak of its popularity, having successfully left its roots as a good-time Two Tone band who didn't take themselves too seriously and having gained credibility within the serious music press without ever losing its original fan base. The band's second album, *Absolutely* (1980), was also a top ten hit in the United Kingdom but struggled to reach #146 in the United States, where the band was dropped by Sire. In October 1981 the band's third album, *Seven*, proved that the group was in no danger of losing popularity at home as it entered the charts at #5. By 1982 the regard in which the band was held in the United Kingdom reached a peak when "House of Fun" hit #1 and the following compilation album, *Complete Madness*, released in May 1982, also reached the top of the charts. An album of original material, *The Rise and Fall*, released in November of the same year, hit the #10 spot. By now the band had found another recording contract in the United States through Geffen; its debut for the label, *Madness*, reached #41 in April 1983. Two months later the band had its biggest stateside hit when "Our House" reached #7. Back in the United Kingdom in September, "The Wings of a Dove" reached #2. By now the group's music was beginning to undergo a change, however. Although the humor was still evident, it was changing from good-natured to a much darker tone. "Grey Day" in 1981 hinted at the change, which was confirmed by the 1984 single "Michael Caine," which hinted at schizophrenia. Although the single reached #11 on the U.K. charts, it replaced the guitar chops and ska/reggae beat of the group's earlier recordings with a more conventional 4/4 rhythm. The March 1984 album *Keep Moving* reached #6 in the United Kingdom, but it proved to be the beginning of the end as the public struggled with the new, darker tone of Madness. (*Keep Moving* reached only #109 in the United States, the band's last placing on the American charts.)

In October 1984 the band announced the formation of its own record label, Zarjazz. The first release, "Yesterday's Men" in September 1985, continued to reflect the band's downbeat approach in both title and style. Although Madness's fan base pushed the single to #18, the enthusiasm appeared to be on the wane. *Mad Not Mad*, released in October, reached #16. In September 1986 the band announced it had split up.

Although Madness was active as a group only for the first half of the decade, its popularity in the United Kingdom is reflected by its third-place listing among artists that spent the most weeks in the U.K. singles charts during the 1980s. Madness totaled 218 weeks, outdone only by Madonna and Welsh Elvis Presley impersonator Shakin' Stevens.

After Madness fragmented into splinter groups (one being The Madness), recriminations began to surface about use of the name and material. These differences lasted for a few years, but a successful re-formation in 1995 led to a sell-out concert in London's Finsbury Park and a "best of" album took the band to the top of the charts in the middle of the 1990s. Today, Madness still releases songs but rarely gains any commercial success, although the group's occasional live shows, showcasing the band's original mainly early material under the banner Madstock, still sell out and are received with the same enthusiasm that greeted the band's re-introduction in 1995.

References

www.madness.co.uk

Total Madness by George Marshall (London: ST Publishing, 1993). ISBN 0951849743

Majid, Sheila (Malaysia)

Born Shaheila Binti Abdul Majid into a family of seven brothers and sisters in Malaysia on January 3, 1965, Sheila Majid initially showed little desire to forge a career in music. But at the birthday party of a friend in 1982 she was coaxed onto the stage to sing. A fellow guest at the party was Roslan Aziz, a songwriter and producer. Aziz invited Majid to an audition, was impressed, and offered her a recording contract, even though he had no company to sign her with. Majid accepted the offer. By 1983 she had completed her first album, *Dimensi Baru*, but no local record labels were interested because the music was unlike the predominant "rock" style that saturated the market in Malay at the time. Majid's style owed more to jazz and R&B.

For two years Aziz attempted to get the album released and eventually succeeded in convincing a skeptical EMI to take a chance. The album went gold within weeks. In the following year Majid consolidated her place in Malaysia with her follow-up, *Emosi*, which also won great critical acclaim in Japan, where she has remained a hugely popular artist. (A Japan-only release, *Wanita*, hit the nation's charts in 1995.) *Emosi* continued to showcase Majid as a predominantly jazz artist, though elements of pop were evident. The album won a release in Indonesia, where Majid won the BASF award for best female artist, the first time a non-Indonesian had taken the title. In 1987 she released her third album, *Warna*, and became the first Malaysian artist to release a recording on compact disc. In the same year she won an award for the bestselling album in Indonesia.

At this time Majid married Aziz, and three years later she released *Lagunda* (1990). The album went triple platinum after a series of live shows to promote it. A mature blend of the jazzy pop Majid was becoming known for, the album stayed in the Malay charts for two years. Early in 1993 she released a compilation album, *Gemilang*. Majid then spent time away from performing, until, in 1995, she recorded a duet with fellow Malay artist Nora. The song they performed together, "Jentayu," won the duo the best performance in a group award at the AIM awards. She followed the success of "Jentayu" with the release of her fifth album, *Ratu*. Although it followed the formula of her early work, it was another major success, and Majid was presented with the AIM award for best female vocal performance and best album in 1997. Following the release of *Ratu*, Majid visited London for the first time. After a series of successful concerts, she considered plans to record an album in English but remained skeptical about the success of the project. The plans were soon shelved.

Although her musical career was thriving, Majid's private life was suffering as she began a complicated and bitter divorce from Aziz. At this time Majid suffered from negative press attention, both for the divorce and for her 1999 comeback album, *Ku Mohon*. The bad reviews from the tabloids did not affect the music critics, however, and in April 2000 Majid received two more AIM awards for best pop album and song of the year (for the single "Ku Mohon"). In July she celebrated her fifteenth year in the industry by performing in front of the Prime Minister and First Lady of Malaysia before embarking on another series of live concerts, both at home and in Indonesia, which took her into the early months of 2001. The profile of Majid in her home country was assured after she was given the Rotary Club of Padu award in November for being "recognized, respected and acknowledged as a leader in her field." *Sheila Majid 15* (2001), a compilation album featuring material spanning her career was then released, celebrating her fifteen years in the music business and as a preview of her next fifteen.

In 2002 Majid visited Singapore for a series of concerts and personal appearances before returning to Malaysia for more live shows.

References

www.sheilamajid.com

Mana (Mexico)

Toward the end of the 1970s in Guadalajara, Mexico, Fernando Olvera, Juan Diego Calleros, and his brother Ulises, formed a rock band, Green Hat, that began playing bars around the city. Initially singing in English, they changed their name to Sombrero Verde and began performing in their native Spanish. They soon attracted the attention of record companies and released a debut album, *Sombrero Verde*, in 1981. The record received little attention, and the follow-up, *A Ritmo de Rock* (1983), suffered the same fate. Undeterred, the band continued to write new material, still focusing on straight rock songs. In 1985 Alejandro Gonzalez joined as drummer and brought Cuban-Colombian influences. In the following year the band became Mana. Recognition continued to elude them until, at the end of 1986, Warner Music Mexico signed the band.

It took another three years of playing small gigs and honing their by now accomplished rock music before a first album was released. *Falta Amor* (1989), although well received, initially failed to sell; it took two years before the album became widely recognized by the public. It was the release of the single "Rayando el Sol" that finally brought the band success in Mexico. An upbeat, optimistic and life-affirming tune, the song raced to the top of the charts and a new interest in Mana appeared, and *Falta Amor*, released two years previously, became an "overnight" success.

To take advantage of its new popularity in 1992 the band released its second album. *Donde Jugaran Los Ninos?* featured two new members, Ivan Gonzalez and Cesar Lopez, as Ulises Calleros stopped performing to concentrate on the management of the band. By the end of the year the album had sold one and a half million copies (three and a half million by 1997) and had a record eight singles charting during the year. Although the band continued to play a heavy schedule of concerts, it was now appearing in stadiums rather than tiny clubs and was a regular on TV and radio. In 1993 the group played concerts across Latin America, as well as in Spain and in Spanish-speaking communities in the United States. By now the group's success had made Mana idols to many, and it became the first Mexican act in twenty-six years to top the charts in Argentina and Spain with the single "Vivir sin Aire." In July of the same year a Mana concert at the Palacio de Los Deportes in Mexico became the second highest-grossing concert of the month in the world. *Donde Jugaran los Ninos?* remained in the Latin charts for almost two years.

As the band's fame continued to escalate, Ivan Gonzalez and Cesar Lopez suddenly left. Initially it seemed that Mana was finished, but the songwriting team was based solidly around the efforts of Olvera and Gonzalez, so the band set about auditioning new members. More than eighty musicians put themselves forward for the vacant positions, and the band finally settled on Mexican guitarist Sergio Vallin. A long and arduous series of rehearsals resulted in the release of *Cuando Los Angeles Lloran* in 1995. The album, which showed Mana settling into a niche as a straight rock act, went gold and platinum in over twenty-one countries as well as selling 500,000 copies in the United States alone. After the record won the Billboard award for best Latin album, another extensive tour began and the band played to 25,000 people in Spain, a new record for a Mexican group. The tour encompassed more than 400,000 fans watching the band over a series of fifty-two concerts.

Always aware of the environment, the band founded Selva Negra ("Black Forest"), an organization to promote the needs of the planet and its ecological system. In 1996 a calendar highlighting endangered areas of the world was produced and sold in the thousands. More touring continued, and in 1996 Mana became the first Mexican band to appear on the popular U.S. TV show *Regis and Kathie Lee.* Presenting the group as the world's biggest Latin rock band, the show helped Mana sell out a fifteen-date tour of the United States.

Returning to the studio, the band released its fourth album in October 1997. *Suendos Liquidos* became another huge success, earning gold and platinum discs around the world and winning a Grammy for best Latin rock album. As the music of Mana was slowly developing, a new term, "Rock n Español," described the genre of music that bands like it were making. The 1998 tour that followed earned the band record attendance in Los Angeles and Chicago; the eight-week tour became the fifty-fourth highest-grossing tour for the year anywhere in the world (figures that would usually only be reached by a tour lasting four months or more). Mana invited the ecological organization Greenpeace into the concerts to distribute material, as well as Amnesty International, which highlighted cases of human rights abuse in Latin America. Always socially and politically aware, Mana then took time away from music to concentrate on working for charities concerned with Mexican children. In 1999 the band was invited to perform on *MTV Unplugged*; the concert gave Mana the chance to prove itself in an acoustic environment, away from its usual loud and upfront stage shows. The album *MTV Unplugged* was released shortly thereafter and served as testimony to the group's musical ability.

In October 2001 a boxed set of four albums, *100% Mana*, was released as the band continued to work on its first new material in five years, due to be released in summer 2002. Mana continues to use its position to highlight injustices against both the planet and its citizens, while maintaining its status as the most popular Latin rock band in the world.

References

www.mana.com.mx

Manic Street Preachers (Wales)

Nicky Wire (b. January 20, 1969), James Dean Bradfield (b. February 21, 1969), Sean Moore (b. July 30, 1968), and Richey Edwards (b. December 22, 1968) grew up together in the Welsh mining community of Blackwood. After leaving university, Wire formed a band with Bradfield and Moore called Betty Blue and played a first gig at the Blackwood Little Theatre in 1988. In an effort to secure shows in London, the trio pooled their money to record a single, "Suicide Alley." Edwards designed the record sleeve and later joined as a full-time member. Immediately prior to the release of the single, the band changed its name to Manic Street Preachers. Only three hundred copies of the single were made, but it was enough for the group to secure its first London gig. The owner of Damaged Goods Records attended the gig, and the group's energetic stage show and punk-styled guitar songs impressed him enough to offer the band a deal at the beginning of 1990. The subsequent release, "New Art Riot," early in 1990, won the band recognition from music critics, many of whom made the record their single of the week. Two more singles, "Motown Junk" and "You Love Us," followed, attracting a growing audience for the band's highly charged political stance and "spiky" music that consisted of the twin guitar attack of Bradfield and Edwards.

In May 1991, however, Steve Lamacq, a journalist with the British rock magazine *NME*, questioned the authenticity of the group, claiming it was not "for real." Unable to make an impression on the skeptical Lamacq, Edwards took a razor blade and carved "For Real" into his forearm. The action made front-page news, and six days later the band signed with Sony. Two more singles followed before the re-release of "You Love Us" earned the band a slot on

Britain's most popular TV music show, *Top of the Pops*. The group's debut album, *Generation Terrorists* (1992), was a modern take on the punk rock phenomenon of the late 1970s with song lyrics that attacked all aspects of government and society. The record was released to mixed reviews but sold more than 750,000 copies. The band then embarked on its first U.S. tour early in 1992. In September a cover of "Suicide Is Painless," the theme music from the film *M*A*S*H*, helped the band reach the top ten for the first time.

After another album, *Gold Against the Soul*, was released in June 1993, the band undertook a world tour opening for Bon Jovi. The first six months of 1994 were also dominated by a hectic touring schedule with the Manics playing in Europe, Asia, Australia, Japan, and the United States. In August the band released its third album, *Holy Bible*, but in the same month Edwards was admitted to the hospital suffering from nervous exhaustion. After Edwards returned a few weeks later, the band once again began touring to promote the record. Although lyrically still spitting vitriol, musically the band had begun to mature. In January 1995 the band re-entered the studio to begin recording material for its next album. At the beginning of February the group was due to fly to America for a short promotional visit, but Edwards could not be found. He had disappeared from his London hotel room, and his car was found near the Severn Bridge on the border of England and Wales. With no word as to his whereabouts, the band had to decide on its future. After talking to Edwards' parents, the group decided to carry on as a trio. The band's sound was becoming more polished and the production on the album gave it a "rehearsed" sound as opposed to the chaotic, almost improvised music of its earlier recordings.

In April 1995 the Manics released "A Design for Life." The song, based around Bradfield's incendiary guitar, included a string section in the chorus that was very different from the punk ethic of the group's early releases. The single entered the chart at #2, winning the band an Ivor Novello Award for songwriting. The album *Everything Must Go* was released in May 1996, turned double platinum, and won a number of best album awards from music magazines. It also became the basis for a play, titled "Everything Must Go." With the play being set among the disparate youth of South Wales who, since the closure of the coal mines in the late 1980s, had no work and very little hope, the Manics' music was judged the perfect soundtrack. Although there were no releases in 1997, the band consolidated its position in British music by winning best album and best band at the Brit Awards.

This Is My Truth Tell Me Yours (1998) continued to show the band maturing as songwriters and lyricists. Although the music was based around the traditional rock three-piece of guitar, bass, and drums, the band added more keyboards and orchestration to give the album a fuller sound. By the end of the year it had secured its first #1 single with "If You Tolerate This Your Children Will Be Next." In magazine polls for 1998, the Manic Street Preachers were voted #1 for band, single ("If You Tolerate This . . . "), album (*This Is My Truth . . .*), video ("If You Tolerate This . . . "), and live act. *Q* magazine called the group "the best act in the world today." The Brit Awards nominated it for best British group, best British album, and best British single. The group won the first two categories. The Manics then became the subject of a BBC TV documentary detailing the band's career to date. Setting out on another world tour at the beginning of 1999, in February 2001 the band became the first Western act to play in Cuba, with the concert even being attended by Cuban leader Fidel Castro. In March 2001 the album *Know Your Enemy* hit the charts as the band continued to question political policies and ideals in its lyrics with songs such as "Freedom of Speech Won't Feed My Children." (Despite numerous reported sightings of Richey Edwards from around the world, there has been no proof as to his whereabouts or whether he is still alive.)

References

www.manics.co.uk

Everything: A Book About the Manic Street Preachers by Simon Price (London: Virgin, 1999). ISBN 0753501392

Marlin, Lene (Norway)

Born in Tromso, Norway, on August 17, 1980, Lene Marlin Pederson's earliest memory was of visiting a music shop with her parents and being distraught when she had to leave behind a guitar she had been playing. She was fifteen before she got a guitar of her own, as a Christmas gift. Marlin soon began writing her own songs and performed them for her family and friends in her bedroom. Marlin's friends first contacted the local radio station, NRK, which invited her into the studio to perform over the air. The station later introduced her to the record label Virgin Norway, which signed the seventeen-year-old to a record deal.

As she began recording her debut album, Marlin was still studying in Oslo, and her dual efforts won her a Karolineprisen, an annual award presented to a student who achieves good grades while at the same time contributing to the Norwegian cultural scene. In October 1998 she released her first single, "Unforgivable Sinner." A gentle tune underpinned by acoustic guitar, the song reached #1 and stayed there for eight weeks. It became the fastest-selling single in Norwegian history. It was her second release, though, that made Marlin an international star. "Sitting Down Here" (1999), similar in arrangement to her debut single, was an instant hit across the world, receiving heavy exposure on MTV in the United States as well as in Europe and East Asia. The accompanying album, *Playing My Game*, sold 50,000 copies in just three days in Norway (equivalent to 10 percent of the entire country owning the album). In November 1999 the success earned Marlin an MTV award for best Nordic act and also won her a local award, the Spellemannsprisen. Surprisingly, despite the success of "Sitting Down Here," her record company decided against releasing the album in the United States.

At this point Marlin was appearing across the world to promote the single but then decided to return to Norway to work on new material, refusing to succumb to the heavy touring and promotional schedules needed to keep a new artist in the public eye. As a result the third single from the album, "Where I'm Headed," not released until March 2001, failed to achieve the same success as her previous release even though the album itself has, to date, sold 1,350,000 copies worldwide. The Norwegian daily newspaper *Dagbladet* reported in April 2001 that Marlin had earned nearly $5 million from *Playing My Game*. Later, Marlin was nominated at the 2001 Brit Awards for best international newcomer following sales of over 100,000 copies for her debut album in the United Kingdom. She also contributed to songs for the new album, *In Symphony*, of fellow Norwegian singer **Sissel**, released in November. Marlin remains in Norway, where she is still heavily involved in the music industry and is still working on new material. An album has been tentatively scheduled for release in 2002, although Marlin remains determined to follow a career path that is not overly stressful.

References

www.lenemarlin.com

Playing My Game by Lene Marlin (International Music Publishing). ISBN 1859097596

MC Solaar (France)

Born in Dakar, Senegal, in 1969, Claude M'barali moved to France with his family as a young child. Growing up in the Paris suburb of Villeneuve St. Georges, M'barali showed a typical child's interest in TV but could just as often be found reading novels and listening to music. With parents whose native country was Chad, it was only natural that M'barali listened to traditional African music, but his parents also exposed him to American jazz. At age twelve he spent a year in Egypt, where he heard the rhythms of northern Africa. As a teenager M'barali began to listen to the American rap and hip-hop artists who were getting air time on the radio stations and TV programs in France. Through his combined love of words and music, M'barali embraced these new musical forms and began to write his own material. Performing in French under the name MC Solaar, his ambition was to show that rap was a musical style that could transcend language.

By 1989 he had joined with Parisian deejay Jimmy Jay, singer Melaaz, and rapper Soon EMC, and they performed as The 501 Special Source. Within a year MC Solaar was performing solo, playing shows in the clubs of Paris. He soon signed with Polydor Records and released his first single in 1991. "Caroline" reached #1 in the French chart, an unheard-of feat for a rap artist. The album that followed, *Qui Seme le Vent Recolte le Tempo* (1991), became the first rap/hip-hop album in France to go platinum, eventually selling over 400,000 copies. The album also became a benchmark for other French rappers. Solaar's answer was to release the single "L'histoire de l'Art," in which he sang about others stealing his style.

MC Solaar
Pictorialpress Ltd.,
London, UK

In 1992 he was voted best upcoming act at the Victoires de la Musique awards ceremony. His growing success in France led to tours in Europe and Japan and also led to him signing in the United Kingdom with the influential "Talkin' Loud" label. In the United States he was a guest on Guru's *Jazzmatazz* album (1993) and was a featured artist on a compilation released by Tommy Boy records. Unlike many of the rappers at the time who were using suburban violence as the main inspiration behind their music, Solaar's lyrics dealt widely with pacifist themes. *Prose Combat*, released in November 1994, showcased his beliefs and dealt with ideas of love and camaraderie. The album eclipsed his debut release and sold over a million copies.

Although Solaar was well known for his pacifist stance, he was invited to record a song for a new French movie, *La Haine*. The film followed the lives of three young men living on the outskirts of Paris and dealt with the violence and racism that were rife in the suburbs of the French capital. The song that Solaar presented, "Comme dans un Film," reflected the same themes and led Solaar into a new dimension of thought culminating in the album *Paradisaque* (1997). It featured the "gangsta rap" that was being imported from America, but with a unique Gallic slant. The single "Gangster Moderne" carried on these ideas and became another chart hit.

In 1998 Solaar released his fourth, self-titled album. Here the rapper returned to the laid-back style that had originally won him a legion of fans and admirers, both among the public and in the music business around the world. The year ended with a double album, *La Tour de la Question*, recorded over a series of concerts around France.

In summer 2001 Solaar released *Cinquième As*. Focusing on the political history of France and autobiographical stories, the record offered a relaxed mood, a style of hip-hop that Solaar has made his own. Although selling well in France, the album failed to live up to expectations across Europe. As Solaar undertook another tour of France in November and December, a series of singles was released including "Solaar Pleasure" and "Hasta La Vista." These songs have remained in the French and European charts as MC Solaar continues to fly the flag for Gallic hip-hop and rap.

References

www.solaarsystem.net

MTV-Cyclopedia by Nick Duerden, Ian Gittens, and Shaun Phillips (London: Carlton, 1997). ISBN 185868336x

Mecano (Spain)

Jose Maria Cano met Ana Torroja at university in Spain, and although musically Cano wanted to be a solo artist, he invited Torroja to join him. Jose's brother, Nacho, who always had a keen interest in music and had played in a band previously, joined the others and the trio became Mecano. Although they were unsuccessful in securing gigs, they presented their bombastic rock to various record companies. In 1982, they signed with CBS. After recording their first single, "Hoy no me Puedo Levantar," the band members began to promote it themselves after being given no funds by the record company who were unsure how the song would be greeted. The band distributed the record to anyone willing to play it, including radio stations, bars, and restaurants. When the reaction to the standard rock song was encouraging, CBS put money into the promotion that resulted in sales of 35,000 copies. Although the follow-up single, "Perdido en mi Habtacian," did not perform as well, Mecano was now recognized by the public.

Although relying on a traditional rock line-up, the band was beginning to be viewed as a group that tried to bring innovation into their work. Mecano recorded videos (one of the first Spanish groups to do so) and wrote lyrics that reflected the angst of their generation. A subsequent single, "Quiero Vivir en la Civdad," became a national anthem for Spanish youth. As the band gained increasing numbers of fans, the record company sent the group to London to record a debut album. The result, *Me Cole en Una Fiesta* (1982), sold 100,000 copies within the first three months of its release. Mecano was now the most popular band in Spain and was appearing regularly on TV and radio, as well as undertaking its first tour of Spain. In summer 1982 the band released "Maquillaje" as a single, which went straight into the charts at #1. In an attempt to break into the English-speaking market, the group re-recorded its debut album. Although the album did little in the way of sales, the band gained valuable experience about how to promote to foreign markets. This was useful when Mecano began to perform in other areas of the world, especially Latin America.

Mecano
Pictorialpress Ltd., London, UK

Mecano had come to be seen by the press as the most important rock band in Spain.

In December 1982 the group recorded its second album, *Donde Esta El Pais de las Fiadas*. Released in April of the following year, the album was a success. Now that the members of Mecano were national heroes, the Cano brothers decided to take time off to write for other artists. After the band's third album, *Ya Viene el Sol*, was released in 1984, Mecano spent the rest of the year on the touring and promotional circuit. Although the band members took more time off to begin solo careers, in 1985 they released a live album (*En Corcierto*) to satisfy the demands of their huge fan base. *Entre el Cielo y el Suelo*, Mecano's fifth album, was released in 1987; with the band staying true to its rock beginnings, the single "Entre el Cielo y el Suelo" was named song of the year at the Spanish music awards and became the group's best-selling record. By now Mecano was achieving recognition in other countries. The band's next album, *Descanso Dominical* (1989), not only continued the group's popularity in Spain but sold well in Latin America and East Asia, as well as being recorded in Italian and French. The single "Mujer Contra Mujer," released in France under the title "Une Femme Avec Une Femme," sold over 400,000 copies.

The band's seventh studio album, *Aidalai*, was released in 1991, but the members of Mecano were by now deeply involved in their own solo projects.

After touring the album for nearly two years, and with Troja's voice suffering from the strain of playing so many concerts, the band took time off. A "best of" album, *Ana Jose Nacho*, released in 1992, signaled what seemed to be the end for the group. However, it wasn't until 1997 that Jose Cano finally left Mecano to pursue other musical projects. Although there continue to be rumors that Mecano will play again, there is little evidence to support them.

References

www.mecano.net

Mehndi, Daler (India)

Born in Benares in the north of India, Daler Mehndi began singing at age five. When he was ten years old he met a group of artists who were passing through his town on the way to perform in Jaunpar. Without telling his family, he joined them and found himself performing in front of 10,000 people. His family found him standing center stage, enjoying the applause of the huge audience. The experience heightened Mehndi's appetite for music, and when he was fourteen he heard Ustad Raahat Ali Khan (now deceased) on the radio and left home in an attempt to find Khan's whereabouts. Mehndi ultimately located Khan, who in turn agreed to take Mehndi on in a traditional *Guru-Shishya* relationship. (*Guru* means "teacher, spiritual guide, mentor"; *Shishya* means "student.") Mehndi then immersed himself in the traditions of Hindustani classical music and learned to play the tabla, harmonium, and tanpura as well as how to sing *ghazaals*, songs inspired by Indian poetry. In 1995 Mehndi changed his focus and began to experiment with pop music.

The experiment was an immediate success. Mehndi's debut album, *Bolo Ta Ra Ra* (1995), recorded for the Magnasound label, sold over half a million copies within the first two months of its release. His high-energy singing style and his appearance, complete with bejeweled turban, made him an overnight sensation. The album is still the biggest-selling non-soundtrack album in Indian history. Toward the end of the year India's most popular music station, Channel V, named Mehndi best male pop singer for 1995, a success that was repeated in 1996 and 1997.

Dard Di Rab Rab (1996) secured Mehndi's position. Soon his concerts were populated by audiences "on the brink of hysteria." Roles in India's famous Bollywood movies—full of dancing and singing and always containing a leading man (more often than not Mehndi), a leading lady, and a villain with the expected storyline and happy ending—followed. Films such as *Mrityudata* and *Arjun Pundit* filled cinemas for months and kept Mehndi in the public eye as he began work on his third album. Released in 1997, *Ho Jayegi Bale Bale* continued to feature Mehndi's high-energy style as traditional Indian instrumentation blended with Western dance beats. The album earned Mehndi the Screen Videocon award for best male pop singer. He also became the first Asian artist to perform at the industry-only Tam Tam festival in France.

Always an outspoken advocate for charities concerned with health issues, in 1998 Mehndi began his Green Drive campaign. Aiming at improving the quality of the environment, the Green Drive campaign planted more than 2 million trees around the streets of Delhi, financed entirely by Mehndi. As he toured the country in support of his 1998 album, *Tunak Tun Tun*, Mehndi promoted issues related to the Green Drive and encouraged local and national welfare organizations to become involved as part of his wish for Green Drive to become a "people's movement." During 1999 and 2000 another two and a half million trees were planted. Although many new bhangra-pop singers have emerged since Mehndi introduced the genre, he still commands huge audiences. In fact, the 2000 release of a "best of" album sold over a million copies. Mehndi is currently negotiating a new contract before recording material for a fifth album.

References

www.indianmelody.com/dalermehndi

Mercury, Daniela (Brazil)

Popularly known as the Queen of Axé (pronounced "ah-shay"), Daniela Mercuri de Almeida was born in the city of Salvador in the Bahia region of Brazil on July 28, 1965. After finishing her education, Mercury trained to become a dancer but began singing on *trios elétricos* at the end of the 1980s. (The *trios elétricos* are trucks wired up to sound systems that drive around the streets of Salvador during the carnivals that take place through the summer. Each truck has a band or deejay playing the reggae-samba style of Axé.) Mercury soon became one of the most sought-after singers. In the last years of the decade she released two albums with the band Comanhia Clic. Though neither record had much commercial success, it did introduce Mercury to the general public, and a record deal with Sony Brazil soon followed. By the end of 1991 she had recorded her first album, *Swing da Cor*, which became a surprise hit with its light pop and big ballads. Although she was already well known in Salvador, now the wider Brazilian public noticed Mercury's fresh, dynamic style and made her an instant success.

Concerts were arranged to promote the album, and the next twelve months were taken up performing across Brazil. By 1993 a new album was ready for release; *O canto de Cidade* was also based on the Axé style and confirmed Mercury as an established artist. As well as breaking records in Brazil, the album sold over a million copies in neighboring Argentina before Mercury had even performed a concert there. Later in the same year she was admitted to the hospital with appendicitis and fans held a 24-hour vigil while TV news bulletins broadcast regular updates on her well-being. Toward the end of the year she made her U.S. debut at the Ritz in New York, and in 1994 she became the only Brazilian to be invited to play at the annual Sony Music party (where the staff followed their president's lead by dancing in the aisles to Mercury's performance). By now Mercury had begun to make a mark in Asia.

The release of *Musica de Rue* in 1994 once again broke records for a Brazilian artist in Japan, where she was so popular that she agreed to record a track in Japanese. Although Mercury was still the biggest name in Axé and she loved performing in her native city (the local government proclaimed her "the greatest Bahian tourist attraction"), she was beginning to move away from the solid rhythms of the genre. To reflect her growing international stature, she enlisted the help of a group of songwriters to produce a sound she thought would have more international appeal. Her next album, *Feijao com Arroz* (1996), was of a more languid style than any of her offerings to date, but the change proved popular as the album outsold all her previous releases. She continued to produce new material, which eventually was released as *Electrica* in 1998.

After the *New York Times* called Mercury's music "international pop with finesse and power" and *Billboard* wrote that she had "made Bahian music accessible without compromising its artistic essence," she returned to the studio to record *Sol da Libertade* (2000). Then a European tour was arranged as well as shows in South America and Asia. In January 2001, Mercury appeared at the Rock in Rio festival, sharing the stage with, among others, Sting and **Silverchair**. Later in the year she released *Sov de Qualquer Lugar*. The album was a collection of up-beat, rhythmical songs, heavily reliant on percussion to push the numbers along. Since the release of the album, Mercury has continued performing at festivals and in theaters in Brazil and South America.

References

www.vol.com.br/danielamercury

Moist (Canada)

David Usher (b. April 24, 1966) was born in Oxford, England, to a Canadian father and a Thai mother. He moved to Canada as a young child, attended Simon Frasier University in Vancouver, and then began playing in bands, where he met keyboard player Kevin Young (b. September 18, 1966), a former student of Queens University in Kingston, Ontario. Usher and Young began auditioning, with little success, for musicians to form a band to play the songs they had been recording. Bass player Jeff Pearce (b. April 25, 1967) and guitarist Mark Makoway (b. September 12, 1966) had also been students at Queens and had been playing in bands together when they met Usher and Young at a party in 1992. After realizing they had much in common they formed a band, naming it Moist for no reason other than "it sounded good." After drummer Jamie Kaufman was enlisted, the group began rehearsing and playing the clubs of Vancouver. Before long Kaufman was replaced by Paul Wilcox (b. February 13, 1969) a friend of a friend, who had been working as a chef and who had not played drums for over a year. Performing regularly for the next twelve months, the band began to attract fans in increasing numbers to its solid rock music, but record labels seemed uninterested. By April 1994, the band had recorded a tape of its songs that sold well at shows; but the recording had taken up most of the band's resources, to the point that breaking up was considered an option as money and enthusiasm began to wane. EMI then stepped in and offered the band a deal, seeing in Usher, with his long hair and exotic looks, an ideal front-man and selling point.

The first fruit of the association was the single "Push." Receiving heavy air-play on Canada's most influential radio station, MuchMusic, the single sold 5,000 copies in a little over a month, a significant achievement in Canada. The band's debut album, *Silver* (1994), allegedly recorded in three days, was re-leased soon thereafter. The intense guitar-based songs helped the record to sell almost half a million copies, earning the band a four times platinum disc. As a result the band won a Juno Award for best newcomers despite one review berat-ing them as "a disparate and odd assortment of human beings." By 1995 the band had moved to Montreal, stating that the mixed culture of the city would give the group new inspiration for its next album.

Creature (1996) quickly equaled the success of *Silver*. By now Moist had become the biggest rock act in Canada, and an in-store appearance in Calgary had to be cancelled when almost 5,000 fans turned up at the shop to catch a glimpse of their idols. The band was now beginning to gain recognition in other countries, including England (where "Push" reached the top twenty) and Thai-land (helped partly by Usher's Thai connections and partly by EMI's marketing department, which made the most of Usher's maternal family connections). While on tour in Thailand the band found its fans camping in the lobby of the hotel twenty-four hours a day. In the same year the group played in the town of Tuktoyaktuk, in the Arctic Circle, with rock band Metallica to 500 people, and then toured with Neil Young, playing to 15,000 people per show at arenas around Canada. Although the band's 1997 album release was available only to its fan club, it still won at the MuchMusic Awards for the video to the single "Tangerine." The band was now engaged in touring across the world, with vary-ing degrees of success, and preparing material for a fourth album. During this period Usher recorded a solo album, mostly in the kitchen of his apartment in Montreal; he released *Little Songs* in March 1998. Mellower than Moist records, the album earned a gold disc while Usher undertook various promo-tional duties.

After the band's fourth album, *Mercedes Five and Dime*, was released in June 1999, the first single taken from it, "Breathe," immediately charged to the #1 spot in Canada. A similar round of concerts followed, and once again Usher took time off to begin recording a solo album. In December it was announced that drummer Paul Wilcox was going to leave the band. Having suffered from a back problem for some time, he decided to take up a career as an actor. Mark Makoway, who was also involved in other projects, wrote *"The Indie Band Bible,"* an account of how to break into Canada's music scene.

By May 2001 Usher had recorded another series of reflective, acoustic lead songs and released his second solo album, *Alone in the Universe*, followed in July by another album, *Morning Orbit*. He then toured for four months, beginning in Canada before visiting Southeast Asia with Moist, minus Makoway, as his backing band. (Makoway during this time became involved in a series of other projects, including working with Ellen Reid from **Crash Test Dummies** on her debut solo album, *Cinderella*.) The albums were nominated for three Casby awards before Moist released a singles collection, *Machine Punch Through*, in November as a precursor to new material in 2002.

References

www.http://listen.to/moist

Morthens, Bubbi (Iceland)

Asbjöern Morthens was born in the Icelandic capital, Reykjavik, on July 6, 1956. Known familiarly as Bubbi, as a child he moved to Denmark, the home country of his mother, to attend school. Although he had been reading the works of classical authors such as Alexander Dumas and Victor Hugo from the age of six, he was diagnosed as dyslexic, which led to a difficult school life. When he reached age fifteen he left school and returned to Iceland, where he found work in one of the many fish processing factories on the island. While there Morthens began writing songs and performed them for his fellow workers in the hostels where the migrant workers lived.

In 1980 he released his first album, *Isbjarnarblus*, a collection of folk songs about the hardships of factory work. Later that year he met two Englishmen, brothers Mike and Danny Pollack, and two natives of Reykjavik, Rúnar Erlingsson and Magnús Stefánsson, and formed the band Utangardsmenn. The first punk band in the country, the group released four influential albums during 1980 and 1981—*Rækju-Reggea, Geislavirkir, 45RPM*, and *I upphafi skyldi endinn skoda*—before Morthens left to form the group EGO. His new band managed to release three albums in two years (*Breyttir timar, Imynd*, and *EGO*), but Morthens also continued to release solo work during this period, with *Fingraför* and *Línudans* (both 1983).

After the breakup of EGO, Morthens concentrated on his solo career. However, the drug consumption that had been a feature of his earlier bands began to overwhelm him, and in 1984 he was admitted to the hospital. As he was weaned off drugs, he wrote the material for *Kona* (1985), a collection of introspective and autobiographical songs that was regarded by many critics as his best to date. He subsequently released more albums, both solo efforts and collaborations with other Icelandic musicians, including the album *Skytturnar* (1987), which he recorded with members of **The Sugarcubes**. He also wrote the soundtrack for the film *White Whales*. Morthens's prolific output continued, and in 1988 he composed the music for another movie, *Foxtrot*. Still writing prolifically, between 1988 and 1992 Morthens released eight solo albums, including a "best of," *Sögur af landi*, in 1990. By now he was Iceland's most popular performer, as he continued to release an album a year of his folk/punk with *Lifid er ljuft* (1993), *3 Heimar* (1994), and *I skugga Morthens* (1995). The latter album was a tribute to his uncle, Hauser Morthens, a popular singer/songwriter in the country.

Although he was a mainstream musical success, Morthens was always already to court controversy. In 1997 he organized a boxing match, a sport that had been illegal in Iceland since 1956, to promote his latest album, *Truir thu a engla*. Although he did not actually take part in the fighting, during the bout he was arrested and later given a two-year suspended prison sentence. In the same year Morthens introduced new musical styles into his album *Allar áttir*. The blend of rock, soul, folk, and pop gave a new dimension to his solo work. In the following year he returned to a more sparse, acoustic sound for *Arfur*, which reflected the country's social landscape with downbeat black humoured songs. In 1999 he released a compilation album containing music from his first ten years, *Sögur 1980–1990*; this was followed in 2000 by another album dealing with the latter half of his career, *Sögur 1990–2000*. In 2000 he was also invited to put the words of Sweden's leading eighteenth-century poet, Carl Michael Bellman, to music. He performed the work later in the year at the Reykjavik Arts Festival, after which he released the album *Bellman,* which introduced orchestral arrangements to Morthens' work. To celebrate the new millennium, Iceland held an awards ceremony at which Morthens's first group, Utangardsmenn, was named band of the century.

References

www.members.aol.com/skugga607/velkomir

Murat (France)

Jean-Louis Bergheaud was born in the tiny village of La Bourboule, in the heart of the French countryside, on January 28, 1954. By the time he was seven years old he had mastered the harmonica, but music was only a peripheral interest until, when the boy was fifteen, an English teacher introduced him to jazz and R&B. Soon thereafter he formed his first band, Clara, and began performing in the local area. After he left school he traveled around France, finding jobs where he could and learning any musical instrument that came to hand; then, in 1977, he returned to Auvergne, the area where he was born, and began to concentrate on music.

In 1981 he released a single, "Suicidez-vous, le peuple est mort," but the downbeat song (which stated that France was dead and people should commit suicide) was banned by some radio stations and disappeared. It was enough for him to be noticed by EMI, however, and in the following year he signed with the company. An album, *Murat*, that reflected his early musical passions was released in 1982 under the name Jean-Louis Murat, but it failed to sell. The follow-up, *Passions Privées* (1984), fared no better, and Murat and EMI parted company. By 1987 he had signed with Virgin Records, and two years later he released *Cheyanne Autumn*. Despite no marketing strategy or promotional concerts, the album's gentle, moody ambience helped it immediately go gold, selling in excess of 100,000 copies, as a single from the record, "Sentiment nouveau," climbed high in the national charts. This was an indication that Murat was being taken seriously by the critics (the newspaper *Liberation* stated that he "breaks down the boundaries between rock, pop and pure poetry") and the public alike, who empathized with the reclusive singer.

In 1991 he released *Le Manteau de Pluie* to critical acclaim and also recorded a duet with singer **Mylene Farmer**; "Regrets" became another chart hit. Despite the relative success of his albums, Murat had yet to play any concerts. It wasn't until after the release of his next R&B influenced album, *Venus* (1993), that Murat put a band together and set off on a tour of the country. While on the road he wrote the music for a feature film, *Mlle. Personne*, that opened in French cinemas later that year. Some of the concerts he performed during that period were recorded, and an album, *Live*, was released in 1995.

In 1996 Murat released *Dolores*. Taking on a rock-oriented feel, the album was regarded by many critics as his best to date and included his version of a poem by the nineteenth-century French poet Baudelaire, "Reversibilité." Murat toured behind the album, but instead of being backed by a full band, he was joined by Denis Clavaizolle. Clavaizolle had produced much of Murat's work to that point and played keyboards during the shows. Shortly after the tour ended, Murat took part in the recording of a tribute album to Leonard Cohen, *I'm Your Fan*, where he appeared alongside REM, Nick Cave, and The Pixies. Another live album, *Live in Dolores*, was released in 1998 before Murat moved to the United States to begin work on his tenth album. *Mustango* had a vague country and western feel that incorporated Murat's downbeat, poetical lyrics. The album was recorded in New York and Tucson, Arizona, before being released in France in 1999. In next year Murat appeared at festivals across France while writing new material.

Continuing to involve himself in projects that took him away from the mainstream, in April 2001 Murat released *Mrs. Deshoulières*. The album was based on the work of Antoinette Deshoulières, a radical poet in seventeenth-century France. She was a member of a group of women writers known as Les Précieuses, who sought to bring feminine issues to the forefront of society. The French actress Isabelle Huppert was the voice of Deshoulières on the record, and she appeared on TV with Murat to perform songs from the album, which later became a top ten hit in France. In March 2002 Murat released *le moujik et sa femme*. The record used piano and harmonica to give the songs a mellow feel, and it became another chart success.

References

www.jlmurat.com

Mutton Birds, The (New Zealand)

Singer/guitarist Don McGlashen, guitarist David Long, and drummer Ross Burge had all been involved in the New Zealand music scene for many years, playing in various bands and being veterans of many album releases, when they formed The Mutton Birds in 1991. In the following year, after bass player Alan Gregg became the band's fourth member, the group released its debut, self-titled album. The records folk/pop style made it a favorite with college radio, and before long New Zealand's mainstream stations added it to their playlist. Within twelve months the album went platinum, and EMI Australia offered the band a contract. Accepting, the group returned to the studio and began recording the follow-up, *Salty*. Although the album was released in April 1994, a single, "The Heater," had already hit the stores in February and entered the charts at #1. *Salty* became the band's second platinum album, continuing The Mutton Birds' take on upbeat, folky pop. A subsequent single, "Anchor Me," released in September, saw McGlashen win New Zealand's top songwriting award.

Now well established at home and in Australia, in 1995 the band made regular trips to the United Kingdom, where, later in the year, the group released *Nature*. The album was a compilation of the best songs from the band's first two albums. Although it did not fare too well in the charts, it won the band enough critical acclaim to encourage it to begin to spend more time in England—and London soon became the group's second home. Appearing at all the major European festivals during the summer of 1995 helped establish the name of the band in Europe, and in order to keep its profile high at home, it released a box set of its first two albums, *Box of Birds* (1995). As the band felt more at home in England, it decided to record a third album in London: *Envy of Angels* was released in November 1996. Variously described as "deliriously tuneful" and "breathtaking" by critics, the album's tone of claustrophobia and melancholy, although turning triple platinum at home, failed to capture the imagination of the mainstream music fans in Britain. However, it earned the group a dedicated and growing number of core supporters. It also introduced the band to an audience worldwide, with sales in South America and Canada as well as mainland Europe.

Although Long left the band in 1996 to return to New Zealand (he was replaced by Chris Sheehan), the group's profile continued to grow in its native country. Early in 1997 the band reached the top twenty with a cover of U.S. rock band Blue Oyster Cult's "Don't Fear the Reaper," recorded for the soundtrack of the movie *The Frighteners*. Despite the group's critical success, the band's U.K. company, Virgin, dropped it because of poor album sales. Undeterred by this setback, the band released a live recording of a London show, *Angle of Entry* (1997), on its own Gravy Train label. In January 1998, The Mutton Birds played a series of small shows in the south of England before returning to New Zealand in the summer, where they performed a series of a sold-out concerts across the country.

As the band was committed to touring, it released a compilation album in the United Kingdom in June. *Too Hard Basket—B-Sides and Bastards* satisfied the group's growing fan base but failed to show on the British charts. Later in the year Gregg left the band and began working with **Bic Runga**; Gregg was replaced by a non–New Zealander, the Englishman Tony Fisher. The band released its fourth studio album, *Rain, Steam & Speed*, in September 1999. The album won favor in the press as it showcased the band's intelligent and sensitive songwriting, but it did little to introduce the group to a mainstream audience in the United Kingdom even though it kept the band at the top of the charts at home. A second live album, *The MB's Live in Manchester*, was released in December, but it only satisfied the group's hardcore audience. Throughout 2000 the band played regular concerts across Europe and the United Kingdom, as well as major shows in New Zealand and Australia. In a chart released in 2001 listing New Zealanders' favorite songs, The Mutton Birds placed #23 with "Dominion Road." In 2001 the group returned to the United Kingdom to begin more recording and touring.

References

www.muttonbirds.com

N

Namie, Amuro (Japan)

Amuro Namie was born on the small Japanese island of Okinawa on September 20, 1977. As part of her education she enrolled in the Okinawa Actors School and began performing in school concerts. In 1992, at age fifteen, she and four friends, Ameku Minako, Takushi Namako, Aragaki Hisako, and Makino Anna, formed the pop band Super Monkeys and signed with EMI before releasing their debut single, the synthesizer-heavy "Mr. USA." Shortly thereafter the band relocated to Tokyo, where Namie was soon regarded by the record company as the most talented singer in Super Monkeys. In fact, the group's fourth single, "Paradise Train" (1994), was released under the name Amuro Namie and Super Monkeys and continued the trend for up-beat pop dance tunes. The following January the group's next single, "Try Me," sold over 750,000 copies. Super Monkeys was now going through a period of disruption, as Minako and Hisako left and were replaced by Ritsuko Matsuda and Reina Miyanchi. By April, Namie was looking to develop a solo career, however, and left the band after the release of "Taiyo No Season." Super Monkeys then became SM4 before finally developing into Max, the name under which they achieved more success.

In June 1995 Namie released her first solo single. "Stop the Music" developed the sound of Super Monkeys with more depth in the production and it raced to the top of the charts. A month after her nineteenth birthday, Namie released her first solo album, *Dance Tracks Vol. 1*, a collection of synthesized pop tunes that sold over 2 million copies in Asia. It brought her to the attention of Japan's top producer, Tetsuya Komoro, who took her under his wing and signed her with the Avex-Trax label, where together they produced some of the biggest hits ever seen in the country. The first single of the collaboration was "Body Feels Exit," which hit #1 in Japan in October 1995. Over the next six months Naime released three more multimillion-selling singles, "Chase the Chance,"

"Don't Wanna Cry," and "You Are My Sunshine." *Sweet 19 Blues*, released in July, was notably similar to her debut album and sold 3.7 million copies within the first week of its release, a record for the country at the time. In November an album of Namie's solo songs and Super Monkey tracks, *Original Tracks Vol. 1*, sold over 2 million copies. At the end of the year Naime became the youngest person ever to win the Japan Records award for selling over 10 million records for the year.

The year 1997 started out with the release of another #1 single, "Can You Celebrate," as she began her first tour. Named "A Walk in the Park," the tour took her across Asia into Taiwan and Hong Kong, as well as Japan. Naime was also appearing in TV commercials for cosmetics, dairy produce, and hair products, among many others. Her next album, *Concentration 20* (1997), almost a copy of her earlier work, became another massive seller. Three months later Naime announced plans to marry; in December, to celebrate her wedding, she re-released "Can You Celebrate," which again occupied the #1 spot in the country. The following year the single won the grand prize at the Japan Records awards.

In January 1998 Namie released a compilation album covering her work of the previous three years. The album, *181920 Best Collection*, became her second solo #1 album. Namie later announced she was pregnant and was going to take a year away from the industry. In December she became a mother and released the first of her new material which, although again driven by keyboards, showed that Naime had achieved a maturity in her voice. "I Have Never Seen" also became a #1 hit. The following year tragedy struck: On the same day that Naime released the single "Respect the Power of Love," her mother was killed by Naime's sister's husband in an argument, allegedly over money.

In July 1999 Naime released a single, "Toi et Moi," taken from the Pokemon movie *Pocket Monster*, and followed it in September with "Something about the Kiss." After the birth of her son and the death of her mother, Namie began to appear less frequently on TV and stage. However, on New Year's Day 2000 she released the single "Love 2000," and later in the month she released the album *Genius 2000*. Two more singles issued at the end of the year, "Never End" and "Please Smile Again," reached #1, as did her first single release in 2001, "Dreaming I Was Dreaming." Namie continues to balance a career and motherhood. In December 2001 Namie released *Break The Rules*. The album was a collection of R&B numbers that were recorded with U.S. producer Dallas Austin, who gave the songs a smooth pop feel. The album was another huge hit in Japan.

References

www.amuro.com

Nena (Germany)

Gabriele Susanne Kerner was born on March 24 1960, in the small town of Hagen, Germany. In 1979, after school and college, she met Rainer Kitzmann,

Nena
Pictorialpress Ltd., London, UK

who played guitar in the rock band The Stripes, along with Carlo Karges (guitar), Uwe Fahrenkrog-Peterson (keyboards), Jurgen Demel (bass), and Rolf Brendel (drums); Kerner joined as vocalist. After playing shows around Hagen, in 1980 the band relocated to Berlin, where it had its first hit, "Just A Dream," which reached #1 in Germany. An album, *The Stripes*, followed and achieved a small amount of success for the group. In the following year The Stripes broke up and Nena was formed, with Kerner becoming the public image of the band. A debut single, "Ner Getraumt," became an instant success, but it was in the following year that Nena had its most spectacular breakthrough. In 1983 the band released a self-titled album that included the song "99 Luftballons." Released as a single, it became #1 all over Europe and Asia and in the United States.

The band toured Europe on the strength of "99 Luftballons," and, although its 1984 album, titled simply, was a huge hit in Germany, its synthesizer and guitar soft-rock songs failed to chart anywhere else. Another album was released in the following year, *Feuer und Flamme*, but the band had run its course split up in 1987. By now the German public identified Nena as being Kerner, not the group. For the next two years Kerner remained out of the public eye but returned with *Wunder gescheh'n* (1989), a collection of self-written songs that were slower and quieter than the former band songs. The album sold over a million copies.

In 1990 Nena released a solo album *Komm Lieber Mai*, dedicated to her recently born twins. The album, a collection of sentimental songs about childhood written from her memory of growing up, was the first of a series of best-selling albums that shared the same theme. In 1993 she released *Bongo Girl*. The tour that accompanied it and the single "Manchmal ist ein Tag ein ganzes Leben" were received enthusiastically by press, TV, and her fans. With the birth of her next child in 1995, Nena released her second album of childhood songs, *Unser Apfelhaus*. The release touched a nerve with the German public and sold well.

It wasn't until 1997 that she released her next album, *Jamma Nich*, a record that harked back to her rock roots. Nena undertook a tour with a new band to promote it, playing to sold-out venues across Germany. In the same year she released *Nena's Weihnachtreise*. It became another #1 album and marked her change from being a pop icon to being a family entertainer. In 1998 she consolidated her position, as the single "Was hast Du in mei nem Traum gemacht" was used to introduce the German Grand Prix of that year, a program she also co-presented. In the same year she undertook her biggest tour, playing eleven open-air concerts to over half a million people. Between 1999 and 2001 she continued to play across Germany, until in October 2001 she released a new album, *Chokmah*. This release showed Nena tiring of her image as a family entertainer, as it continued her rock sensibility; and in November she appeared in a sultry pose on the front cover of Germany's *Maxim* magazine. In 2000 the single "99 Luftballons" was covered by both a German girl duo, Pleasure Deluxe, and the U.S. band Goldfinger. In April 2002 Nena released another album of songs for children, *Tausend Sterne*. During the summer she performed at a number of festivals across Germany and then undertook a tour that kept her on the road until October.

References

www.nena.de

Rock On: The Illustrated Encyclopedia of Rock n' Roll: The Video Revolution by Norm N. Nite (New York: Harper & Row, 1985). ISBN 0061816442

New Order (England)

Vocalist and guitar player Bernard Summer (b. January 4, 1956), bass player Peter Hook (b. February 13, 1956), and drummer Steven Morris (b. October 28, 1957) all were members of the alternative indie band Joy Division in Manchester, England, in the 1970s. Although the band was respected by the United Kingdom's music press and was winning a growing fan base, as well as planning a major tour of the United States, it came to an end when singer Ian Curtis committed suicide in May 1980. The three remaining members of the band decided to carry on as New Order and undertook a small tour of the United States before returning to England, where keyboard player Gillian Gilbert (b. January 27, 1961) joined the band. Although the group was viewed by many as merely an imitation of Joy Division, by spring 1981 the band had its first top ten single, "Ceremony," and released its debut album, *Movement*. Although Joy Division was based on a traditional musical line-up of guitar, bass, and drums, New Order was experimenting with new electronic technology, introducing samples and drum machines which was reflected in the May 1982 single "Temptation." This new technology was responsible for the "Acid House" craze that was beginning to take U.K. club culture by storm. Later the band, along with local Manchester record label Factory, opened a nightclub, the Haçienda, which became the breeding ground for the "Madchester" scene of the late 1980s, led by **The Stone Roses**.

In March 1983, New Order released the single "Blue Monday." The track, largely based around Hook's lead bass line, was available only as a 12″ disc and became the biggest selling 12″ in the United Kingdom ever. The song also became the catalyst for a new genre of music in the United Kingdom that blended dance beats with the traditional four-piece band line-up. Two subsequent singles, "Confusion" and "Thieves Like Us," were also only released as 12″ discs. The length of the tracks (both over six minutes long), coupled with the 12″ format, meant they received little airplay on radio and TV. Although the band failed to make any impression on the charts, it was becoming one of the most respected in the country by the press. New Order continued to release singles, but it wasn't until 1987 that it once again appeared in the charts. "True Faith," released in July and accompanied by an award-winning video, reached the top five and gave the band its biggest hit to date. (The following year the group's re-mix of "Blue Monday" by U.S. producer Quincy Jones also made the top five.)

In 1989 the band released *Technique*, which became its first #1 album. A chart of the same year, showing the most popular songs of the decade, revealed New Order to be in thirteenth position with "Blue Monday," which had spent forty-nine weeks on the chart. As the band grew in mainstream popularity it was invited to write a song for England's national soccer team, which was about to travel to Spain for the World Cup of 1990. "World in Motion" featured vocals by some members of the English team and reached #1, causing critics to dub it "the best [soccer] song of all time." Instead of capitalizing on the commercial success of "World in Motion," the band parted to spend time on other projects. Hook formed the group Revenge; Sumner joined with **The Smiths'** guitarist, Johnny Marr, to form the group Electronic; and Morris and Gilbert became The Other Two. Although all this activity resulted in rumors of a split, in 1993 the band released *Republic* and headlined the Reading Festival in England. *Republic* went on to sell more than 500,000 copies in the United States. Four singles were released in 1993 ("Regret," "Ruined in a Day," "World," and "Spooky"), but the next two years saw only re-releases of "True Faith" and "Blue Monday" as the band members returned to solo projects. In 1998 the band re-emerged with its first new material in five years, "Brutal," which later appeared on the soundtrack to the Leonardo Di Caprio movie *The Beach*. ("True Faith" appeared on the soundtrack to *American Psycho*).

In 2001, New Order released *Get Ready*, a more guitar-based effort still relying on the punchy bass lines of Hook. It settled in the top ten. In October the band won a special award at the British Dance Music Awards for its outstanding contribution to dance music. During the summer of 2002 the band played festivals across Europe. In July *Before & After,* a double album of live material featuring both Joy Division and New Order material, was released.

References

www.neworderonline.com

Nievera, Martin (Philippines)

Martin Nievera was born in the Philippines on February 5, 1962, the son of Bert Nievera, a popular singer of the 1950s and 1960s. When Nievera was three years old, his father moved the family to Hawaii as Bert became the singer in the band S.O.S. Although his mother tried to discourage Nievera from pursuing a singing career, the influence of his father proved overwhelming. While Martin was still a child, Bert opened a restaurant and the two of them would often sing together as they were cooking.

After he finished his schooling, Martin Nievera returned to the Philippines at age eighteen to try to establish himself as a singer. Initially, he enrolled in business courses at college, but through the influence of his father soon found live engagements. By the end of 1982, after the release of his first successful album, *Martin . . . Take One,* he had earned the title of most promising entertainer by the Aliw Awards Foundation. The record became the blueprint for Nievera's future releases, as it mixed cover versions with highly orchestrated and highly produced original ballads. The following year a single, "Pain," earned him first place at the 6th Metro Manila Popular Music Festival. In 1984 and 1985, he was named entertainer of the year and most outstanding male performer respectively, following the release of albums *The Best Gift* (1984) and *Martin* (1985).

In 1986 he married another popular Filipino singer, **Pops Fernandez**, and the couple began to tour as a duo, as well as appear on TV together. By now Nievera had been christened the "Concert King of the Philippines" by the press, while his wife won the title of "Concert Queen." In the following year Nievera began a successful acting career in TV and movies, as his natural charm and "gift of the gab" made him come across as a natural performer on the screen. More awards followed as he released more powerful ballads in 1987, with the single "You Are To Me" and album *Ikaw and Lahat sa Akin* among them.

Following on from his acting, Nievera began to host TV variety shows, and in 1986 introduced a new singer, **Regine Velasquez**, to the Filipino public on the show "Penthouse Live." Velasquez soon became known as "Asia's Songbird," helped by the contribution of Nievera and Fernandez. Over the next few years Nievera released a string of albums, including *Say That You Love Me* (1988), *A New Start* (1991) and *Roads* (1994), which included a duet, "Forever," with Velasquez. The albums all followed the same formula of original material and cover versions, and rarely contained songs other than ballads. Nievera continued to appear in concert theatres across the country and visited

Canada and the United States where, in 1998 in California, he was given the media achievement award at the Philippine American Convention.

It was during this time that the pressures of recording and live work began to have an effect on his marriage and, in 1987, Nievera and Fernandez split up. He recorded an album of songs in only two days which was dedicated to his wife, and although the 1998 album *Forever* was initially meant to be a personal gift to Fernandez, it was released commercially and has since become the second best-selling album ever in the Philippines. The success of the record convinced Nievera to release two more as part of a trilogy and *Forever, Forever* and *Return to Forever* (both 1999) went on to top the charts.

The following year Nievera became the first pop singer to perform with the Philippine Philharmonic Orchestra. The album that was released from the concert, *Martin Live at the CCP,* sold over 20,000 copies on pre-orders before it had even been released, and when he appeared at the Tower Record store in Manila, thousands of fans descended to get a glimpse of their idol. In November 2001 he released another album, *More Souvenirs,* featuring both standard covers such as "Send In The Clowns" and "What A Wonderful World," as well as medleys by writers such as Rodgers and Hammerstein. It was a song on this album, however, that showed Nievera in a negative light for the first time in his career. A single released from the album, "To Say Goodbye," was credited as having been written by Nievera but was actually recognized as a re-write of the song "We Don't Know How To Say Goodbye" by American songwriter Diane Warren. The scandal made front-page news in the Philippines. Nievera protested his innocence throughout, but the album had to be withdrawn and was later re-issued with the song removed. The album later reached the top of the local charts without "To Say Goodbye." In March and April 2002 Nievera had another successful tour of the United States and then began a string of concerts in Makati City in the Philippines. The performances took place every Friday and Saturday night during the month of May, and created a new sales record for a concert series as Nievera continues to be the most popular male entertainer the country has ever produced.

References

www.martinnievera.com.ph

Noa (Israel)

Achinoam Nini was born in Israel on June 23, 1969, from Yemenite roots but was raised in New York. She returned to her native country as a seventeen-year-old and, a year later, was drafted into the Israeli army as part of compulsory national service. She spent two years playing in the army band, performing hundreds of concerts, and decided, on leaving the armed services, to pursue a career in music. After enrolling in music school in 1990 she met Gil Dor, who later became her musical partner. Although Nini was influenced by Western rock and pop music, Dor took responsibility for the direction of her work, introducing local rhythms and instrumentation and taking control of the arranging and production as well as offering musical and lyrical contributions. In 1991 Nini released her debut album, *Mishaela*, which reflected her love of Western music without compromising her Eastern roots. The album sold moderately well, and Nini began to perform in the clubs of Tel Aviv, the Israeli capital. In 1993 her follow-up album, *Achinoam Nini*, was released, again only in Israel. The album showed a marked change in direction, as it was sung mainly in English, and Nini began to win an audience in western Europe. By now she called herself Noa and released an album of the same name in 1994. In the following year she released her first single, "I Don't Know," and was invited to sing at a peace rally in Tel Aviv. During the rally the Israeli prime minister, Yitzchak Rabin, was assassinated. The experience had a major effect on Noa, and she became more politically aware, both in her life and in her career.

In 1996 she released *Calling*, an album sung in English. By now Noa was contributing her own material to her records, which gave them a more autobiographical and personal lyrical content. A second album, *Noa* was released in 1997, the majority of which was written by the singer, including the single "Too Proud." As her reputation continued to grow, she recorded an album with the Israeli Philharmonic Orchestra and in the same year (1998) released her first album in the United States, *Both Sides of the Sea*. The record was a collection of old songs, but she sang entirely in Hebrew as the album was aimed mainly at émigrés from Israel rather than the U.S. market itself. Her profile in America began to rise, however, after she sang at the White House and at a concert in memory of the murdered Rabin, both in the presence of President Clinton.

Noa's ninth album, *Blue Touches Blue* (2000), highlighted her gift for melody. It was released as she began a year-long, 150-date tour of Europe. A song from the album, "Beautiful That Way," was used in director Roberto Benigni's Oscar-winning movie *Life Is Beautiful*. Later in the year Noa, was the recipient of a special award for the advancement of Israeli music across the world. A "best of" album, *Osef Rishon*, was released early in 2001 before she toured Europe during July and August. Noa briefly visited the United States in November 2001 and she is currently in Israel recording new material for future release.

References

http://universal-vhost.capcave.com/noa/site.htm

Nylon Beat (Finland)

Jonna Kosonen (b. September 3, 1977) and Erin Koivisto (b. July 2, 1977) were born in the Finnish capital Helsinki. After finishing their education, they formed Nylon Beat specifically to enter the local Kiitorata music competition in 1995. After winning the contest, they were immediately signed to a record deal and sent into the studio to record their debut album. A pop record of up-tempo dance tracks, it contained the band's first single, "Teflon Love," released in 1996. The single reached the top of the local charts, as did the album itself, *Nylon Beat*, later in the year. More singles followed, including "Rakastuin Mä Looserin," which was covered by the Estonian band Best B4 and became the most popular song of the year in Estonia. By the end of the year *Nylon Beat* had become a platinum album, as the group won best new band and best debut album at the Finnish music awards. The follow-up, *Satasen Laina* (1997), was as upbeat as the group's debut album had been and was soon a platinum disc, becoming the band's second #1. Three singles released from the record, "Satasen Laina," "Kuumalle Hiekalle," and "Jus," all reached the top five.

Although the band was among the most popular in their country, it had ambitions of gaining a wider audience. In an attempt to introduce itself to the rest of Europe, it released its first English-language album, *Nylon Moon*, in 1998. The album earned an international release but sold well only in Finland, where it turned gold, and in other Scandinavian countries. Another series of hit singles taken from the album was released throughout the year: "Like a Fool," "Umm Ma Ma," and "Viimeinen." As Nylon Beat toured constantly to promote its records, it began to play with a live band rather than backing tapes. Partly because of the live shows the band's popularity soared, and in 1999 it released *Valehtelija*. The album became the band's biggest seller, as it reached double platinum while the group was named band of the year at the annual Finnish music awards. Nylon Beat had now become the biggest band in Finland.

In 2000 the group set a new precedent in Finland as its fifth album, *Demo*, went gold on advance orders from an eager public before it had even been released. Following this the group appeared in the *Guinness Book of Records* as well as on the front page of the *Wall Street Journal*. Then the group released a tune, "Syytön," initially as a ring tone for cell phones that fans were able to download from the Internet. At concerts the audience would play the single on their phones before the band joined in. The song, which appeared on general release as a CD a week after it was released for fans, immediately went to #1. Toward the end of the year the band released an English-language single in Japan. However, the song, "Like a Fool," failed to win an audience in the already saturated pop arena of the country. Taking advantage of new technology, Nylon Beat is working on new cell phone ring tones and a daily comic strip available on WAP, the technology that allows a cell phone to access the Internet. The band is planning a second, as yet untitled, English-language album, although no release date has been set.

References

www.mediamusiikki.fi/nylon_llbeat

P

Paradis, Vanessa (France)

Born in St. Maur, France, on December 22, 1972, Vanessa Paradis sang on the TV show *L'ecole Des Fans* at the age of eight. When she was thirteen her uncle taped her singing at home, and the demo was sent to composer Frank Langloff and lyricist Etienne Roda'Gil. Later that year Paradis released her first single, "La Magie des surprises Parties," but it won little notice. Only in 1987, when Langloff and Roda'Gil presented Paradis with "Joe Le Taxi," did she become known in France. The song, a jokey number that featured a simple saxophone riff and the pubescent Paradis plaintively singing a tribute to a taxi driver, became #1 all over Europe. It also reached the top of the charts in England, where it became the first song in a foreign language to reach #1 since the 1960s. Three more singles ("Manolo Mandete," "Maxou," and "Marilyn and John") did well in France, and then Paradis released her debut album, *M & J* (1987), a collection of light pop numbers that sold well throughout Europe.

Although she was still releasing singles, in 1989 Paradis won her first acting role in the movie *Noche Blanche*. The movie won the aspiring actress a Caesar, the French equivalent of an Oscar. It was to be her only film appearance until 1995. In 1990, however, she released a second album, *Variations sur le meme t'aime*. A collection of smokey ballads and pop numbers, the album found itself in the upper reaches of the French pop charts. Throughout this time Paradis was becoming more than just a pop singer. Following her successfull acting debut, she won a modeling contract from the French company Chanel worth 3 million French francs. The contract with Chanel raised her profile in the United States, and in 1992 she moved to New York to record her third album. It was the first to be sung in English, with rock musician Lenny Kravitz. The album had a more American feel than the very French style of her earlier recordings, which were more melodic and idiosyncratic. The record, called simply *Vanessa Paradis* (1992), was followed by a world tour. Called the "Natural High" tour, some of

Vanessa Paradis
Pictorialpress Ltd., London, UK

the shows were recorded; in 1993 the album *Natural High Tour* was released. The record was accompanied by two singles, "Gotta Have It" and "Les Cactus," which proved to be her last for almost seven years.

After the Natural High tour, Paradis returned to the movies in *Elisa* (1995). Between 1997 and 1999 she released three films, *Un Amour de Sorcière, Une Chance Sur Deux*, and *Une Fille Sur Le Pont*, while commuting between France and the United States. In May 1999 she became the mother of a baby girl fathered by U.S. actor Johnny Depp. As the baby demanded Paradis's time, a compilation album, *French Collection*, was released in 2000. The album was followed later in the year by her first new material since 1993. The album, *Bliss*, again found Paradis an audience in Europe, and France in particular. During October she began filming for a new movie, *Don Quixote*, before visiting France for a series of concerts in March and May 2001. A new single emerged in July, "Que Fait La Vie," before an album, *Au Zenith*, which was much more rock based than her previous work, was released in November. Taken from a series of live concerts, *Au Zenith* sold well in France. Although her albums sell by the million in her home country, Paradis has failed to gain international recognition for her music and is best known as the "face" of Chanel. She currently lives in Manhattan.

References

welcome.to/vanessa.paradis

Pausini, Laura (Italy)

Laura Pausini was born in Solarolo in the Emiglia-Romagna region north of Italy on May 16, 1974. Singing from an early age, she began performing in the piano bars in her hometown accompanied by her father. After moving to Milan she attended college and entered the Castrocaro Song Contest but was disqualified for singing the Frank Sinatra tune "New York, New York" (only original songs were permitted). In 1992 the songwriter Angelo Valsiglio discovered Pausini and wrote a song for her that was entered in the prestigious San Remo song festival in 1993. The song, "La Solitudine," was an immediate success and lead to the release of her self-titled debut album later in the year. Entering the charts at #1, the album sold over 2 million copies but was not well received by critics, who considered the simple pop music of the eighteen-year-old to be "adolescent" and were scornful of the fact that she did not write her own material.

However, the Italian public ignored the press and flocked to see Pausini as she performed in a series of concerts across the country. While on tour, Valsiglio and writer Marco Maratti were busy preparing material for a second, more rock-oriented album, *Laura* (1994). It immediately built on the success of her debut album by selling over 4 million copies across Europe. Pausini then made a Spanish-language album that featured a number of songs from her previous albums. After being released in Spain, it sold over a million copies. It also opened up the Latin American market, whose sales helped make Pausini the bestselling Italian artist for 1994 in her home country, albeit with help from the Spanish-speaking population. The album won her the World Music Award for bestselling Italian artist in 1995. She also won the Lo Nuestro (known as the "Latin Grammy") in Miami and was awarded a Golden Globe by the Italian ambassador in Madrid for her contribution to Italian culture in Spain.

Although Pausini was now one of the biggest stars in Italy, she felt her contribution to her recordings was not substantial enough. As a result she split with Valsiglio and Maratti and began working with her fiancé, Alfredo Cerruti Jr., and Dado Parasini. Pausini's growing confidence in her own ability was widely appreciated by the critics, who praised the album *Le Cose Che Vivi* (1996) for its growing maturity. The album was also recorded in Spanish and included three tracks sung in Portuguese, enabling the album to be successfully marketed in Brazil to complete her triumph in South America.

As she continued to contribute material to her recordings, Pausini's personal concerns with violence against children were reflected in some of her lyrics; this led UNICEF to invite her to become an ambassador. Although Pausini declined, she appeared on behalf of the agency many times, not as a singer but a personality, and a percentage of profits from *Le Cose Che Vivi* were donated to the organization. A song she wrote for UNICEF, "Il Mondo Che Vorrei," was performed as part of a Christmas concert in 1996, attended by Pope John Paul II. During 1997 and 1998 Pausini appeared in concert halls across Europe and South America until, late in 1998, she returned to the studio to record *La Mia*

Laura Pausini
Pictorialpress Ltd., London, UK

Riposta. Released in October 1998, the album featured Pausini's first song in English, written for her by Phil Collins, a former Genesis member and a successful solo performer. During a tour to promote the album, Pausini performed in front of 20,000 fans in the Basque region of Spain to promote peace. (The Basques are fighting for independence from the rest of Spain and are viewed either as "terrorists" or "freedom fighters," depending on your point of view.) In 1999 Pausini was invited to sing at the annual Pavarotti and Friends event that the operatic tenor produces for charity. She also recorded a song, "One More Time," for the soundtrack of the movie *Message in a Bottle* starring Paul Newman and Kevin Costner.

At the beginning of 2000 she began writing for her new album, *Tra Te e Il Mare*, which was released in September. It continued to reflect Pausini's more confident and mature arrangements and lyrics. April and May of the following year were taken up with a tour of North and South America before the release of *Volvere Junto A Ti* in October 2001. The album featured more songs written by Pausini as her pop sensibility continued to grow. After more concerts in the United States and South America in October and November, Pausini returned home to play her only Italian show of the year in Milan in December. To date Pausini has received eleven platinum records in Spain; ten in Italy; six in Holland; four in Chile; three in Mexico; two in the United States, Switzerland, Portugal, Belgium, Brazil, and Colombia; and one in Guatemala, Bolivia, Paraguay, and Uruguay. She is well on the way to selling over 16 million albums.

In January 2002 she began a European tour that was scheduled to end in August, when she was due to begin recording new material.

References

www.laurapausini.com

Powderfinger (Australia)

In 1989 in Brisbane, Australia, bassist John Collins (b. April 1970), guitar player Ian Haug (b. February 21, 1970), and drummer Steven Bishop formed a band that they named Powderfinger (after a song by legendary U.S. artist Neil Young). The three musicians were still in high school. When Haug began to study economics at the University of Queensland, he met Bernard Fanning (b. August 15, 1969), and invited him to join the band as main vocalist. At the same time Jon Coghill (b. August 26, 1971) replaced Bishop on drums, and Darren Middleton, guitarist/keyboard player (b. October 4, 1972), became the final member of the Powderfinger ensemble. The band played numerous shows in the pubs and clubs of Brisbane, continually improving on its mix of folk, rock, and pop that reflected the influence of Neil Young. Early in 1993 the band released its first, self-titled single. It immediately won interest from major record companies. When the second single, "Transfusion," replaced U.S. grunge band Nirvana at #1 in the Australian Alternative chart, the band signed with Polydor at the end of the year.

In June 1994 the band released its first major label single, "Tail," which was followed by the album *Parables for Wooden Ears* in August. The album was a collection of folky rock tunes led by Fanning's lilting vocals, but it was not well received and Polydor contemplated dropping the band. As Powderfinger was still pulling in the crowds for live shows, the band was granted a reprieve; but the group released only two singles during 1995, "Save Your Skin" and "Mr. Kneebone," although it continued to tour heavily and its fan base grew in response. Powderfinger's busy schedule of live concerts continued into 1996, and when the band's second album, *Double Allergic*, was released in September the live work appeared to have paid dividends: The album was a collection of solid rock tunes that entered the chart at #7 and remained in the top ten for three months. The single "Pick You Up," which reached #22, also won two nominations at the ARIA awards for song of the year and best Australian single, although it failed to win either one.

Double Allergic had by now reached #4 in the national chart. Bolstered by this success, the band set out on another series of tours that took up most of the year and included visits to the United States and Canada. By the end of 1997 the band had received five more nominations in the ARIA awards for best album, best single, best group, best song, and best alternative release—but, once again, the group failed to win any of the categories. After so many near misses, 1998 became the year when Powderfinger turned its work into mainstream success. The group spent the first six months in the studio and reappeared in August with the single "The Day You Come." Reflecting the group's musical roots and displaying obvious influences from Neil Young, by the end of the year the song had become the most-played single on Australian radio. When the band released its third album, *Internationalist*, in August, it entered the chart at #1 and remained in the top twenty for over a year. "The Day You Come" became the eighth bestselling single of the year.

The year 1999 began in the usual way for the band with lengthy tours, plus in February the group released a single, "Already Gone," and contributed a song, "These Days," to the soundtrack of the movie *Two Hands*. In April the band returned to the United States and played shows in, among other cities, Los Angeles and New York, as well as Canada and England. At the end of the year the band finally won recognition from the critics when it was presented with awards for best song for "The Day You Come" and best album for *Internationalist*. Once again nominated for a string of ARIAs, the band finally won in the categories of best rock album, best album, best single, and best cover art. "These Days" was named Australian song of the year.

In June 2000 the band recorded "My Kind of Scene" for the *Mission Impossible 2* soundtrack before releasing a new single, "My Happiness," in August, that entered the chart at #4. In the following month the album *OdysseyNumberFive* entered the chart at #1, going platinum in its first week and four times platinum within three months. After touring Australia, Powderfinger returned to the United States in February 2001 for a series of eight concerts and appeared on "The David Letterman Show" on March 26. In April the group played England and visited Europe before returning home to begin writing new material for release later in the year. In November the band became involved in a cancer charity, performing fundraising concerts. To date *OdysseyNumberFive* has turned five times platinum in Australia.

References

www.powderfinger.com
The Encyclopaedia of Australian Rock and Pop by Ian McFarlane (St. Leonards: Allen & Unwin, 1999). ISBN 1865080721.

Puffy (Japan)

Yumi Yoshimura was born in Osaka, Japan, on January 30, 1975. Although she was a talented athlete, by the time she reached college she had decided to study fashion design. The college life, however, was not to her liking, and she soon left to work as a sales assistant in a clothes shop and as a waitress. In 1996 she attended an audition for Sony Music, where she met Ami Ohnuki. Ohnuki was born in the Japanese capital, Tokyo, on September 18, 1973. When she was in the fourth grade her family moved to Korea, but after her brother died in an accident they returned to Japan in 1986. By the time she was in her third year at senior high school she had set her mind on becoming a singer. With a group of friends she sent a demo to Sony and attended the audition that brought her into contact with Yoshimura.

Ohnuki and Yoshimura were both chosen by Sony at the audition, and the company began schooling them in the art of being in a pop band. The duo was soon noticed by Japanese rock star **Okuda Tamio**, who began to write material for them. Named Puffy by American musician Andy Sturmer (from the rock band Jellyfish, who had been working with Tamio on Tamio's forthcoming solo album), the band released its first single in May 1996. "Asia no junshin" was a guitar-based song with a 1960s feel much in the style of Tamio's band **Unicorn**, and it differed substantially from the sampler and drum machine–based techno that was dominating the Japanese charts at the time. When the local beer company Kirin signed the band to promote its product, the Puffy craze began.

The singers undertook a series of live shows to promote "Asia no junshin," and soon thereafter they released a short, seven-track album, *AmiYumi*. Although the release won favor from the critics, it was the Beatles-influenced single "Kore ga watashi no ikiru michi" that catapulted the band to stardom. After selling over a million copies, a cosmetics company, Shiseido, used the track on its TV commercials and signed the duo to another promotions contract. By the end of the year the Puffy duo were cover stars on every youth magazine in Japan, and their habit of wearing jeans and college sweatshirts began a new fashion craze among the young women of the country. A new single released in March 1997, "Circuit no musume," was used by Yamaha to promote its new line of Vino scooters. During the year that followed, virtually every Japanese magazine ran an advertisement showing Puffy astride Yamaha's Vino scooters or promoting another Shiseido product. A video of the tour they had undertaken was released and sold over a million copies.

In August 1997 the duo released another album, *Solo/Solo*. It was a double release with Ohnuki and Yoshimura each appearing exclusively on her own CD. Now freed from the chores of songwriting, Ohnuki and Yoshimura were able to concentrate on concerts, commercials, and TV shows, keeping the Puffy image high on the agenda of the nation's youth, while Tamio began work on their next release. *Jet CD*, released in April 1998, became widely acknowledged as Puffy's best work. Tamio, an unapologetic lover of Western 1960s music including that of The Beatles and The Beach Boys, recorded some of the songs in mono, a puzzling decision to the technology-obsessed Japanese. The album consisted of all the Puffy singles to date, combined with new material. Tamio's trademark blend of Western styles, traditional Japanese melodies, and idiosyncratic production made *Jet CD* a unique record for a J-pop band. ("J-pop" is a generic term for the indigenous pop music that dominates the Japanese music charts.)

At the beginning of 1999 the band released *Fever*Fever*, which, although not reaching the heights of its predecessor, still sold well. It featured a mix of different musical genres, including rockabilly and country, due to the musical skills of Tamio. An experimental re-mix album, *PRMX*, released later in the year appeared to confuse many of Puffy's fans. It was accepted with grace from critics, however, who again saw Tamio's influences in the production. As Tamio began to concentrate on his own solo material, a compilation album was released during 2000 to keep the Puffy image in the public eye in the heavily competitive area of J-pop bands. By the end of the year a new album, *Spike*, had been released under the name Puffyamiyumi, and two singles, "Umi e to" and "Boogie Woogie No. 5," both topped the charts. In October a film by French director Luc Besson (who also directed *Betty Blue* and *Leon*), *Wasabi*, featured Puffy on its soundtrack. In December the band released another Japanese top-selling single, "Aoi Namida." More concerts in Japan are due early in 2002 as Puffy continues to win success with its guitar-based music and to maintain its place at the top of the Japanese pop market, helped by the writing and production skills of Okuda Tamio.

A new album, *An Illustrated History*, was released in summer 2002. The album focused more on keyboards, to give the up-tempo pop songs a light feel.

References

www.puffyamiyumi.com

Pugacheva, Alla (Russia)

Alla Borisovna Pugacheva (b. April 15, 1949) first tasted success in 1974 when she won third prize at an All Union pop competition in the former Soviet Union and has since become Russia's top woman pop star. Pugacheva's prolific career began with *Mirror of the Soul* (1977). The songs on the album became the blueprint for her success, offering sentimental lyrics reflecting a woman struggling with her passions. She later began an acting career in *The Woman Who Sings*, the first of her five feature films in the same year. Having begun her career studying at the Department of Variety Direction at the Lunacharsky Institute, she quickly moved on and won various awards both for her music and her involvement with the politics of her country. These have included the Golden Microphone (1981), The Medal for Input in World Affairs (1981), Golden Disc (1984), and the Medal for Input in World Affairs by Means of Harmony and Music (1987). Boris Yeltsin, then-president of the Soviet Union, presented her with the Order of Service to the Fatherland, Second Class, explaining that only the president can have First Class. She was the last-ever People's Artist of the Soviet Union, as the Union broke up shortly thereafter with the fall of Communism.

In 1995, after receiving negative publicity in the Russian press for her unashamedly sentimental songs and lack of progression, Pugacheva released the album *Don't Hurt My Feelings, Ladies and Gentlemen*. The critics were ignored, and have continued to be ignored, by the Russian people; as a result, to date Pugacheva has sold somewhere between 150 and 200 million albums. (Figures on the exact number of sales are difficult to ascertain due to the lack of a "proper" chart in Russia.) These albums have mostly been sold on the strength of her concert programs rather than on her previously recorded material. Pugacheva has starred in some of the top-grossing live shows for a woman in Russian pop, with "The Monologues of Single" (1981), "I Came and I'm Talking" (1984), and "Christmas Reunions" (1988–1992). The singer's fame began to grow outside of Russia when a Finnish ocean liner was named after her in 1985. A perfume in her name was on sale in France in 1991, and she designed her own line of shoes and edited and published her own magazine in 1993. Also in 1994 she married fellow Russian superstar **Philip Kirkorov**, making them the most celebrated and biggest-selling partnership in Russia. A documentary about Pugacheva, made by her husband, was watched by 85 percent of the Russian population when it was broadcast on TV.

After the fall of Communism, Pugacheva's career blossomed again through her relationship with Russian émigrés. To Russians living outside of their native country, Pugacheva embodied the part of the old Russia that can still be remembered with fondness. Thus she released a succession of albums heavily indebted to rose-tinted memories of the past: *Primadonna* (1997), *Yes!* (1998), and *The Selected One* (1999). In February 2000 she toured the United States, visiting Miami, Los Angeles, Chicago, and Atlantic City, and played to sold-out concert halls. *The New York Times* described her as "Tina Turner with a hint of Edith Piaf." She also found time to release two new albums, *White Snow* and *Madam Broskina*, as her theatrical style and bombastic tunes continued to endear her to Russians both at home and abroad. *River Ferryman* was released in November 2001, and her recorded output appears to show no sign of either changing or diminishing. The Prima Donna, as she is popularly known in Russia, continues to perform throughout Europe. She also appeared in Mongolia a few months after her husband was the first pop star to appear there.

References

www.angelfire.com/ma3/alla/en/index

R

Ramazotti, Eros (Italy)

Eros Ramazotti was born in Rome, Italy, on October 28, 1963, and received his first guitar at the age of eight. After spending his early teenage years mastering the instrument, his singing career began in earnest. Between 1982 and 1984 he recorded various demos, but it was not until 1984, when the twenty-one-year-old won the young artist category at the San Remo music festival, that Ramazotti found himself with a record contract. The success song "Terra Promessa," featuring politicized lyrics across a rock backing that were unheard of from a young singer at the time, immediately became a cult hit with the country's teenagers. In the following year, Ramazotti released the album *Cuori Agitati* to widespread acclaim throughout Europe and began his first major concert tour throughout Italy.

In 1986 Ramazotti again appeared at the San Remo festival with "Adesso tu," which helped to make his second album, *Nuovi Eroi* (1986), become double platinum with sales in excess of 500,000 copies across Europe. The following years were taken up with the familiar formula of tours and releases, but with each album Ramazotti achieved more widespread acclaim. In 1987 he released his third album, *In Certi Momenti*, another record of sumptuous ballads and rock-oriented mid-paced numbers that featured a duet with English singer/actress Patsy Kensit. The album sold more than 2 million copies across Europe. By 1988 Ramazotti's live performance schedule left him with little time for writing new material, and he released a mini-album, *Musica e*, consisting of material from previous records. Its sales exceeded anything he had done to date, over 3 million copies in Italy and Spain, and also opened the door to the lucrative Latin American market. There Ramazotti employed his knowledge of the Spanish language; after recording a Spanish version of the album, he undertook a tour across South America and played to over 3 million people.

Eros Ramazotti
Pictorialpress Ltd., London, UK

Another tour of Europe and Latin America followed in 1990, and a show at Radio City Music Hall in New York quickly sold out, drawing heavily on the Italian community in the city. The show signaled the beginning of the second phase of Ramazotti's career, as he began to work with well-established artists— including Spike Lee, who directed a video for the single "Cose della vita," taken from Ramazotti's album *Tutte Storie* (1993). The video was shown heavily on MTV Europe and became another bestseller, convincing Ramazotti that he should establish his own production company, Radiorama.

By the summer of 1995 Ramazotti was playing festivals across the world, sharing the bill with Elton John, Rod Stewart, and Sheryl Crow. Although he was becoming recognized as a major artist, Ramazotti was still underachieving in the English-speaking markets and decided to record his next album, *Dove c'e musica* (1996), in Los Angeles. Although he employed a number of well-respected American session musicians, Ramazotti's decision to continue singing in Italian and Spanish hampered the album's progress among English-speaking Americans. The album did produce his biggest hit to date, "Aurora," a sentimental ballad celebrating the birth of his first daughter. The album sold over 6 million copies and reached the top ten in fifteen countries, earning him MTV's best Italian singer award and a German Echo award for best international singer of 1996. The year ended with a sold-out concert at the Royal Albert Hall in London.

A "best of" album, released in 1998, included duets with Andrea Bocelli and Tina Turner. Ramazotti's next album, *Eros* (1998), had the same sound as his previous releases and reached the top five across Europe and Latin America (where he was now a superstar in Mexico and Argentina), winning many platinum discs on its way to selling over 6 million copies. The album also took first place in the continental album of the year category and fourth place in the world album of the year category from the industry magazine *Music and Media* and won the best album award at the World Music Awards. Ramazotti then began a sixty-date tour during which he performed to more than 1 million people. The tour included a duet with Italian tenor Luciano Pavarotti as well as concerts in New York City and Los Angeles, where he sang with Stevie Wonder and Celine Dion.

In April 1999, Ramazotti won his second Echo award for best singer of the previous year, defeating Eric Clapton, Joe Cocker, Bryan Adams, and Phil Collins. During the event, which was televised across Germany, Ramazotti shared the stage with Cher and REM. His first new material in four years was released in 2000 under the title *Stilelibero*; once again, Europe and Latin America saw the album reach the top of the charts. Following a series of concerts in 2000 and 2001, Ramazotti began to write more material. The single "Per Me Per Sempre" continued his success as he once again toured Europe during October and November, presenting his AOR (Adult Oriented Rock) style to thousands of admiring fans.

References

www.erosramazotti.com

MTV-Cyclopedia by Nick Duerden, Ian Gittens, and Shaun Phillips (London: Carlton, 1997). ISBN 185868336x

Raptor (Thailand)

Joni Anwar was born in the Thai capital, Bangkok, on August 30, 1981. While attending the Bangkok Pattana International School, he met Louis Scott, born in Kenya on March 4, 1982. The pair sang together in school productions (Anwar also appeared in commercials for the beverage Ovaltine, and Scott advertised soda) and were soon noticed by producers from the country's biggest music label, RS Promotions. Although only ages thirteen and twelve, respectively, the young singers were taken into the studio in 1994 and emerged as the youngest band in the country. Named Raptor, the band's self-titled debut was a pop/dance album with Anwar and Scott rapping in Thai. In the following year RS teamed the band with a host of other up-and-coming Thai stars on its label and released *Superteens*. Raptor had little input in the album, but it sold well because it featured some of the most sought-after teen stars together on one album.

With Anwar and Scott now being a relatively mature and experienced fifteen and fourteen years old, respectively, the second Raptor album was released in

March 1996. *Waab Boys* featured another RS artist, Pookie Prisnana, although Raptor sang most of the songs. The album won an unusual award from the Thai recording industry for "best background effects" as the group undertook selective promotional concerts that invariably sold out well in advance as its up-tempo, rap/dance numbers mainly about girls continued to excite the Thai youth. At each show the band was requested to sing its biggest hit, "Yah Pood Leaw," and the group duly obliged. After a year of concerts supporting the album, another record was released in 1996: *Day Shock*. It was the first Raptor album sung in English, but "Yah Pood Leaw" was still the band's most requested song, and on the album they re-recorded a faster version of the tune to appease their fans. While recording and playing concerts, Anwar and Scott both appeared in successful movies. Anwar starred in *Dek Rabaed Yeed Laew Yid* and Scott in *Tho Laew Tong Tho* and *Bullet Teens*. Both artists were cast as the heroic young love interest.

In 1997 RS put together another compilation of its artists, and this time Raptor had a much larger role because it had become one of the biggest bands in the country. As Scott and Anwar advanced in years, their maturing voices added depth and subtleties to the band's melodies, although the musical backing remained largely the same. The compilation album, released in November, became the most successful in the country for 1997 and sold over a million copies in Thailand. A single, "Kum Deaw," reached #1 and stayed on the charts for over four months. By the beginning of 1998, however, Scott was beginning to develop health problems. A long-term sufferer of migraines, he was finding the live shows difficult to take part in because the effects of the lights and strobes made him ill at the end of each performance. In May 1998 Raptor's last album was released. *Raptor Goodbye* brought the band's career to a premature end as Anwar went on to a solo career and Scott went back to the university to continue his education. In May 2000 Anwar released his debut solo album, *Joni Bad Boy*, and began helping his younger brother to break into the Thai pop scene.

References

www.geocities.com/Broadway/Booth/4416

Rein, Trine (Norway)

Trine Rein was born in San Francisco on November 7, 1970, but within twelve months, she returned to Norway with her mother. Throughout her school career Rein sang in plays and other productions and finally joined a band, Sound of Silence, in 1985. In the following year, as a solo artist, she entered a local talent competition and won through to the national finals, eventually taking second place. Any opportunities that the competition presented were lost, however, when she returned to America in 1987 to live with her father and attend high school. By 1988, though, Rein was back in Norway, where she finished her education, joined the guitar pop band Saturn, and played gigs all over the southern part of the country. The exposure she received through these concerts won Rein work in various studios, singing backing vocals for other artists and recording radio jingles.

Still unable to find success in her own right, Trine joined her third band, WIP (World In Peace), in 1991 and released an album of acoustic and electric guitar pop songs. The single "Ghost Jam" topped the charts, and the follow-up single, a cover version of the Everly Brothers' "All I Have to Do Is Dream," found an international release. Her work with WIP brought her to the attention of the Norwegian branch of EMI, and in 1992 the recording company offered her a solo contract. Her 1993 album, *Finders Keepers*, continued the guitar pop vein of her previous bands and became a bestselling record. The album's success continued into 1994 and reached #1 in February, holding the position for four weeks. Rein was awarded the Spellemanspris for best newcomer as album sales reached 180,000 copies. The interest the album created lead to a wider release throughout Scandinavia, where the record sold over 400,000 copies, and into Japan, where Rein undertook a comprehensive promotional tour.

In 1995 Rein returned to the studio and began work on her second album, *Beneath My Skin*, which was released in the spring of the following year. The record entered the charts at #1 and stayed there for three weeks. It was the single released from *Beneath My Skin*, however, that pushed Rein into the international spotlight. "Torn," a song about heartbreak pushed along by a busy acoustic guitar riff, had already been a successful release in Norway by another artist before Rein took it to #1. The song was also picked up by Natalie Imbruglia, a former Australian soap opera actress who was beginning a career in music. Imbruglia's version of "Torn" reached #1 in many countries, including the United States and the United Kingdom in 1998. However, as news began to appear in the press that the song was not an Imbruglia composition, Rein suddenly was portrayed in music papers across the world as the victim of "song theft." As Imbruglia told the press that she had never claimed the song as her own, Rein's version began to win radio play in competition with the more successful version. It was a brief taste of widespread fame for Rein, though, as the scandal was soon forgotten. Her next record, *To Find the Truth*, was not released until September 1998—too long after the scandal for the U.K. and U.S. record-buying public to remember Rein. Although the album reached the top of the chart in Norway, it did not find a wider audience. In 1999 she released an album, *Greatest Hits*. She then returned to the studio to record more material but has not released a new album, though she did contribute vocals to Chicago jazz band Liquid Soul's song "I Want You To Want Me" in 1999.

References
Home.swipnet.se/psw/trine.html

Rita (Israel)

Born in Iran on March 26, 1962, Yahan Farouz took part in *aliyah* (immigration of Jews) with her family and moved to Israel in 1970. Although she studied singing, it was acting that brought her onto the stage, where the appeared in Israeli performances of "Cat on a Hot Tin Roof" and "My Fair Lady." In 1986 she was chosen as a prospective Israeli entrant in the Eurovision song contest; although her song, "An Escape Route," was not chosen to represent the country, her performance won the attention of the public and the media. By now Farouz had married the popular Israeli singer Rami Kleinstein, whom she first met in 1978, and taken the name Rita. Her debut album, *Rita* (1986), was a collection of slow numbers featuring many piano-based songs written by her husband. It sold over 100,000 copies, a huge volume in Israel. It has since become the third best-selling Israeli album ever.

As Rita's popularity continued to grow, at her many concerts the audience would bring bouquets to the front of the stage and take over singing the choruses of her songs. A second album, *The Days of Innocence* (1988), cemented her popularity. In 1988 she also released her first international album, *Breaking These Walls*, in Holland, but it failed to make any impression. As Rita's fame soared in Israel, she was asked to represent her country in the Eurovision competition. Although Israel failed to win Rita was still a star at home. When a compilation album, *Milestones*, was released, it won a gold disc. In 1994 she released the album *Great Love* and began a series of sold-out shows that played weekly at a theater in Jerusalem for over three years. Rita was now performing her gentle love songs regularly across the country. She began a tour in 1997 that lasted, intermittently, for three years, as she performed to ever-growing audiences. When she was invited to perform Israel's national anthem, the Hatikva, at the 1998 Independence Day concert, the strength of her following in the country revealed itself. Criticized by the press and politicians when it was reported that she was to be paid $20,000 for the performance, Rita threatened not to attend the event. Fans inundated her home with flowers begging her to reconsider. The concert organizer, Shuki Weiss, called her "our [Israel's] Barbra Streisand." It took a personal phone call from the Israeli prime minister, Benjamin Netanyahu, to persuade Rita to perform at the celebrations. She later donated her fee to charity.

By now it was five years since Rita had released any new material. The album *Open the Window* (1999) was considered by many critics to be too long, containing twenty songs, and too similar to her previous work, but the Israeli public disagreed and bought over 20,000 copies within the first twenty-four hours of its release, setting an Israeli record. The album won Rita the vocal performance of the year award at the newly inaugurated Tamuz awards. In the following year Rita won another Tamuz award for best video (for "Open the Window"), and a poll by Radio Israel, designed to find the top Israeli records of the twentieth century, placed the song fifth in the chart. Rita continues to perform many shows, and toured Israel in summer 2001 in the company of her husband. She is still one of the biggest women stars in Israeli pop history.

A two-album set of their shows, *Rita and Rami on Stage*, was released at the end of 2001.

References

www.us-israel.org/jsource/biography/rita.html

Rossi, Vasco (Italy)

Vasco Rossi was born in the tiny Italian village of Zocca on February 7, 1952. After school he went to live with his aunt in Bologna and entered the university to study economy and commerce. In 1975, with a group of friends, he founded a radio station, Punto Radio, where he served as a deejay. During this time he began to write songs and in 1978 released *Ma Cosa Vuoi Che Sia Una Canzone*, an album of rock tunes that gained very little attention. In the following year, after the release of the musically similar-sounding *Non Siamo Mica Gli Americani*, Rossi undertook his compulsory military service before releasing three rock albums in three years: *Colpa d'Alfredo* (1980), *Siamo Solo Noi* (1981), and *Vado Al Massimo* (1982). Although the title track to *Siamo Solo Noi* won him some recognition, it was *Bollicine* (1983) that took Rossi to the forefront of the Italian music scene. The album reached #1 and sold over a million copies as it turned a relative unknown into a national star, albeit with little change in style or content from his previous albums.

Although Rossi had toured constantly during his formative years, he was now playing to audiences of over 10,000 people per show. In 1984 he released a live album, *Va bene, ve bene cosi*, recorded during his last tour across the country. During the same year, however, Rossi was arrested for cocaine possession. After a short spell in jail, he began a detox program that kept him away from music for over a year until he released *Cosa Succede in Città* in 1985. Two more studio albums followed in 1987 (*C'è Chi Dice No*) and 1989 (*Liberi, Liberi*), during which time he again toured constantly, his traditional rock format winning him an army of new fans. By the end of the concerts he had enough material to release two more live albums, *Fronte Del Palco* (1990) and *10.7.90 San Siro* (1991), both of which sold well. Rossi's thirteenth album, *Nessun Pericola Per Te* (1996) became his bestseller. Although it showed almost no change and merely confirmed Rossi's love of guitar-driven rock songs, it sold half a million copies during the first week of its release. In the same year he became the first Italian to release a video via the Internet; it was for the single "Gli Angeli," directed by Roman Polanski. Rossi ended the year with a concert in Palermo attended by over 200,000 people.

In 1998 he performed another huge concert to 130,000 people in Imola as part of a tour where he played to over 600,000 fans and where he introduced material from his newest album, *Canzoni Per Me* (1998). In the following year he was nominated in six categories at the Italian Music Awards, including best tour, best album, and critics' favorite. Later in the year his live album of the Imola show, *Rewind*, entered the Italian charts in the top ten. As Rossi began the new millennium, he released *Hotel Stupido* (2001). In June it was announced that over 1,000 tickets for a planned show in Turin had been stolen to sell on the black market, such was the demand to see Rossi perform. He later appeared at the Heineken Jammin' Festival in June 2001, headlining the show above **The Stereophonics**, The Offspring, and Alanis Morissette.

References

www.vascorossi.net

Roxette (Sweden)

Marie Fredriksson was born on May 30, 1958, in Sweden, and Per Gessle was born on January 12, 1959. Gessle began playing in bands at age eighteen, becoming a major star in Sweden with rock act **Gyllene Tider**, while Fredriksson began singing in the clubs of Sweden. The pair met in 1981, when Fredriksson sang backing vocals for a Gyllene Tider single. Soon thereafter Fredriksson recorded an album with Martin Sternhufvud under the name Mamas Barn. The album, *Barn som barn*, was released to poor reviews, and the band split up soon thereafter. While Gessle was winning national acclaim, Fredriksson returned to the studio to record a solo album, *Het Vind*, in the summer of 1983. The album lacked direction and met with a lukewarm response. Fredriksson then was invited to tour with Gyllene Tider early in 1984, but within a year the band had split up, leaving Gessle to concentrate on a solo career. Toward the end of 1985 Fredriksson released her second album, *Den sjunde vagen*, which sold in reasonable numbers. At the same time EMI's Kjell Andersson convinced Gessle that he should record with Fredriksson, and the first album from the newly christened group Roxette, *Pearls of Passion* (1987), was released. A single, "Never-Ending Love," reached the top ten.

Gessle continued to write new material for Roxette, while Fredriksson released her third solo album, *Efter Stormen*, in 1987, and it sold 200,000 copies. In June 1988, Gessle and Fredriksson traveled to London's Abbey Road studios to record *Look Sharp*. The album was Roxette's first internationally released record. Fredriksson's short, bleached hair and black leather pants became as much a trademark of the band as Gessle's synthesizer- and guitar-driven pop songs, and they reached #1 across Europe, selling 350,000 copies in Sweden alone. A single, "The Look," followed and reached #1 in the United States as well as all over Europe, Asia, and Australia. The album went on to sell more than 8 million copies worldwide.

"The Look" was followed by "It Must Have Been Love" and "Listen to Your Heart," both of which became #1 in the United States as well as the rest of the world. A tour of the United States had to be postponed when the Gulf War erupted, but in March 1991 the *Joyride* album was released and a world tour began. *Joyride* contained more rock tunes written by Gessle, based around his guitar playing, a synthesizer backing, and Fredriksson's powerful vocals. The album sold more than 10 million copies, and the single "Joyride" became the

Roxette
Pictorialpress Ltd., London, UK

band's fourth U.S. #1 hit. It also topped the charts in twenty-six other countries. In October, Roxette was featured on a Swedish stamp that sold over 5 million copies. During a world tour Fredriksson began work on another solo project that later became the album *Den stangiga resan* (1992). While promoting her album, Roxette took a break and the record company released a live album, *Tourism* (1992). The album failed to make the top hundred in the United States, and the next single, "Queen of Rain," did not get an American release.

The band spent the summer of 1993 recording its next album, *Crash! Boom! Bang!* Due for release in April of the following year, it was delayed for a week amid press speculation that the pair had fallen out. Although this appeared to be confirmed in June, when Fredriksson got married and Gessle was not invited, the band began another world tour—this time to South Africa instead of America. The lack of shows in the United States was reflected when the single "Crash! Boom! Bang!" reached only #104 on the Billboard chart. The popularity of the group in Europe, however, continued, and the band was invited to place handprints on the Walk of Fame in Rotterdam, Holland. By the end of the year Roxette received a platinum disc for sales of the album. The decision to tour South Africa was vindicated when the country presented the band with a quadruple platinum disc for *Joyride*, a double platinum disc for both *Look Sharp!* and *Tourism*, and a platinum disc for *Crash! Boom! Bang!* At the same time the group played four sold-out shows in Johannesburg in front of 125,000 fans. In 1995 Roxette took another break, this time for Gessle to rejoin Gyllene Tider, which had once again become popular as a result of Gessle's success in Roxette. To fill the gap while Gessle was away, Roxette's record company released a greatest hits package, *Don't Bore Us, Get to the Chorus* (1995), which sold over 4 million copies. At the end of the year, Fredriksson was named Sweden's richest woman pop star.

Although Roxette spent the beginning of 1996 appearing on TV and in the press, Gessle was committed to another tour with Gyllene Tider that kept him occupied until August. At the same time Fredriksson recorded her next solo album, *I en tid som var* (1996), a collection of songs similar to Roxette's that reached #2 in the Swedish chart, selling 40,000 copies. As there was no time to record new material, the band re-recorded some of its best ballads in Spanish and released *Baladas En Espanol* (1996) in Spanish-speaking countries, where it sold a million copies. As the duo's personal projects kept them from performing as Roxette, in June 1997 the band found itself without a U.S. record label. Gessle and Fredriksson then decided to spend more time on Roxette and moved to Spain to begin work on *Have a Nice Day* in January 1998. The recording of the album, however, took most of the year as Gessle kept returning home to spend time with his wife and son.

During the early part of 1999 the band was involved in interviews to promote the new album, which was due for release in February. The album went on to win gold discs in South Africa and Germany, and platinum in Spain. Away from Roxette, Fredriksson recorded a duet with fellow Swedish star Totta Näslund, and the single "Ett minne bättre glömt" reached the top ten. Beginning in October 2001 the band toured Europe for two months as it promoted *Milk, Toast and Honey* (2001). The album spawned three singles, "The Centre of the Heart," "Real Sugar," and the title track, which led to Roxette becoming the most-played Swedish group of the year in Sweden. A Danish TV show was dedicated to the band as it began to tour Sweden in November. Although still a major band in Scandinavia, Roxette has struggled to relive its former glories elsewhere.

In May 2002 Gessle recorded a song for a tribute album dedicated to U.S. punk rockers The Ramones. The track, "I Wanna Be Your Boyfriend," was released as a single in Scandinavia. The following month Swedish radio station Mix Megapol conducted an internet poll among its listeners to find the best song ever. "It Must Have Been Love" came first.

References
www.roxette.co.uk
Roxette by Milton Okun (New York: Music Sales Ltd., 1995). ISBN 0895248433

Run Rig (Scotland)

Run Rig performed its debut live show in Glasgow, Scotland, in 1973 as a three-piece band and released an album, *Play Gaelic*, shortly thereafter. It wasn't until 1979, however, with the formation of the group's record label,

Run Rig
Pictorialpress Ltd.,
London, UK

Ridge Records, and the release of its first album, *The Highland Connection*, that Run Rig began to win recognition. Initially formed by brothers Rory (b. July 27, 1949) and Calum (b. November 12, 1953) MacDonald and Blair Douglas, Run Rig began as a part-time student holiday hobby. However, with the release of *The Highland Connection*, featuring rock tunes with a Gaelic flavor, the band expanded into a six-piece and became a serious endeavor. With the release of its next album, *Recovery* (1981), Run Rig's musical identity began to form. The group's songs dealt with the history of Scotland, both musically and spiritually, and began to find an audience outside of the band's native country. Buoyed by its increasing popularity, the band headed south to London but disliked the dictates forced on it by an industry requiring greater commerciality and less "Scottishness" in the group's music style and lyrical content. As a result Run Rig released only two singles, "Dance Called America" and "Skye," for the independent Simple recording label. In 1985 the band released its fourth album, *Heartland*, with the opening track, "O Cho Mealt," sung in Gaelic.

By 1987 Run Rig began to play larger festivals, including a successful tour of Canada and as support to Irish superstars U2 at Scotland's biggest sports stadium, Murrayfield, in the Scottish capital of Edinburgh. Another album was released on Ridge Records, *The Cutter and the Clan* (1987), but the band was beginning to realize that it would never gain the exposure it deserved by staying with its own label. After the group signed an international deal with Chrysalis, it mounted another unsuccessful attack on the singles chart with "Survive." Run Rig and Chrysalis, though, realized that the band's greatest strength was its live shows, so they released a live album, *Once in a Lifetime*, in 1988. More recording yielded more singles, "News from Heaven" and "Every River," in

1989. In the following year a new album, *The Big Wheel*, was released, and a series of dates culminated in an open-air show on the banks of Loch Lomond, in the heart of the Scottish countryside, that was attended by an audience of 20,000 fans. In 1991 Run Rig increased its popularity as it played more concerts in Europe, achieving great success particularly in Germany and Denmark. After more time in the studio Run Rig released its ninth album, *Amazing Things*, in 1993 to commemorate twenty years of the band's existence. The tracks featured the band's trademark Gaelic rock sound that had won many fans at home and in Europe; but although selling albums in vast quantities, the band never broke into the singles market. In 1994 the group released *Transmitting Live*. In the following year the band finally won a place in the United Kingdom's top forty singles chart.

When the brewing company Carlsberg used a Run Rig song, "An Ubhal As Airde," on a TV commercial, Chrysalis took advantage of the exposure by releasing the track as a single—which ultimately earned the band an appearance on the United Kingdom's most popular TV music show, *Top of the Pops*. The band's next single, "Things That Are," failed to make any impact on the charts; and its eleventh album, *Mara* (1995), was released to a mixed reception. A compilation followed, but in 1997 the band was "put on hold" as singer Donnie Munro ran for Parliament as a member of the Labour Party. (Although he came in second in that election, Munro decided to pursue a career in politics that he continues to this day.) It wasn't until 1998 that a replacement for Munro was found in Canadian Bruce Guthro. A new album, *In Search of Angels* (1999), featured the group's first new material in four years, and once again the band toured heavily to promote it. In 2000, Run Rig performed as part of the Celtic Connections festival in Glasgow, the setting for its first performance twenty-seven years earlier. The show was recorded and released as an album in September. The band played a short tour of the United Kingdom in March 2001 before a new album of Gaelic-influenced folk/rock, *The Stamping Ground*, was released during summer.

The band visited Europe for a series of concerts in December and continued to play live in the United Kingdom in June 2002.

References

www.riggies.org.uk
The History of Scottish Rock And Pop: All That Ever Mattered by Brian Hogg Enfield (Enfield: Guinners Publishing, 1993). ISBN 0851127231

Runga, Bic (New Zealand)

Born Briolette Kahbic Runga in Christchurch on the South Island of New Zealand in 1976, Runga was surrounded by music from an early age. Her mother had been a singer in Malaysian nightclubs in the mid-1960s, and her father and sisters also played in bands. A budding drummer at age eleven, Runga turned to singing in jazz bands by her mid-teens and toyed with the idea of becoming a poet before learning the guitar and keyboard and deciding to attempt a career in music. As a result she moved to Auckland, on New Zealand's North Island, as an eighteen-year-old in 1994. The city was popularly known as the center of the country's music business. Initially Runga played small clubs in Auckland, where, finding herself short of material in the minutes preceding a show, she wrote "Drive" on an acoustic guitar. The song was to have a marked influence on her career. Before long Runga signed a record deal with Sony (in September 1995); three months later she recorded "Drive" and took it into the top ten. The song a solo performance by Runga on acoustic guitar and vocals, also won her the prestigious Silver Scroll, awarded in New Zealand for excellence in songwriting (and previously won by other New Zealand stars such as **Dave Dobbyn**), as well as led to her being named most promising woman vocalist at the 1996 New Zealand Music Awards.

The year 1996 was taken up with a string of shows across the country both as support to legendary New Zealand names such as Tim Finn and Neil Finn from Crowded House, and as a way of headlining her own concerts. By now Runga was starting to develop her very personal lyrics and folk-based songwriting skills, as more singles followed in September 1996 ("Bursting Through") and May 1997 ("Sway"). During the intervening months Runga prepared material for a debut album. Recording began in May and was completed only three weeks later with Runga herself producing the album, as well as playing many of the instruments herself. The album, *Drive*, was released late in 1997 and entered the top ten with extensive critical acclaim. The album went on to become the biggest-selling album in New Zealand by a native New Zealander ever. At the end of the year Runga was named top woman vocalist; and "Bursting Through" was nominated as best single by the New Zealand music industry, although it narrowly failed to win. As a result of her growing reputation, she was invited to contribute to the soundtrack of the movie *American Pie*. Runga recorded a duet, "Good Morning Baby," with Dan Wilson of the U.S. band Semisonic and had her own song, "Sway" (taken from the album *Drive*), also included on the album. "Sway" became the most played song of 1997 in New Zealand.

Much of her time throughout 1998 and 1999 was spent contributing to other artists' records. For example, she sang vocals on New Zealand band **Stellar***'s album *The Underwater Melon Man* (Stellar* includes Runga's sister Boh). She also contributed vocals for another New Zealand band, **Strawpeople**, to use in its cover version of The Cars' late-1980s hit single, "Drive" (a different song from Runga's own). By the end of 1998 Runga had won album of the year as well as best single and best songwriter for "Sway." Runga also wrote some music for the movie *Channelling Baby* (produced in New Zealand), including the single "Night Will Close Us Down." She continued to play shows throughout her native country and established herself firmly as a favorite of critics and the public alike. Her single "Dust" was nominated for song of the year in 1999. She also won the title of solo artist of the year three times in succession (1998, 1999, and 2000) from the magazine *Metro*.

In March 2000, Runga won an international achievement award for her music. She then joined Dave Dobbyn and Tim Finn in August 2000 for a tour of New Zealand. All twenty-six dates sold out in advance, and an album of the tour, *Together in Concert: Live*, was released in November. By May 2001, Runga had recorded enough new material for an album but scrapped all the songs because she was unhappy with the content. Instead she embarked on a series of live dates, all of which sold out. Although she is a relative newcomer to the New Zealand music scene, Runga appeared twice in a chart, published in 2001, of New Zealand's all-time favorite songs with "Sway" (#6) and "Drive" (#21). In June 2002 Runga released a new single "Get Some Sleep." The song was a delicate acoustic number that set the tone for a new album, *Beautiful Collision*, released in July.

References

www.bicrunga.com

S

Seo Taiji & Boys (South Korea)

Jeong Hyun Chul was born in Seoul, South Korea, on February 21, 1972. Throughout school his main interest was the study of music, and he formed his own band, Haneul Byuk, when he was just fourteen years old. While playing in the band he was noticed by Shin Tae-Chul, a respected figure in the Korean music scene, and was invited to play bass for Sinawe, a well-known heavy metal group. Although joining the group would mean the end of his education, Jeong had no hesitation in accepting the offer. Within a year the newly named Seo Taiji left the band to form his own group. At this time two other young artists, Yang Hyun Suk (b. December 2, 1970) and Lee Juno, were dancers and choreographers, and Seo Taiji saw them as the perfect foil to the music he was writing, which owed more to the hip-hop/rap culture of the United States than the rock songs and ballads that dominated the Korean music scene.

Seo Taiji & Boys, as the new band became known, released its first eponymously titled album in 1992. The band's blend of rap and rock was a completely new phenomenon in Korea, and the group suddenly found itself the #1 act in the country. The album sold in excess of one and a half million copies within months of its release, a record for any Korean band to date. By November, as he wrote material for the second album, Seo Taiji made a deliberate decision that the band was not going to make any TV appearances. Of course, the lack of publicity created an even bigger market, as the band's mainly teenager following speculated as to the content of the new album. Released in 1993, *Hayeoga* quickly emulated the success of its predecessor and sold almost 2 million copies. On the album Sao Taiji introduced traditional Korean instruments into his mixture of Western genres and created yet another new sound for Korean ears. By now Seo Taiji & Boys was being hailed as the creator of "Shinsedae" ("New Generation"), and books were written about the new feeling among Korean youth—or, as one book title put it, "The Seo Taiji Generation." Magazines and newspapers in Korea carried stories about the band, calling the members "Fathers of the Korean Music Industry" and Seo Taiji "The President of Teenagers."

So far the content of Seo Taiji's songs had been innocuous, the music being more important. But for the band's third album, *The Classroom Idea* (1994), Taiji returned to his rock roots and the lyrical content took a dramatic turn. As the lyrics spoke about unification (with North Korea), education, and politics, topics not usually addressed in Korean pop, the band was soon in trouble with the government (which, in 1994, was still able to censor public material.) As the government exercised its censorship right, many lyrics were cut and one song released as a single, "Regret the Times," was banned by the Korea Broadcasting Ethics Committee. Although the committee decided that the lyrics might be harmful to the youth of the country, the banning caused such an outcry that by the time the argument had been settled, the song was allowed to be played on the radio and the committee itself had disbanded. The album was also said by the government to have secret messages dealing with Satan and death hidden within the tracks. As the band waited for the controversy to pass, Taiji began work on new material. When *Come Back Home* was released in 1996, the fans and critics delighted in the record. Introducing "gangsta rap" to Korea, it confirmed the group as the pioneers of music in the country. Seo Taiji & Boys was now at the peak of its talents; but, declaring a wish to remain at the top, Taiji announced that the band was splitting up. Almost immediately Seo Taiji retired to the United States, seen off at the airport by over 5,000 grieving fans. He remained in America for the next four years.

At this point Yang Hyun Suk moved into production and management. His first project was to team a solo singer with a moderate career called Jinu with an energetic newcomer, Sean, to create the group Jinusean, which went on to reach #1 in the Korean charts. Lee Juno, in a move that echoed his partner's, also created a band of former dancers and added a popular singer, Lim Sung Eun, from the defunct band Two Two, and renamed the group the Young Turks Club. The new band also topped the charts. However, the efforts of Yang Hyun Suk and Lee Juno only acted as reminders to the Korean public of the greatness of the former band. When it was announced that Seo Taiji was releasing a solo album, *Take Two*, in 1998, it sold out in Korea on the day of its release, regardless of the fact that Taiji remained in America. Two years later Taiji returned to Korea with a second solo album, *Taiji*, which sold over a million copies. Now Taiji began to take on the loud and aggressive nu-metal genre that was being extolled by rock bands such as Limp Bizkit in the United States. Taiji's June 2000 album, *Ultramania*, reflected this influence. During the summer of 2001, Taiji toured across Asia under the banner of the "Summersonic" tour. A live album of the concerts was released soon after. Seo Taiji has recently been working with Japanese artists **Chage & Aska** with a view to releasing new material, although no date has yet been fixed.

At the end of 2001, a compilation of the band's early work, *Seo Taiji 1992–1996 Best*, was released in Korea.

References

www.taijizone.com

Shevchuck, Yuri (Russia)

Yury Shevchuck (b. May 16, 1957 in the village of Yagodnoe) discovered his love for pop music through The Beatles when he first heard the band as a ten-year-old in his hometown of Ufa in the former Soviet Union. By 1980 he was an art teacher, guitar player, and budding poet/songwriter who subsequently formed the rock band DDT (named after the insecticide) with Rustam Asanbaev, Gennedy Rodin, Vladimir Igachev, and Rustan Karimov. (Throughout the history of DDT Shevchuck has used over twenty-two musicians and a wide range of instruments including flutes, slide guitar, harmonica, mandolins, and violins.) In 1982 the band got the chance to record some material as part of a talent contest. Booking some time in a local studio, the group recorded its first album, *Pig on a Rainbow*, in three days. The group won a prize for the anti-military song "Don't Shoot," but it was later in the year that DDT began to win notice. At the end of its first public concert, at the Ufa Oil Research University, there was a scandal as the audience, all members of the Communist Party, were shocked at the material they heard: not generic rock music, but challenging lyrics. As a result of the concert the group's songs were banned by the state, and subsequently the band's popularity soared.

Political scandals followed the band at every turn. After a successful performance at the Rock for Peace festival, the group was edited out of the TV broadcast that appeared shortly thereafter. The album *Periphery* (1984) found Shevchuck in more trouble for his outspoken and non-conformist lyrics, this time with the Soviet secret police, the KGB. As he wrote controversial material for a new album, he was threatened with imprisonment if it was released. Subsequently he left Ufa and relocated to Sverdlovsk and then to Moscow in 1985. Later that year he gave his first solo concert in Leningrad and released an acoustic album—*Moscow. Heat.*—written with fellow musician Sergey Ryzhenko; the album highlighted his politicized lyrics unencumbered by raging guitars. In 1985 he released *Time*, recorded with itinerant players. By 1986, Shevchuck began to audition for new members to re-form DDT in Leningrad. The new band differed little musically from its former incarnation, as it continued to play politicized heavy rock. This led to a performance at the V Rock festival in 1987 to great acclaim. The album *I Got This Role* (1988) was DDT's first government-sanctioned album, released under the new policy of *glasnost* that was introduced under the leadership of President Mikhail Gorbachev.

For the next three years DDT undertook a punishing schedule of concerts, releasing albums when it could. It wasn't until the 1992 release of *Actress Spring* that the band began to favor studio work over live work, as it gave the musicians more space to experiment with its sound and introduce new instrumentation and musical ideas. Ironically, its next album (released the following year) was a live recording of a concert in Moscow. In 1993 the band received the title of Best Group by the Russian music press, while Shevchuck won best rock singer.

In 1994 DDT released a new album, *This Is It . . . ,* which was built on a solid rock foundation but introduced brass and woodwind to give the songs a more melodic feel. *Love,* in 1996, was similar in style though Shevchuck's lyrics introduced a romantic air. In January 1996 Shevchuck began a tour of Chechnya, where he gave over fifty concerts to the Russian army, at the time involved in a bloody civil war with Chechnya. It was after the visit that he wrote what became one of his most popular songs. "Dead City" was a plaintive ballad dedicated to the fledgling country's capital, Grozny.

Later in the year a new radio series, "Jingles," began in Russia. The series was a collection of thirty- to ninety-second soundbytes aimed primarily at Russian youth. The programs contained information about various social issues including AIDS, government elections, and ecology. Shevchuck, as an icon of Russian rock music, was chosen as one of the early presenters.

In 1997, DDT visited the United States and played a series of six concerts, including one at Georgetown University in Washington, D.C., that included a full choir. (Although the band had previously visited the United States when it recorded the *Love* album in Massachusetts, it had not previously played live in the United States.) Also in 1997 the band visited Australia to promote the *Born in the USSR* album. In November 1998, Shevchuck visited Jerusalem to give a series of solo concerts. Early in the following year DDT released its sixteenth album, *World Number Zero,* and plans were made to tour Russia once again.

After playing a series of "unplugged" shows in 2000, Shevchuck appeared at the International Festival of Russian Arts and Culture in Las Vegas in November. At the festival, named "Cold War–Hot Culture," Shevchuck gave poetry readings of material he had written some years earlier. During April 2001 the people of Ufa apparently forgave Shevchuck for any earlier indiscretions, as they collected signatures as part of a petition calling for the government to give the artist honorary citizenship after he fled in the 1980s. It has yet to be granted. DDT prepared for a winter tour of the United States in 2001 before returning home to concentrate on new projects. The same year DDT released *August Snowstorm.* The lyrical content was typical of Shevchuck, as he continued to find fault with the political and social situation in Russia.

References

www.vlink.ru/rock/eng/bands/ddt

Silence 4 (Portugal)

Singer/guitarist David Fonseca knew drummer Tozé Pedrosa from the local music scene in their hometown of Leiria, 50 miles north of the Portuguese capital, Lisbon, when he invited him to join a band he was forming. Fonseca saw

Sofia Lisboa perform in local bars almost a year earlier and decided that she would be the perfect singer for his as yet unnamed band. Subsequently bass player Rui Costa was invited to hear the group play, and he joined soon thereafter. Once the band began to rehearse, the resulting rock songs were not to anyone's liking. Pedrosa then suggested they try some acoustic numbers rather than using amplifiers. The band was more pleased with the results and named itself Silence 4 due to the "quiet" nature of its music.

As the band retreated to a rural farmhouse to concentrate on building a body of material, Fonseca began writing in English. Although the group was winning a growing following in Leiria, when it tried to interest publishing and record companies with its material it was turned down. The record industry in Portugal thought it would be difficult to promote a band in Portugal that sang in English. The band's material was also heavily acoustic, a style that was accepted as part of the flamenco genre but unusual in Portuguese pop. In 1996, however, the band was offered a record deal after winning the Festival Termóro Unplugged. In the following year the band contributed a song to an album, *Sons de todas as cores*, released as part of an anti-racism project. Silence 4's contribution was a cover of English band Erasure's "A Little Respect" (a song also covered by U.S. rock band Wheatus in 2001). The song received heavy radio play and, as a consequence, reached #1 on the Portuguese charts.

As the group began to record its debut album, the record company insisted that at least some of the material be in Portuguese. Fonseca relented and wrote "Eu nao sei dizer" and "Sexto Sentido," both of which appeared on the gentle, acoustic-based *Silence Becomes It* (1998). Released in June, the album quickly rose to the top of the local charts, where it stayed for twelve months, selling five times platinum by the end of the year. Silence 4 had always put great stock in playing concerts, and during 1998 it played in excess of 100 shows across the country as well as major European festivals. As a result it wasn't until June 2000 that the band released more material. Its second album, *Only Pain Is Real*, continued to downplay heavily amplified rock music; in fact, the introverted nature of Fonseca's lyrics helped the record to become a platinum disc in Portugal within two weeks of its release after it entered the chart at #1. A single from the album, "To Give," spent five months on the charts at #1. Between August and December the band played another tour of Portugal that was preceded by a TV special dedicated to the group's music, ending with two shows at the Coliseu de Lisboa.

In April 2001 the group played some small concerts in London before returning to Europe to perform more shows throughout the summer. Although no new material has been released since *Only Pain Is Real*, the band continues to perform in Portugal. Despite the heavy English bias in the lyrics of Silence 4, the group has yet to establish itself outside of Portugal.

References

www.silence4.net

Silverchair (Australia)

Guitarist Dan Johns (b. April 22, 1979), bassist Chris Joannou (b. November 10, 1979), and drummer Ben Gilles (b. October 24, 1979) were only thirteen years old when, in 1992, they formed the band Innocent Criminals, rehearsing in their parents' garage in Newcastle, Australia. Soon they became Silverchair and began performing small shows, playing covers of Led Zeppelin and Deep Purple songs. The band entered a nationwide talent contest in 1994 and won first prize, a trip to a professional recording studio. There the group produced its first single, "Tomorrow," based on the type of music they had been influenced by in their pre-teens. Sony Music heard the track and decided to release it. Within weeks it was #1 on the Australian charts and stayed there for six weeks. The band's debut album, *Frogstomp*, which reportedly was recorded in just nine days, hit the charts in June of the following year. Although criticized for imitating the "grunge" sound made popular in the United States by bands such as Pearl Jam and Nirvana, the record went double platinum in Australia and sold over two and a half million copies worldwide. The band toured as much as the members' educational commitments would allow, supporting the Red Hot Chili Peppers in the United States and Hole in Australia.

By now, Silverchair was receiving some unwelcome publicity in the press. Lyrics from *Frogstomp*, often dealing with negativity and death, were quoted in a 1996 trial when two teenagers were accused of murdering family members. However, the publicity appeared to help raise the profile of the band nationally. The follow-up album, *Freakshow* (1997), also reached the top of the Australian charts. By now, each member of the band had graduated from high school and was able to spend more time in the studio and on tour, which proved crucial in helping Silverchair to create its own guitar heavy sound as its technical expertise grew. Although still heavily influenced by rock and grunge, the songs showed the band maturing at a rapid rate. In 1999, the group released *Neon Ballroom*, an album that included the single "Ana's Song," which sold over a million copies. The album also featured "Emotional Sickness," on which celebrated pianist David Helfgott (the subject of the motion picture *Shine*) played, which gained the group huge critical success. The heavy schedule of concerts helped the album sell more than one and a half million copies, as the band was named Australian artist of the year at the 1999 ARIA awards. By the end of the decade Silverchair had more top twenty hits in the 1990s than any other Australian artist or group.

Early in 2000 the band's record company released a compilation album, *Silverchair: The Best of—Vol. 1*. Despite the band's refusal to promote it, stating it "ripped off" the group's fans because it included no new material, the album went gold with in the first week of release. In January 2001 the band performed in front of its biggest audience to date, at the Rock in Rio festival in Brazil, when 250,000 people watched the show.

In the summer of 2002 Silverchair released their fourth studio album, *Diorama*. Although still based around the band's three-piece formation, the songs explored genres other than rock with the soul-like "Luv Your Life" and the more pop sound of "The Greatest View." The band also introduced brass, wood-wind, and an orchestra to give the album more variety musically than its previous releases. The album reached the top ten of the local chart as the band performed at festivals across Australia and Europe.

References

www.chairpage.com
Silverchair by Matthew Reid (London: Omnibus Press, 1998). ISBN 0949789585

Sissel (Norway)

A native of Bergen, Norway, Sissel Kyrkjebo was born on June 24, 1969. By the time she was fifteen years old she was a veteran of TV music shows, and in 1986 she released her first album. *Sissel* was a collection of pop ballads and up-tempo numbers very different from the operatic style that suited her soprano voice and that was to win her recognition later in her career. After its release it sold over 300,000 copies in Norway. In the following year Sissel released an album of Christmas songs, *Glade Jul*, that sold over half a million copies.

After the success of her two albums, Sissel decided to expand her talents and agreed to take on the role of Maria in a stage production of *The Sound of Music*, a role made famous by Julie Andrews in the film of the same name. With her acting debut critically well received, Sissel returned to the studio in 1989 and by October had released *Soria Moria*. As her performing experience increased and her voice continued to mature, her appearances both live and on TV helped her create an expanding fan base. She met Danish singer Eddie Skoller on the set of a music program in fragment August 1991, and by the end of the year the couple were engaged. In 1992 Sissel released the album *Gift of Love*. The singer's love relationship at the time gave the album a personal feel and offered fans a brief insight into her life. In August of the following year, two years after meeting, Sissel and Skoller were married, and thousands of fans went to the church to offer their support.

When the Winter Olympic Games of 1994 took place in Lillehammer, Sissel was invited to perform at the opening ceremony. It was timely exposure for her, as she had just released her fifth album, *Inert I sjelen*. (The album also gained a Japanese release as *Deepest in My Soul* but faired poorly.) The operatic qualities in her voice were now well developed, and in December she appeared with tenor Placido Domingo in a TV concert, "A Christmas in Vienna." Then, in the following year, she sang for Prince Charles in London as part of the show "A Royal Gala." Although she was able to perform in a classic style, she released a new album, *Vestland, Vestland* (1994), that featured her own style of ethereal vocals. Another Christmas album, *Christmas in Vienna III*, was released at the end of 1995.

By now Sissel was a household name in Norway, and she soon broke into the international market. In 1997 she came to the attention of filmmakers working on the soundtrack for a new movie to be directed by James Cameron called *Titanic*. Sissel's ethereal, haunting music, with its roots in traditional Celtic sounds along the lines of Irish singer **Enya**, was deemed by the filmmakers to be exactly what the film required. She recorded seven songs that appeared on the soundtrack, an album that later became #1 across the world. Due to the international exposure afforded her by *Titanic*, Sissel began to divide her time between Scandinavia and the United States. She recorded material with West Coast rapper Warren G, but the album, *Prince Igor the Rapsody,* failed to sell because audiences were puzzled by the eclectic mix of rap and Sissel's distinctive vocals. After the failure of the album, she returned to what she did best: *Back to Titanic* was a collection of songs that were similar to those in the original soundtrack. A stop-gap album, *Fire in Your Heart—The Best of Sissel*, was released in 1998 while she took time off to raise a family. She collaborated with fellow Norwegians **Lene Marlin, Abel Morten**, and **Espen Lind** on material for *All Good Things* (2000). Although the album could have been disjointed with so many writers contributing, Sissel's vocal style held the project together.

After the release of *All Good Things* in 2000, the album turned gold in her native country as it sold over 100,000 copies within the first month of its release, as well as reaching #5 in the Danish chart and achieving a gold disc. In May of the following year Sissel appeared at a children's film festival, "Barnefilm," after playing a minor role in the movie *Flyvende Farmor*. Later, in September, she performed in Washington, D.C., as part of the Norwegian Visions concert. In November 2001, Sissel released her most ambitious album to date. Recorded live at the Drammers Theatre with the Norway National Orchestra, *Sissel in Symphony* (2001) included contributions from fellow Norwegian artists Lene Marlin and Espen Lind. The album did well in Norway but has yet to gain an international release.

In January 2002, *All Good Things*, was released in the United Kingdom as Sissel continues her attempt to break into a wider market.

References

www.sissel.net

Smiths, The (England)

When guitar player Johnny Marr (b. 1963) was looking for a lyricist to put words to his music in the spring of 1982 in Manchester, England, he approached Steven Morrissey (b. May 22, 1959), who readily agreed. Over the next six years the combination of Marr's sparkling guitar riffs and Morrissey's apparently-doom-laden lyrics won them a huge following among teenagers. Although often accused of being humorless, the band constantly argued it was misunderstood and misrepresented, claiming that its music was packed with humor, irony, and sarcasm that both critics and fans overlooked. Yet song titles such as "Girlfriend in a Coma" and "The Boy with the Thorn in His Side" and

Morrissey's lyrics (which seemed to express depression and a sense of "me against the world"), did not stop the band from becoming one of the most popular groups in the country.

Giving themselves the name The Smiths as a direct response to the more exotic names that were prevalent in the U.K. charts of the time, such as Duran Duran and Spandau Ballet, the group soon recruited bassist Andy Rourke (b. 1963) and drummer Mike Joyce (b. 1963). After only its seventh live show, the band signed a record contract with the independent label Rough Trade that allowed it to release one single. The result, "Hand in Glove," divided the music press, who thought it was either genius or stunningly boring and reached #1 in the independent music chart. Although it was two years before the release of the group's second single, "This Charming Man" (1983), the band had already been surrounded by controversy. Some critics read into Morrissey's lyrics suspicions of child abuse, especially in the songs "Reel Around the Fountain" and "Handsome Devil," an accusation strenuously denied by the singer. ("Reel Around the Fountain" was allegedly about Myra Hindley, who was convicted of the abduction and murder of schoolchildren in Manchester in the early 1960s. She died recently while in jail in England.)

"This Charming Man" reached #25 in the national chart with Marr's chiming guitar riffs coming to the fore, and the band began to attract a devoted following that pushed the group's third single—"What Difference Does It Make?"—to #12. The band's eponymous debut album, released one month later, showcased the juxtaposition created by Marr and Morrissey. The album climbed to #2. It was the start of a period in which The Smiths were regarded as one of the most important bands of the 1980s by the U.K. music press. Although the group refused to make videos, as a reaction to what it saw as the superficiality of many of the bands of the time (once again citing Duran Duran and Spandau Ballet), the band's fan base continued to grow. A compilation album of the group's early work for radio shows, *Hatful of Hollow* (1984), reached #7. By February of the following year the band's second album, *Meat Is Murder,* entered at #1, and concerts across the United Kingdom sold out within days.

Morrissey and Marr were now being talked about as the finest songwriters in the country. Although subsequent singles "Shakespeare's Sister" and "Bigmouth Strikes Again" barely reached the top thirty, in June 1986 the band released *The Queen Is Dead* to almost unanimous acclaim. By now The Smiths' songwriters had reached the apex of their creativity, as Marr overdubbed guitar on guitar and Morrissey's wit sparkled. Reflecting the success of their debut album, the new album reached #2 and began a period where The Smiths were the country's most influential musicians. A series of singles released from the album consolidated the band's position over the next year: "Panic" (#11, July 1986), "Ask" (#14, October 1986), "Shoplifters of the World Unite" (#12, January 1987), and "Sheila Take a Bow" (#10, April 1987). A compilation, *The World Won't Listen*, released in February 1987, became the band's third #2 album.

Although The Smiths had successfully toured across Europe the group had yet to make an impression in the United States. So a compilation album, *Louder Than Bombs* (1987), featuring the group's successful U.K. hits, was released for the U.S. market. Although it failed in America, the interest in the United Kingdom was sufficient for the record label to release the album there, and it reached #38. The band's fourth studio album, *Strangeways, Here We Come* (1987), was a more downbeat effort musically, but it still managed to reach #2.

By now, however, internal tensions were beginning to manifest themselves, particularly between Marr and Morrissey, as articles in the music press claimed the quality of the band's creative output was diminishing. In August 1988, before an official announcement could be made, Marr left the band. By the end of September the band had split up. A live album, *Rank*, was released in the same month and also reached #2 in the charts. Another "best of" album, *The World Won't Listen*, was released four years later in August 1992 and became the band's first #1 in nine years. Morrissey then began a successful solo career until he was accused of racism; although he constantly denied the accusations, his career never fully recovered. Johnny Marr played with other musicians and in other bands, including Electronic with Bernard Summer of **New Order**, before forming his own band, The Healers, in 2000. Although Andy Rourke and Mike Joyce continued to play in other bands, including Sinead O'Connor's, they took Morrissey and Marr to court in the late 1990s for uncollected royalties and won. In 2002 Morrissey began a series of solo concerts while nothing new has been heard from Marr, Rourke or Joyce.

References

www.cemetrygates.com
Morrissey and Marr: The Severed Alliance by Johnny Rogan (London: Omnibus Press, 1995). ISBN 0711918384.

Soda Stereo (Argentina)

Forming a band in Buenos Aires, Argentina, in 1982, Gustavo Cerati (b. August 11, 1960), Charly Alberti (b. March 27, 1963), and Veta Bosio began playing music that had a strong reggae influence, unusual in South America. The band spent two years playing the clubs in its native city before it finally landed a record deal and released its self-titled debut album in 1984. An immediate success in Argentina, the band began to play concerts across Latin America; after the release of *Nada Personal* (1985), the group started playing to larger audiences. While on the road, Soda Stereo continued to write upbeat material and began to take on the style of the new romantic movement that was becoming popular in the United Kingdom. The combination of synthesizer and guitar masked the increasingly dark lyrics of the group's third album, *Signos* (1985). *Signos* reached the top of the charts across South America and introduced the band to the Spanish public in Europe. By now, Soda Stereo was playing to capacity audiences of 25,000 people in stadiums across the Spanish-speaking countries of South America, and the title track from the album became a huge hit in the wake of the band's live shows.

For the next two years the band members concentrated on their own individual projects, producing new records and collaborating with other, established musicians. To fill the gap in their creative output, a live album, *Ruido Blanco*, was released in 1987. Feeling frustrated by the group's lack of success in North America, Soda Stereo decided to record its 1988 album, *Doble Vida*, in New York with producer Carlos Alomar, who was already well known for his work with John Lennon, David Bowie, and Mick Jagger. The record showed the band moving away from the synthesizer and developing into more straightforward rock. Although the album was another great success in Latin America, it failed to gain much notice in the English-speaking world, despite the band touring North America. The band was popular enough in South America, however, for Pepsi to sign it to a promotional deal. TV commercials helped raise the profile of the band even further.

By 1990, Soda Stereo had become a rock band, but its need for experimentation continued as it employed a 7/4 time signature on the track "En el Séptimo Dia" from its new album *Canción Animal* (1990). More concerts and TV appearances followed before Soda Stereo members again took a break, as their solo work demanded more time.

It was another three years before the release of *Dy'namo* in 1993. As their own work had been taking them away from the Soda Stereo "sound," *Dy'namo* was a complete departure for the band. More aggressive than the group's previous work, the album appeared to show Soda Stereo struggling to find a new direction. Following the release of the album the band members once again turned to their solo projects, and in 1994 they only released a "best of" album and *Zona De Promesas*, a re-mix album of old material. In 1995, *Sueño Stereo* became another chart topper as horns and strings were added to create a lighter pop feel, but it was the band's last album of new material. Still enjoying huge success, the group performed a concert as part of the "MTV Unplugged" series later in the year. A final album, *Comfort Y Música Para Volar* (1996), contained some of the songs from the unplugged session and cover versions of other artists' material. Another stadium tour of South America was undertaken, but these appearances proved to be the last for Soda Stereo. Already finding it difficult to combine the requirements of the band with their solo work, Cerati, Alberti, and Bosio decided that the time had come for Soda Stereo to end. A final double live album, *El Ultimo Concierto 1&2,* was released in 1997. Containing songs from the band's final tour, the album was a fitting tribute to Argentina's biggest band. The three members of Soda Stereo continue with their solo projects and have won varying degrees of success in South America while still failing to affect the English-speaking market.

References

www.accessglobe.com/rock/bands/soda

Soulsister (Belgium)

Jan Leyers and Paul Michiels had been part of the Belgian music scene for several years before working together as The Soul Sisters in 1986. Born in the town of Heist-op-den-Berg, Michiels tasted success in the band Octopus between 1974 and 1980, as well as attempting a solo career in the early 1980s that spawned a top thirty hit, "Females." The Soul Sisters' first release, the single "You Get to Me," was a slick piece of synth pop based on drum machines and smooth keyboard riffs that won steady airplay on Belgian radio. Although further releases "Talk about It" and "Like a Mountain" won the duo a reputation in the media as excellent songwriters, it took another two years, and a change of name to Soulsister, before they finally made their mark. "The Way to Your Heart" (1988), another slick pop song, became a huge hit in Belgium, Holland, and Germany and reached the top fifty on the U.S. Billboard chart. As a result, the planned album *It Takes Two*, a collection of well-produced pop, had its release date brought forward by two months to cash in on the success.

After spending the next months touring Europe, the duo returned to the studio to begin work on its second album. When *Heat* was released in 1990, the band was now called Leyers, Michiels, and Soulsister, reflecting the fact that Leyers and Michiels were the foundation of the band and employed other musicians when in the studio or on tour. *Heat* was a collection of Europop tunes that eventually produced seven singles released over a period of eighteen months. The album stayed in the Belgian chart for over two years. While *Heat* was enjoying its extended run in the chart, the band continued to tour and Leyers and Michiels continued writing. As the touring came to an end, they had amassed enough material to once again enter the studio to begin work on a third album, *Simple Rule*. Although it was not a favorite of the critics (*Humo* magazine called the album "11 pieces of digitally recorded civilized music, dipped in aftershave"), the Belgian public once again flocked to the nation's music stores and helped the album reach the top of the chart. More touring followed, and in view of the group's growing reputation as a live act, the almost inevitable live album was released in 1993. *Live Savings* was recorded over a series of shows at which the band opened for the singer Sting across stadiums in Europe.

But the constant round of tours was having a negative effect on the group. By now, Leyers and Michiels were unable to break away from the routine imposed on them. The band's next album, *Swinging Like Big Dogs* (1994), showed little progression in the bands' musical style and was accompanied by Leyers giving interviews stating, "It feels like the story has been told . . . this may well be our last album." Although the band continued working together, there was no new material; and when a "best of" album, *The Way to Your Heart*, was released in 1997, it was announced that Soulsister was no more.

Leyers went on to form My Velma, a three-piece band that played a more rock-oriented style, while Michiels returned to his solo career and released a string of singles that sounded like the Soulsister of old. Through the new careers of Leyers and Michiels, the legacy of Soulsister continued to grow; another compilation, released at Christmas 1999, *Try Not to Cry—The Singles Collection*, again saw Soulsister at #1. In 2000, Leyers was invited to write the soundtrack to the movie *Team Spirit* by Belgian director Jan Verheyen. Leyers asked Michiels to contribute, and the duo released two singles, "Only Your Love Will Do" and "Forever Young," both of which reached the top of the national chart.

Although My Velma is nominally still together, Leyers has described the project as "running on the slowest possible break." During 2001 Michiels released *Forever Young*. The album was a collection of cover versions on which Leyers contributed vocals. Later, Leyers undertook a short solo tour in January 2002 in Belgium theaters.

References

Members.aol.com/geert1302/soulsister

Split Enz (New Zealand)

Formed in Auckland, New Zealand, in 1972, Split Enz went through a myriad of personnel changes but was always based around the songwriting partnership of Tim Finn (b. June 25, 1952) and Phil Judd. Beginning as Split Ends, the band released its first single in 1973, "For You," followed by a TV appearance on the talent show *New Faces*. The band finished second to last in the voting, as its guitar pop failed to impress the judging panel. In the following year the group became Split Enz. In 1975 the band toured Australia for nine months, gaining a small but fanatical following and a record deal with the Mushroom label. Recorded in two weeks, the debut album, *Mental Notes* (1976), was based heavily around synthesizer riffs that preceded the music of the New Romantics that dominated the charts of Europe in the early 1980s. The album made a small impression on both the Australian and New Zealand charts.

During this period the band caught the attention of Phil Manzanera, guitarist in Roxy Music, who offered to help with the recording of some material. As a result the group moved to England in 1976 and signed a worldwide deal with Chrysalis Records; but without an agent, the band found it impossible to get any live shows. Meanwhile the songwriting partnership between Finn and Judd was not producing anything new, and although an album, *Second Thoughts* (1976), was released, it was essentially a re-recording of *Mental Notes*. Judd, disillusioned at playing to uninterested audiences and the duties of promoting the band, left and was replaced by Tim Finn's younger brother, Neil.

Finn, the elder, took up the mantle of songwriter. The album that followed in 1977, *Dizrhythmia*, showed influences from the new wave scene of the United Kingdom that was basically punk, but with more focus on melody and the introduction of keyboards. The album went gold in New Zealand and gave the band its first top twenty hit. In the following year, however, the band was dropped by Chrysalis and found itself without a contract. Improbably, the New

Zealand Arts Council gave the group a grant of NZ $5,000, and the band recorded twenty-eight songs in five days in a small studio in Luton, England, before returning to Australia in the following year. While in Australia the band compiled the album *Frenzy* (1979), using many of the songs recorded in England, but again the band appeared to be creatively stilted.

It was the album *True Colours* (1979) that pushed the band to the musical forefront. The release included a Neil Finn contribution, "I Got You," that helped the record reach #1 in both New Zealand and Australia, selling over 200,000 copies in the latter (the equivalent of one in every ten households owing the album). As "I Got You" continued in the vein of the band's earlier work, the group members began to dress in day-glo suits and flamboyant hair styles reminiscent of the new romantic style popular in the U.K. The success of the single lead to an international deal with A&M, which, in turn, lead to *True Colours* selling well in Britain and the United States and going platinum in Canada. The band received official recognition when a videocassette of *True Colours* was included in a time capsule produced by the Australian government. A hurriedly released album, *Waiata* (1981), disappointed from a sales perspective but produced two hit singles, "One Step Ahead" and "History Never Repeats." After months of touring, the band went into the studio late in 1981 to record *Time and Tide*, an album that brought it once again to the top of the charts in both New Zealand and Australia.

By the time of the release of the next Split Enz album, *Conflicting Emotions* (1983), Neil had taken over the majority of songwriting from his brother Tim and steered the band away from a synthesizer sound toward a more acoustic feel. While the record was another huge success in the band's home territories, it again failed to make any impact internationally. At this time Tim announced he was leaving Split Enz. Neil wrote all the material for the band's next album, *See Ya Round* (1984), but it proved to be their swansong and the group split up in 1984. Subsequently the Finn brothers teamed up once more in the band Crowded House, achieved huge international acclaim, and became one of the biggest bands in the world.

In 1996 the New Zealand Symphony Orchestra performed a tribute to Split Enz, that included contributions from many major New Zealand artists, including Tim and Neil Finn themselves. The resulting album, *ENZSO* (1996), spent several weeks in the charts, eventually selling over 45,000 copies in their home country and 200,000 in Australia. In a chart published in 2001 of New Zealand's most popular songs ever, Split Enz was featured three times with 1979's "I See Red" (#29), 1980's "I Got You" (#11), and 1982's "Six Months in a Leaky Boat" (#5). Split Enz continues to be considered an institution in New Zealand, occasionally re-forming for sold-out concerts.

References

www.frenz.com/splitenz
Neil Finn: Once Removed by Neil Finn (London: Sanctuary Publishing, 2000). ISBN 1860742971

Springbok Nude Girls (South Africa)

Singer Arno Carstens began writing songs with his friend, guitarist Theo Crous, when they formed Springbok Nude Girls with drummer Francois Kruger and bass player Arno Blumer in 1994. In September 1994 they played their first show at a venue in their hometown, Stellenbosch. In the following year, during the Grahamstown Arts Festival, critics began to show interest in the group, alternately describing it as the musical highlight and "one of the most promising bands in the country" as its traditional rock sound won new fans. During 1995 the band became a five-piece when trumpeter/keyboard player Adriaan Brand joined.

The group released its first, self-financed album, *Neanderthal 1*, in August 1995. The record was a traditional rock album, but with Brand's trumpet giving the album a different feel from the rock bands in the country at the time. The energetic live performances of the band transferred well to the recorded format, and the album received extensive radio play. A single, "I Know What I Want," taken from the album, reached #1 on the 5FM Modern Rock Chart. In the following year the Bokkies, as the group had become known, underwent a series of tours and festival appearances that consolidated its popularity and ended with the group signing with Epic Records. The first release for the new label was the five-track single "It Became a Weapon," released in November 1996; by February 1997 the track "Genie" had become the band's second #1. In April the band received the South African Music Award (SAMA) for best rock performance for "It Became a Weapon." The band's second album, *Afterlifesatisfaction* (1997), was described as "one of the most important albums of the year" by South African music critics, who warmed to the group's fractious rock. Then the Australian stadium rock band INXS invited the group on tour in 1997 after which the band undertook more sold-out concerts later in the year as the headline act, including a low-key date in London.

The year 1998 began with more concerts, including a show in Pretoria in front of 16,000 fans. Later in the year the group performed in front of 40,000 people as part of the birthday celebrations for former South African leader Nelson Mandela. Other acts on the bill included Stevie Wonder and Chaka Kahn. On the third Bokkies album, *Surpass the Powers* (1999), Epic brought in producer Kevin Shirley, who had previously worked with Aerosmith and the Black Crowes, in an attempt to give the record a more international appeal. After its release the band undertook a huge European promotional tour. The album was well received by critics—especially in Germany, where German *Rolling Stone* magazine included a song from the album, "Shot," on a promotional CD distributed free among its readership. Other acts on the compilation album included Korn, L7, and Chuck Prophet. *Surpass the Powers* won the Bokkies' the rock album of the year award at the SAMAs in March 2000, partially aided by the band's lyrics that questioned the politics of its native country. At the end of the year the band's fourth album, *Relaxzor*, was another hit on the South

African charts, though the album was simply a continuation of the Bokkies' tried and tested musical formula. In March 2001 it won the band the best rock album of the year award at the SAMAs, the second time the band won the award.

Although the Bokkies appeared to be flourishing, the band's rigid rock sound was beginning to feel restrictive. In September 2001, Kruger, Blumer, and Brand announced they were leaving the band. Crous and Carstens stated that they would continue to work together. A farewell tour was announced for September and October under the banner "The Fat Lady Sings," and a "best of" album of the same name appeared at the end of the year and topped the local charts. To date, no new material has been released by any of the former members of South Africa's premier rock band. In 2002 Carstens began a new career as a model. Blumer is involved with the information technology (IT) industry and Kruger has become a furniture maker. Crous and Carstens still play together as a duo and toured South Africa with a collection of songs called "The Nude Girls Renditions" while Brand has composed music for the Cape Town Symphony Orchestra.

References

www.nudegirls.co.za

Stellar* (New Zealand)

Vocalist/guitarist Boh Runga and drummer Andrew MacLaren moved from their native Christchurch, New Zealand, to the country's music capital, Auckland, in 1992, and there they met guitarist Joel Hanes. Meanwhile, in 1994 director Simon Raby was looking for music for his short film *Headlong*, and Runga and MacLaren offered the song "Ride," which appeared on the soundtrack. For the next few years Runga and MacLaren played with a number of bassists before finding Kurt Shanks, who became a permanent member.

The band, now called Stellar*, continued to play the clubs of Auckland and by 1996 was ready to release a self-financed single, "Happy Gun." The record was recorded and mixed by Chris Van Der Geer, who later replaced Haines as guitarist. Although the single, a light guitar pop number, received little attention, it earned the band an invitation to support the popular local act **Strawpeople** on a number of dates around the country and in Australia. While flying home from Australia, Runga found herself sitting next to a Sony Music executive, and by the end of the flight the man had promised to listen to a demo. In April 1998, Stellar* signed with the label and was in the studio recording material. The band's debut single was due to be released in November but was jeopardized as the band insisted the song be called "Bastard." Sony feared that the name would get the record banned by TV and radio and changed the name to "What You Do." The single received extensive airplay and entered the top ten. During December 1998, Stellar* accompanied **Dave Dobbyn** on tour and then played the prestigious Bay '99 festival in Paihia on New Year's Eve. The rise of the band was so swift that by February it was playing to 6,000 people in Runga and MacLaren's native Christchurch. Following its live successes the band attended the NZ Music Awards in March, where it won the most promising female vocal and most promising group awards. Stellar* also performed its next single, "Part of Me," which was released in April 1999 and reached #4.

More touring and promotional work was undertaken while the band recorded material for its first album, *Mix* (1999). The album showed Stellar* to be thoughtful and intelligent songwriters. Runga's honey-coated vocal became a focal point over the samples and beats that formed the base of the bands music. After its release the band joined first Alanis Morissette and then Garbage on world tours to promote the record. *Mix* reached #1 in New Zealand in September before it eventually sold four times platinum. A single, "Violent," also reached #1. In January 2000, *Mix* was #3 in the music chart posted by the international editor of *Billboard*. The success of *Mix* was reflected at the NZ Music Awards in February 2000 when Stellar* picked up seven awards, for songwriter, single, album, female vocalist, group, producer, and engineer. During the summer the band undertook a series of short tours around New Zealand and Australia in support of the album, which by now had sold five times platinum. While on tour, "Violent" was named the most-played song on New Zealand radio between July 1999 and June 2000.

In February 2001, Stellar* performed one of the biggest concerts in New Zealand history with Dave Dobbyn and **Bic Runga**, younger sister to Boh and a star in her own right. The rest of the year was spent in the studio as the band recorded its next album. A single, "All It Takes," reached the top ten before the album *Magic Line* (2001) entered the New Zealand chart at #1. Although the album featured the band's trademark loops and samples, it focused more heavily on guitars and gave the music a rougher, more natural edge. Another tour of New Zealand was booked for November and December 2001 as Stellar* continued to grow as a force in the country's music scene. In the summer of 2002 the band toured New Zealand before leaving for Europe to appear at festivals across the continent.

References

www.stellar.co.nz

Stereophonics, The (Wales)

Born and raised in the small mining village of Cwamaman, South Wales, Kelly Jones (b. June 3, 1974) and Stuart Cable (b. May 19, 1970) lived on the same street throughout their childhood. Although they chose different, early career paths, with Jones taking a course in script-writing at college and Cable working on building sites, they played in bands together for many years, learning their craft in the working men's clubs of the area. (Working men's clubs, which proliferated in Britain in the 1950s as an alternative to the traditional pub, were private clubs where women and children were not welcome. They offered entertainment such as singers, cards, and snooker.) Covering songs by rock bands (such as AC/DC and Motörhead) they had copied from their elder brothers' record collections, Jones later began writing his own material, based around the characters and society of small-town Welsh life. Jones and Cable later formed a band with sometime electrician and coal worker Richard Jones (b. June 23, 1974) and named their group after their three favorite bands of the time; Tragically Hip, Mother Love Bone, and Bad Company. Tragic Love Company carried on playing the clubs and pubs of South Wales for many years until, in July 1996, the group changed its name to what they saw as the less clumsy Stereophonics.

By August the band was being sought by major record companies in the United Kingdom. After deciding to sign with the newly formed V2, in November the group released a double a-side single. "Looks Like Chaplin" was paired with "More Life in a Tramp's Vest"; both songs were rousing rock numbers featuring Kelly Jones's gruff vocals that were reminiscent of Rod Stewart. Although support shows with **Manic Street Preachers** and The Who followed, the single gained little interest from radio despite being warmly received by the music press. The band's second single, "Local Boy In The Photograph" was released in March 1997. With the help of a touring schedule that took the group all over the country, playing ill-attended shows in small clubs and on university campuses, the record reached #51 in the U.K. charts. A re-released "More Life in a Tramp's Vest" in May took the band to #33 while visiting Scandinavia and playing low on the bill at festivals all over Europe. By now The Stereophonics' constant touring had earned it the sobriquet "Britain's Hardest Working Band" in music magazines and simultaneously laid the foundations for an ever-growing fan base.

The band's fourth single, "A Thousand Trees," released in August 1997, became its first top thirty hit and earned it a place on the music show *Top of the Pops.* In the same month the group released its debut album, *Word Gets Around.* The record was a collection of essays reflecting Jones's view of the world, backed by a basic, three-piece rock sound. As it reached #6 the band visited the United States for a promotional tour before embarking on a sold-out tour of Britain. In the United Kingdom, *Melody Maker* magazine named the group the best new band of 1997. In February 1998, the prestigious Brit Awards named the band best newcomers. *Word Gets Around* had by now reached sales of 100,000 copies in Britain, and The Stereophonics played sold-out shows in Australia and New Zealand. On its return to the United Kingdom it entered the studio to begin work on a second album. Meanwhile, the summer of 1998 was taken up with festivals (the band even became the first act to play Cardiff Castle, in the Welsh capital, since Freddie Mercury's rockers, Queen, in 1978 and the Rolling Stones in 1974). Toward the end of the year the group visited Japan for the first time and played a series of sold-out club venues.

In November 1998 the single "The Bartender and the Thief" was released. Taken from the band's forthcoming second album, *Performance and Cocktails,* the single was another fast-paced, three-minute rock number that gave the band its biggest hit to date. As it reached #3, it was performed in front of 75,000 people before the Rugby Union International match (between Wales and South Africa) at London's Wembley Stadium. Jones's songwriting become more universal on *Performance and Cocktails*; released in March 1999, the album entered the U.K. chart at #1. The album sold over 500,000 copies within the first three weeks of its release, and at the same time *Word Gets Around* reached 300,000 copies. Within two months the band's second album sold over a million copies. As a "thank you" to the Welsh people, the band performed in Swansea to over 50,000 fans. By the end of the year, *Performance and Cocktails* had become the fifth bestselling album of the year.

The year 2000 was taken up with touring across the world and Kelly Jones preparing new material. At the end of the year he undertook a series of solo shows to test out his new songs. The solo shows prompted rumors that The Stereophonics was on the verge of breaking up, but the band denied this and announced two shows in England. In July 2001, The Stereophonics played Donington Castle in England and the Millennium Stadium in Cardiff to promote its third album, *Just Enough Education to Perform* (2000), which entered the chart at #1. Its sound was more mellow, as Jones's previous frustrations seemed to have evaporated as the band became major stars. A series of singles from the album, including "Have a Nice Day," "Mr. Writer," and "Step on My Old Size Nines," reached the top ten in the U.K. charts. As the band continued to grow lyrically, with Jones expanding his views to encompass a wider world, the group's music was criticized for not growing at the same rate despite the introduction of a keyboard player. The criticism failed to diminish the loyalty of the band's supporters, however, and all dates of an arena tour in December 2001 sold out. In the same month the group released a cover of the Rod Stewart number "Handbags and Gladrags" that reached the top ten early in 2002. Another series of open-air concerts took place in the summer of 2002 as Kelly Jones began writing new material.

References

www.stereophonics.com

Stereophonics: Just Enough Evidence To Print by Danny O'Connel. (London: Virgin, 2002). ISBN 0753505274

Stone Roses, The (England)

In Manchester, England, in 1984 vocalist Ian Brown (b. February 20, 1963), guitarist John Squire (b. November 24, 1962), guitarist Andy Couzens, bassist Pete Garner, and drummer Si Wolstencroft formed The Stone Roses. For the next two years the band recorded demos and changed personnel (Alan "Reni" Wren [b. April 10, 1964] replaced Wolstencroft on drums in July 1984) before releasing "So Young" in 1985. Highlighted by Squire's angular guitar parts, it laid the foundation for the band's future sound. However, the single word nowhere, so in the following year the group employed Gareth Evans as its first manager; also, in July, Couzens left. By May 1987 the band had released its second single, "Sally Cinnamon"; despite a chiming guitar lead and Brown's whispered vocal delivery, the song failed to make the charts. But in its native Manchester, The Stone Roses was beginning to build a substantial following, playing sold-out shows across the city. By the end of the year Gary "Mani" Mounfield (b. November 16, 1962) had replaced Garner as bass player.

In June 1988 the band signed a record deal with Silvertone Records that kept the group with the company for eight albums. The band's first single for Silvertone, "Elephant Stone," appeared in October. The single won attention from the national media as the band's local shows were becoming major events in the city. In the following year a gig at the Haçienda Club, in their hometown, was recorded by BBC Television and shown as part of a youth TV series, *Snub TV.* In March 1989 "Made of Stone" became the band's first single to make the charts, creeping into the top hundred. By now Squire's unique guitar style, consisting of a series of overdubs that gave the music great depth, and Brown's almost spoken vocals had become the trademark of the band, a style that was to be copied by numerous groups in the following years, including The High and Flower'd Up.

The Stone Roses' eponymous debut album was released in May 1989 to universal critical acclaim and spent the next year on the chart as the single "She Bangs the Drum" reached #36. By now the band members had become regulars on the front pages of the music press, and their dress of flared jeans and over-sized, baggy T-shirts started a new fashion craze in Britain: the "baggy" look. The Stone Roses were also the catalyst for a new style of music in which the traditional line-up of guitar, bass, and drums was wedded to the burgeoning dance culture, as Wren's hypnotic drumming style was later reflected by the sampled, souped-up version offered by any number of dance tracks. Dance culture was rapidly growing in popularity in the United Kingdom, fueled by new drugs such as Ecstasy. As The Stone Roses grew in popularity, other bands from the group's hometown appeared on the scene; The Happy Mondays and Inspiral Carpets created what the press termed "Madchester," after the drug-fueled lifestyles that the bands were living.

In October 1989 the band released a single that took the British music scene in another direction. At almost ten minutes in length, "Fool's Gold" was a fusion of guitars and dance beats that the band had hinted at in its album but finally perfected in the single. As it reached #8 in the chart, the band was invited to perform on the BBC news program *The Late Show,* which was broadcast live. As Squire began playing the opening chords to "Made of Stone" and Brown began singing, there was a power failure in the studio. As the presenter attempted to talk through the problem, Brown could be seen in the background pacing around and shouting "amateurs, amateurs." Thanks to this event, the place of The Stone Roses in British pop folklore was ensured. The band became so sure of its popularity that it turned down a tour opening for The Rolling Stones and, instead, organized its own show for 30,000 fans at Spike Island in Manchester in May 1990. In the following month the band played in Glasgow, its last show for five years. In July "One Love" became the band's bestselling single, reaching #4; but the record deal the group had signed just two years earlier was beginning to be a point of contention, and The Stone Roses took Silvertone to court in an attempt to free itself from its contract.

While the band was in court it was forbidden to release new material, but Silvertone continued to release, and re-release, old material in an effort to make as much money from the band as possible. In May 1991, The Stone Roses won its case. However, the group remained quiet until February 1992, when it signed with the Geffen label. It was another two years before the band released "Love Spreads" (1994), a single dominated by Squires's bluesy rock guitar that was much "harder" in style than the group's more pop-oriented first releases. The single reached #4 in the chart. It was part of an album, *2nd Coming*, that was greeted by mediocre reviews. Early in the next year the band traveled to the United States to promote the album, which had reached #47 on the charts. But in March, Wren became bored with the band and left. Robbie Maddix, who was brought in to replace him, played a straighter more rock style of drums that worked well behind Squire's new guitar style. The group played some shows in Europe before, in August, playing their first U.K. gig in five years. It was the beginning of the end for the band, though. In 1996 John Squire left; although replaced by Aziz Ibrahim, who neatly replicated Squire's guitar lines, The Stone Roses effectively came to an end as a group. In August the band headlined at the Reading Festival and played what was commonly believed to be the worst show of an erratic live career. The band split up soon thereafter, with Brown issuing a press release on October 29 stating, "Having spent the last ten years in the filthiest business in the universe it's a pleasure to announce the end of The Stone Roses."

Ian Brown went on to have a successful solo career, releasing the albums *More Monkey Business* (1997), *Golden Greats* (1999), and *Music of the Spheres* (2001). John Squire formed the Seahorses, a group that had a period of popularity for two years releasing an album, *Do It Yourself* (1997), but then broke up. He is currently writing new material. Gary Mounfield joined the U.K. indie rock band Primal Scream and continues to gig with them as well as appearing as a club deejay. Alan Wren toured as guitarist in The Rub during March 2001 but has not played since.

References

www.thestoneroses.co.uk
Breaking Into Heaven: The Rise & Fall of the Stone Roses by Mick Middles (London: Omnibus, 1999). ISBN 0711975469

Strawpeople (New Zealand)

Sound engineer Mark Tierney and deejay Paul Casserly first met at university in the New Zealand city of Auckland in the late 1980s. They worked together at BFM, the university radio station, before writing their own material under the name Strawpeople. Focusing more on electronica than on traditional instrumentation, Tierney and Casserly released one single in 1988, "Blue," but then, in need of finances, began writing jingles for commercials. Soon thereafter they signed with the independent label Pagan Records, in 1990, and released the single "One Good Reason." The band's first album, *Hemisphere*, was released in the following year. The record set the blueprint for Strawpeople material: music with a glossy, modern pop feel underpinned by sad, introspective lyrics. Vocalist Fiona McDonald, whom the duo had met while recording commercial jingles, also appeared on the album. The band was determined not to follow the expected route and become a live act, so it remained in the studio instead of touring to promote the record; nevertheless, the album sold reasonably well. Although McDonald was widely regarded as the band's third member, Strawpeople released *Worldservice* in 1992 using a number of guest vocalists to create different moods within the record.

Through the Strawpeople recordings, however, McDonald's reputation was beginning to grow. To satiate her desire to play live, something that she could not do with Strawpeople, she joined the New Zealand bands Headless Chickens and NRA. The exposure afforded her by playing with three bands, and the experience gained by singing different styles of music, was rewarded when she was named best female vocalist at the New Zealand Music Awards (NZMA) in 1991, 1993, and 1995. While McDonald toured across the country, Tierney and Casserly were in the studio recording more of the same for their next album, *Broadcast*, released in May 1994. The album turned platinum and introduced the band to a wider audience. In the following year, though, Tierney left the band to concentrate on his engineering and Casserly began to look for another collaborator. It wasn't long before he turned to McDonald. The following album, *Vicarious* (1996), became the first Strawpeople album to feature only one singer, as McDonald became the sole voice of the band. It was an attempt to put a "face" to the group rather than the succession of vocalists that some fans found a little confusing. *Vicarious* earned the band its second platinum album as Casserly's music and McDonald's voice blended to create melancholy pop, and it was named album of the year at the NZMA. The single "Taller Than God" won a nomination for best single at the same ceremony as the demand for the band to play live grew. Early in 1997 the group performed its debut concert in Australia, sharing the bill with **Bic Runga**. In July the band released *100 Street Transistors*, an album of re-mixes of its earlier songs on which the band invited different artists to feature.

As the Strawpeople project took some time off, Casserly formed his own production company writing music for TV commercials and films. McDonald meanwhile began to record material for a solo album. In March 1999, she released her first single, "Sin Again," which reached #7 in the charts; in September her album *A Different Hunger* reached the top ten. As McDonald concentrated on her solo career, Casserly was recording *No New Messages* with long-term collaborator Joost Langveld. Released in April 2000, the album featured a variety of vocalists, all women. It was also a collaboration with different musicians giving their own input into the project, including Chris Van De Geer, guitar player with **Stellar***. The collaboration made for a rather eclectic album solidly based around Casserly's samples and beats. A single released from the album—a version of the U.S. band The Cars' 1980s classic "Drive," sung by Bic Runga—reached the top of the charts. In October *The Best of 1990–2000* was released and was named as best compilation album at the 2001 NZMA. A compilation album of artists from the Pagan label, *Pagan Gold* (2001), featured the Strawpeople song "One Good Reason." Casserly continues to work with numerous musicians on Strawpeople material, as well as on music for commercials and film soundtracks. McDonald continues to work on a solo career as well as with Strawpeople.

References

www.strawpeople.co.nz

Sugarcubes, The (Iceland)

In 1983 in Reykjavik, Iceland, singer Einer Orn (b. October 29, 1962) formed the group Kukl with fellow vocalist Björk Gudmundsdottir (b. November 21, 1965) and drummer Siggi Baldursson (b. October 2, 1962). The anarco-punks who regarded themselves as iconoclasts played only a few shows before they were joined by Thor Jonsson (b. June 2, 1962) on guitar and Margaret Orloffdottir (b. October 2, 1962) on keyboards. The now unnamed group joined other artists to form a production company called Bad Taste. The members of Bad Taste had all played in punk bands in Iceland that broke up as the movement ran its course. The first work from the newly formed company was a satirical postcard commemorating the meeting of Presidents Gorbachev and Reagan in 1986. The unexpected bestseller earned the company enough money to produce a record by the band that had formed within Bad Taste, The Sugarcubes, to produce a single, "Ammaeli." Released only in the band's home country, it won attention from the small group of critics and fans that listened to "alternative" music. While the single was being released, band member Einer Orn was in London studying and organizing for further Sugarcubes records to be released in England through a record company, One Little Indian, owned by a friend of his. The single, "Birthday" (1987), rose quickly in the charts. Most of its critical acclaim was directed at the unusual vocal delivery of Björk, which integrated her heavily accented English lyric with what can only be described as howls and yelps. The Sugarcubes immediately made the rounds of TV and press interviews, all of which focused on the uniqueness of a pop band from Iceland and a quote by the singer that the band ate puffins, a seabird native to the Icelandic coast and not usually seen as a foodstuff. At the end of 1987 The Sugarcubes played a sold-out tour of the British Isles. The first album, *Life's Too Good* (1988), featured the dark mood of Kukl. It sold over a million copies in Britain alone, making the band the most successful Icelandic group ever.

However, all the attention was having a detrimental effect on the band, which had only begun as a way of having fun. The group's next single, "Hit," was as

The Sugarcubes (Björk)
Pictorialpress Ltd., London, UK

successful as their debut had been, as Björk's vocal delivery became clearer and Orn joined in with a rap. Much lighter in content than anything on the group's debut album, the single featured a catchy keyboard riff and erratic, scatter-gun drumming. The following album, *Here Today, Tomorrow, Next Week* (1990), although featuring more light content, was only a moderate success. After a world tour to promote the album, the band made itself into a jazz ensemble as a way of relaxing from the pressures of the pop industry as well as making music with other musicians on the Icelandic scene.

Although the band had almost split up by 1990, it was contractually obliged to release another album, so the group traveled to Bearsville Studios in Woodstock, New York, to record *Stick Around for Joy* in early 1991. The band did a small tour to promote the record, but the group's collective lack of enthusiasm was evident in the album, whose title was wreathed in sarcasm. Nevertheless the group was still together in the summer of the following year when U2 invited the band to support it on the U.S. leg of its "Achtung Baby" tour. The Sugarcubes accepted, using the shows as a way of saying farewell to the fans. In November 1992 the band played its last gig at the Limelight Club in New York, where, as the group left the stage, they spoke their last words as a band: "Thank you, we were The Sugarcubes."

Although the members of the group all moved on to other projects, they have made little impact on the pop world—except for vocalist Björk, who has become a major international star, releasing many successful albums and recently moving into motion pictures. Her latest solo release, *Vespertine* (2001), led to her becoming one of the first pop musicians to play at London's National Opera House in the fall of 2001. Although little has been heard of the other members of The Sugarcubes, in 2002 Björk released *Björk's Greatest Hits,* with tracks selected by fans over the Internet and, on the same day, the retrospective *Family Tree,* a collection of Björk's own favorite songs from the previous twenty years.

References

www.geocities.com/taosterman/sugar

The Rough Guide to Rock edited by Jonathan Buckley and Mark Ellingham (London: Roush Guides, 1996). ISBN 1858282012

T

Tamio, Okuda (Japan)

Born in Hiroshima, Japan, on May 12, 1965, Okuda Tamio began singing and playing guitar in rock bands during junior high school. Initially a student of computers, in 1985 he became a full-time musician after forming the band **Unicorn**. The group had great success in the late 1980s and early 1990s with its take on 1960s pop music driven by Tamio's sense of fun and wild stage antics.

Although Unicorn continued until 1993, Tamio had already released a single under his own name before beginning a full-time solo career. After the high profile of Unicorn, he spent most of the next two years away from the public eye, concentrating on a new passion for fishing. However, in 1995 he released his first solo album, *29*. The title reflected his age. Although the album featured the guitar/bass/drum arrangement that was the trademark of Unicorn, it showed Tamio in a more reflective mood than when he was part of the previous group. A second album, *30*, released later that year, was taken by critics to be the "other half" of the story that began with *29*: the story of a man reaching a new phase in both his life and career, although still possessing Tamio's trademark humor. Despite the album sleeve showing the artist posing in the classic "John Travolta in *Saturday Night Fever*" dance-floor pose, complete with white suit and finger jabbing skyward, the record was in no way disco; instead, it showed the influences of English beat groups such as The Beatles.

While working on *30*, Tamio discovered two young girls working for his music agency. Ami Ohnuki and Yumi Yoshimura were given the name **Puffy** and soon went on to be a hugely successful pop band in their own right. Although Tamio spent a lot of his time with Puffy, becoming the duo's producer, writer, and backing musician, he also found time to release his own records. In 1997 he released an album called *Shopping* with fellow Japanese star Inoue Yoshui. The single "Shopping" won a huge audience as Yoshui's more modern take on pop complemented Tamio's 1960s style. A mini-album of guitar-based songs, *Failbox*, released later in the same year, found Tamio in his usual playful mood and still using the 1960s as his blueprint. Although he now seemed to put more energy into Puffy than into his own career, his album *Matatabi* (1998) was seen by critics as his finest to date. Described as "a soundtrack to the great American road movie" by critics, the album featured an eclectic mix of pop, rock, country and western, and skiffle. Although many of Tamio's records reflected a Western influence, he was still displaying a unique "Japaneseness," not in instrumentation but in arrangement and execution, that helped to keep him at the top of the J-pop scene when other bands in the genre were duplicating European and American styles. His vocal delivery incorporated the traditional Japanese vibrato. In 2000 he released *Goldblend* and, once again, was credited with helping the Japanese music scene out of what was seen as "a creative slump," as his willingness to explore different genres set him apart from his contemporaries. In January 2001, Tamio released an album that was partly new material and partly re-workings of his older songs: *Car Songs of the Years* was made up of tracks that had a "driving" theme and style as the guitars and keyboards pushed the music along. Once again the critics made reference to American road movies, but Tamio's very Japanese style of singing gave the album a purely Japanese character. In fact, the popularity of the record was testimony to his style. Tamio continued to concentrate on promoting Puffy and fishing but still found time to release two new singles. In July "The Standard" reached the Japanese top ten, and in October, "Custom" also fared well. Both records featured bright, mid-tempo guitar based songs that again reflected Okuda's 1960s influences.

References

www.junkmagnet.com/music/jpop/tamiookuda

Thee Michelle Gun Elephant (Japan)

Vocalist Yusuke Chiba (b. July 10, 1968) and guitarist Futoshi Abe (b. December 16, 1966) met while studying at the Meiji Garden University in Tokyo, Japan. In 1988 they formed Thee Michelle Gun Elephant (named from mishearing the title of a song by U.K. punk band The Damned, "Machine Gun Etiquette") and played with various musicians. In 1991 they settled on a line-up that included two more students from the university, bass player Koji Veno (b. March 27, 1968) and drummer Kazuyuki Kuhara (b. April 3, 1969).

Although the group's brand of British punk rock found a small audience in the clubs of Tokyo, it was another four years before the band released its first recorded material. The band traveled to London, punk's spiritual home, to record *Wonder Style* in 1995. The album was essentially a recorded version of the band's live set, complete with incendiary guitar riffs and Chiba's scorching vocals. In the following month the album was released in Japan but sold only to the band's small fan base. It was enough to get the group noticed by the Japanese arm of Columbia Records, however, and in February of the following year the group released its first single, "World's End." An album, *Cult Grass Stars*, followed in March. Although a more polished effort, it lost none of the band's fire; a tour the group undertook to promote the record sold well as the band played to enthusiastic and growing audiences. Another single, "Candy House," released in August 1996, continued to establish the band as it recorded its next new material, *High Time* (1997). A single from the album, "Lily," gave the group its first chart placing in Japan as it entered at #5. The album itself reached #13 after gaining favorable reviews from the local music press. There followed a sold-out tour as many young Japanese, tiring of the mundane music on the pop charts, saw something in the band that reflected their sense of alienation. On the tour the band visited twenty cities between December 1996 and February 1997. Another top thirty single, "Culture," was released in May.

Having been in London in April to record its fourth single, "Get Up Lucy," the band played some dates in the United Kingdom and around Europe before, in August, releasing the single in Japan, where it reached #24. During the summer of 1997 the group began recording new material. By now the constant touring the band had undertaken over the previous six years had honed their act, and the short, aggressive songs easily transferred onto disc. The group's willingness to appear live and the exposure this afforded it appeared to pay off, as the album *Chicken Zombies* (1997), entered the chart at #5 and a fifty-two-date tour was sold out. During the summer of 1998 the band played its first major festival, the Fuji Rock Festival, in Tokyo, sharing the stage with The Prodigy, Garbage, **The Stereophonics**, and Beck, among others. A year after *Chicken Zombies* hit the charts, the band released *Gear Blues*, an album that became their biggest seller to date. Unwilling to change its style to suit fashion, the band waited for fashion to catch up with it as guitar groups became "flavor of the month." As the record entered the top ten it sold over half a million copies and led to another sold-out tour as the band began playing to audiences of over 5,000 fans per show.

After another summer performing at Japanese festivals, in 1999 the band visited the United States for the first time. The group played a series of shows in small clubs, including CBGB's in New York, to promote its first U.S. release, the single "West Cabaret Drive," in September but it failed to make any impression on the charts. The band's next album, *Casanova Snake* (2000), offered much the same as the group's previous efforts but showed growing confidence. During the year the band's growing reputation abroad led to *Gear Blues* being released in Europe, where a small tour followed. In October it became the group's debut U.S. album release. The band returned home to play another series of shows across Japan before, in June, being on the bill of the Fuji Rock Festival. This time, reflecting the national popularity of the band, it was invited to be the headliner act. In September "Baby Stardust" was released, which preceded a "best of" album. With Thee Michelle Gun Elephant showing no sign of being bored by touring, the group began another visit to the United States in November, where it had released another album, *Collection*, earlier in the year. After returning to Japan the band released a live album, *Casanova Said "Live or Die"* (2000). The album, a recording of a show in Tokyo, captured the energy of the live experience and entered the charts in December 2000. A new single, "Abakareta Sekai," was released in March 2001 as the band continued its prolific output and prepared material for a new album before setting out across the country to play all the major Japanese festivals.

In November the group followed the lead of pop bands across the world and produced a set of bendy toy figures. The Michelle Gun Elephant dolls differed from other figures, however, because their faces were replaced by skulls, which nicely sums up the view that the band members have of themselves.

References

www.tmge.co.jp

Tiro De Gracia (Chile)

Tiro De Gracia was formed in Santiago, Chile, during 1993 by vocalist Juan Sativo and MC Hard Langua. Over the following years the band joined many other musicians on stage, building a reputation within the hip-hop underground of the Chilean capital as one of the more lyrical and thought-provoking groups, as it sang about the political and cultural climate in Chile. Before the group released any material it became a quintet with the arrival of deejay Camilo Cintolesi, keyboard player Patricio Loaiza, and MC Zaturno. In 1994 and 1995 the group released two independently financed singles, "Arma Calibrada" and "Homosapiens," which were available only at the band's live shows.

The group got its break in 1996 when producer Cubo Negro and director Juan Sebastián decided to record a TV program about hip-hop culture and invited Tiro De Gracia to perform. Confident that the nationwide exposure would help the group's career, the band recorded more self-financed songs (record companies remained uninterested despite the hip-hop genre's influence in American music). Only when the recordings were played on local radio stations Rock & Pop and Zero did the band come to the attention of EMI. In November 1996 the group signed with the label, and in May 1997 it went into the studio to begin recording its first major-label record. *Ser Hümano* (1997) immediately became a gold album in Chile as well as being released in Mexico, Venezuela, Colombia, Argentina, and Spain, as hip-hop began to move from the underground to the mainstream in South America.

Although the band had begun to establish itself in Chilean music, it courted controversy. The release of two more singles also brought the group into the spotlight in Chile. "El Perro Pinochet" (1998) criticized the former Chilean leader, General Pinochet; and "Viaje Sin Rumbo" (1999), reported in the press to be pro-drugs, was subject to press censorship (although the band denied the link). These controversies gave the band a growing reputation as a voice for Chilean youth. Late in 1999 the band traveled to Madrid, Spain, to appear at a concert to celebrate the fiftieth anniversary of Amnesty International. In August 2000 the group played an anti-drug charity show for the National Institute of

Youth in Chile. Shortly thereafter the band released its second album, *Decisiones*, which continued to display the group's hip-hop credentials.

Before the album was released, however, Cintolesi left the band to explore new musical avenues. As the singles "El juego verdadero" and "Joven De La Pobla" reached the top ten of Chile's national chart, Tiro De Gracia continued as a four-piece and toured South and Central America, as well as Spain, to promote the album. The group also played some shows among Spanish-speaking communities in the United States. Toward the end of 2001, another album was released: *Retorno De Misericordia* provided proof that the band would be a continuing force in South American music as its aggressive rap questions the status quo. The band is widely recognized as the biggest, and most important, native hip-hop band in Chile.

References
www.tirodegracia.8k.net

Trevi, Gloria (Mexico)

Born in 1970 into a comfortable middle-class home, Gloria de los Angeles Trevino Ruiz grew up in the industrial town of Monterey, Mexico. As a child she received singing, dancing, and piano lessons and later decided to use her talents to make a career in show business. Leaving her hometown at the age of fourteen, Trevi relocated to Mexico City in a bid for stardom but was initially forced to sell chewing gum on the streets to survive. While in Mexico City she continued to study singing and dancing and became a member of an all-girl pop band, Boquitas Pintadas, for a short time in 1985. Four years later Trevi finally got a taste of the stardom she had been yearning for.

After teaming up with producer Sergio Andrade in 1989, Trevi released a single, "Dr. Psiquiatra," that rose to the top of the charts within a week and stayed there for eleven weeks with its Madonna-like pop feel. Her debut album, *Que Hago Aqui* (1990), which featured electronic, unchallenging, danceable pop music, established Trevi as Mexico's number one woman star. But she wrote her own material, which was unusual for a woman pop singer in Mexico, and the controversial topics she introduced in her lyrics brought censure from the authorities. Teenage sex, abortion, and prostitution were not welcome topics in largely Catholic Mexico; Trevi's stage antics were of equal concern. Inviting male members of the audience on stage, she would remove their trousers while dancing around them and finish the show by throwing condoms into the crowd. One song, "Chica Embarazada," was banned by many radio stations because of its overt references to sex and abortion.

Although the government and media condemned Trevi's work, fans flocked to her concerts in the thousands, leading the Mexican writer Carlos Monsivais to dub her "Spokeswoman of Her Generation." Trevi's second album, *Tu Angel De La Gaurda*, was released within months of her debut album, leaving little time for any musical growth. But it brought her to the attention of the Hispanic community in the United States, and a single taken from the record, "Pelo Suelto," became a hit there. In the following year Trevi starred in a feature film, also called *Pelo Suelto*, that broke all box office records in Mexico and became the biggest-grossing film in Mexican film history. The success of the film drew invitations to perform in other countries, where Trevi played to crowds of up to 30,000 people across Latin America (including a concert to 38,000 people in Chile).

In 1992 Trevi released her first calendar, a glossy series of semi-nude portraits. In this Trevi again provoked outrage; nonetheless, the calendar sold over 300,000 copies across the country. In September of the same year she released a third album, *Me Siento Tan Sola*; although stronger in production values, the record was based around the same musical motifs as her previous work and sold almost 800,000 copies. Following the pattern of the previous album, a single, "Zapatos Viejos," reached #1 and became the title of Trevi's second film (which over 30 million people viewed). Another slightly more risqué calendar appeared in the following year and sold 100,000 copies within the first week, eventually selling over 500,000 copies in the United States alone. More polished pop albums and more success followed, until in 1995 Trevi became an apparent victim of a power struggle between Mexico's established TV company, Televisa, and the new TV Azteca. As she was held to old contracts by Televisa but had offers of new contracts from TV Azteca, Trevi "retired" in 1996 as the confusion lead to insinuations that her career was in decline.

Although Trevi's career still appeared to be flourishing, in 1998 an allegation arose that she and her manager, Andrade, were involved in indecent behavior with minors. Although little was made of the case at the time, in June 1999 more allegations came to light, and Trevi and Andrade were sought by the police in connection with the alleged kidnapping and sexual abuse of some teenage girls. Trevi and Andrade were eventually arrested in Brazil in January 2000 and remained in jail for a year while the Mexican government began extradition arrangements.

In October 2001 it was revealed that Trevi had become pregnant while in jail, though she has refused to name the father. The child, a boy named Angel Gabriel, was born in February 2002, while Trevi remains in a Brazilian jail.

References

www.trevi.com

Trompies (South Africa)

Zynne "Mahoota" Sibika, Mandla "Spikiri" Mofokeng, Eugene "Donald Duck" Mthethwa, and Jairus "Kakarumba" Nkwe were school friends in the 1970s in the Meadowlands township of Soweto in South Africa. Determined to make a career in music, the friends went their separate ways in the early 1980s. Mofokeng and Nkwe joined the backing band of established musician Sello

Twala as dancers, and later Mofokeng also played piano for him. Four years later Mofokeng formed his own band, MM Deluxe. Sibika and Mthethwa entered dance competitions together until Mthethwa joined the group Casino. Following their initial experiences they all joined music schools. Sibika and Nkwe studied classical music and jazz, first at Trinity College in London, England, and then at the Wits and Pelmama Academy of Music in Dobsonville, Soweto. Mofokeng and Mthethwa also studied in Soweto. Eventually they all came together at Soweto's Funda Centre. Now armed with technical expertise after years of working in various studios and with various musicians, the group began working in the Phil Hollis studios and started writing and producing as a team. As it worked on what became its debut album, the group needed a name and took it from an Afrikaans cartoon series, "Trompies." (Afrikaans is the language of white South Africans.) The name Trompies, associated with white culture, caused a slight controversy when it was adopted by this group of black musicians, but nevertheless in 1993 they began to perform around the townships of South Africa, building a fan base.

The group's debut single, "Sigiyangengoma" (1994) took the local charts by storm and began the rise of "kwaito" as a musical force. (Kwaito is best described as rap and hip-hop over heavy bass beats and lyrically poses political and social questions.) When the band's debut album, *Sigiya Ngengoma*, was released in 1995, it sold over 80,000 copies. The album brought Trompies into the public eye and made their style of dress, known as "mapantsula," acceptable in South Africa. Before Trompies, the mapantsula style of "sportys" (hats) and "takkies" (training shoes) identified the wearer as a thug. It took the band's success to bring respectability and acceptability to mapantsula.

In 1996 the band formed one of the most successful black-owned record companies, Kalawa-Jazmee, with producer Don Laka and deejay Oscar Mdlongwa to promote its own music and that of other artists. The new label's first release was The Trompies' second album, *Mahoota* (1996). The album followed the success of their debut as the heavy drum beats brought to mind the traditional music of the country. It sold in excess of 80,000 copies. In 1997 the group released a single from the album, "Magasman," which sold double platinum. The band was now being invited to play at festivals all over the country as it became the spearhead of the kwaito movement. *Shoshloza* (1998) continued the band's success, selling close to 100,000 copies, after which the single "Tholakele" (1999) earned the band another gold disc. In October of the same year the band's prolific writing resulted in another album, *Two Cents Ninety Nine*, another slice of bass-heavy kwaito.

After a quiet 2000 with little in the way of live shows, the band reappeared in 2001 with the album *Mapantsula*. The record, a more mature effort, reflected the group's experiences of the past three years as it rose to the top of the country's musical chart. *Mapantsula* became the band's most successful recording, winning three trophies at the Metro FM awards for best album, best song (for "Fohlosa"), and best group. Earlier in the year the band visited London, England, as part of the "Kwaito Storm" tour with fellow artists Bongomaffin, M'du

Masilela, and Mashamplani; on this tour the group performed in small clubs and gave Europe its first taste of kwaito. Although the band still performs across South Africa, it is using its own studio and label to record new artists to ensure that kwaito continues to be a musical force in South Africa.

References

www.musdic.org.za/artists/trompies

U

Unicorn (Japan)

In Japan during the 1980s Nishikowa Koichi, Yoshiharu Abe, **Okuda Tamio** (b. May 12, 1965), Horiuchi Kazushi, and Isamu Teshima blended basic rock with a Japanese sensibility to become one of the biggest bands in the country. Building a fan base by undertaking hundreds of small club concerts, the band, which had formed in 1985, moved to Tokyo two years later after deciding the capital was the best place to expand its career.

Unicorn released its debut album, *Boom*, in 1987. Although the album caught the attention of the public with its melodic, guitar-based music and sold reasonably well, it was the following year's release, *Panic Attack*, that gained the band a place in the hierarchy of the Japanese pop scene. Eschewing the rock formula in favor of an eclectic mix of rockabilly, ska, new wave, and reggae, the album showcased the band's blend of surreal humor, epitomized by bizarre stage outfits consisting of bold colors and strange, clashing styles. *Hattori* (1989) next marked a turning point in the group's career. Although experimenting with musical genres, the album was more focused and sold twice as many copies as the group's previous releases, helping make the band a household name in Japan. With the band's music becoming ever more experimental, they dropped their outrageous stage clothes and began to dress in a more subdued manner, preferring to concentrate on the music rather than the antics. Still displaying musical eclecticism, the band's 1990 album, *Kedamono No Arashi*, became its most successful, both commercially and artistically, as it reached #1 on the Japanese chart and was named album of the year in magazine polls. The album saw Unicorn exploring its more Western musical leanings as vocalist Tamio's love of 1960s British pop came to the fore. Ironically, at the same time the group also began to take on a distinctive Japanese ethnicity, personified by the introduction by Tamio of a traditional Japanese vocal vibrato, a style he continued to explore later within his own work.

With the release of a fifth album, *Hige To Boin*, in 1991, critics and fans alike began to detect a lack of enthusiasm in the band's music. Although the album sold well due to Unicorn's huge fan base, there was a sense that the band was losing the energy that had become their trademark. As the individual members began to perform with other artists, Unicorn was temporarily put on hold. It was 1993 before another album, *Springman*, was released. The record showed no sense of the experimentation that had been a hallmark of the group's earlier release. In September, before any concerts could be organized to promote the recording, the band members decided that their own projects were more important than Unicorn, and the band amicably split up. Before the end of the year a compilation album, *The Very Best of Unicorn* (1993), topped the chart on a wave of nostalgia.

Since the split, the various members have experienced different levels of success. Abe joined the band Sparks A Go Go for a short period in 1997 before returning to solo material. Kazushi released a string of solo albums, and Koichi joined the rock band Vanilla, with which he still performs. The most successful member of Unicorn, Tamio, has become one of Japan's biggest stars as well as an influential producer. He is currently working with the duo **Puffy**.

References

www.limitedsector.com/unicorn

V

Väth, Sven (Germany)

Sven Väth was born in Offenbach, Germany, on October 26, 1964. From an early age he played disco and soul as a deejay at his father's pub, The Queens, in the city of Frankfurt. After finishing his schooling Väth began an apprenticeship in the construction industry, but music was his keen interest. In 1982, while playing at The Queens, Väth was invited to deejay at two of Frankfurt's hippest clubs, The Vogue and Dorian Gray. Building a reputation as one of Germany's best deejays after moving away from disco and experimenting with the embryonic dance scene, Väth joined the band 16 Bit, which released the single "Where Are You?" in 1986. (16 Bit also featured Luca Anzilotti and Michael Münzing, who later formed Snap and had a worldwide hit with "The Power.") 16 Bit soon became the band Off and released *Electric Salsa*, which reached the top of the charts across mainland Europe as Väth's music continued to become more hard edged, with synthetic drum beats pushing the rhythm ever faster. Two more albums followed, *Step by Step* (1987) and *Bad News* (1988), as Väth moved away from the pop-oriented sound and became an influential deejay playing Electronic Body Music (EBM) (which had been recently "invented" by the Belgian band **Front 242**). EBM was an uncompromising, techno-dominated music. To promote his own version, Väth opened a club called Omen that soon became Frankfurt's most celebrated night spot (it closed in 1998).

By 1989 Väth tired of the Off project and formed Mosaic with Mathias Hoffman and Steffen Britzke. Over the next twelve months Mosaic released a string of club hits and re-mixes, including "Is It Serious" and "Dancing with Angels," that encompassed both EBM and the new acid house and trance sound that was taking the United Kingdom by storm and was slowly being introduced to Europe. Väth was seen as a pioneer of these new musical sounds and earned a reputation as Germany's top deejay. In an attempt to have more creative input into his music, Väth formed a record label in 1991: Eye-Q was a partnership with his manager, Heinz Roth, and Mathias Hoffman, who had been in the Off project. The label was divided into Harthouse, playing a techno style, and Recycle or Die, for a more ambient style. Subsequently Väth released numerous records under a string of pseudonyms, including Odysee of Noise, Barbarella, and Metal Master; most of these releases featured hard repetitive beats. At the end of 1992 Väth met Ralf Hildenbeutel, and the pair became inseparable as a musical force. Before the year was over Väth released the first album under his own name after six years in the recording industry: *Accident in Paradise*, a hard-edged dance album, earned him deejay spots in clubs around the world. The record was crucial in helping to distinguish the trance sound from the harder-edged techno. The first single from the album, "L'esperanza," became a mainstream chart hit in Europe and lead to Väth's second album, *The Harlequin, the Robot and the Ballet Dancer* (1993). This release confirmed his reputation as one of the world's leading EBM/techno/trance deejays. The new success gave Väth the space to experiment with new music; through his own label, he then released an album under the name Astral Pilot with Stevie B-Zet. The album, *Electro Acupuncture* (1994), showed Väth searching for an improbably harder edge to his music.

By 1995, however, Väth's numerous side projects had left him short of money. As a result he changed direction and softened his sound for the soundtrack to a movie, *Der Kalte Finger*, which became a hit in Germany. In 1996 he was involved in a project for the Earth Love Fund, an ecological group, and released "Rainforest Is Calling," which reflected his more ambient leanings. Continuing his deejay career, in 1997 financial difficulties finally forced Väth to separate from his partners in Eye-Q, but only after the label moved to Berlin and a petition for bankruptcy was filed. Undeterred, Väth returned to Frankfurt and opened Germany's first booking agency, Cocoon, which became the most important in the country, providing deejays and artists to clubs across Germany.

In 1998, Väth signed with Virgin and released his third solo album, *Fusion*. As the title suggests, the record is an eclectic mix of dance genres. It set Väth on a new creative impulse that resulted in three new albums in 1999 and 2000; *Six in the Mix, Contact*, and *Cocoon Club Ibiza*. At Christmas 2000, Väth released a 12″ single, "Barbarella Remix," and an album, *Retrospective 1990–97*, that highlighted his best work of the period. In the following year he appeared on two compilation albums, *Nu-Progressive Era* and *A Cocoon Compilation*, both of which were available in the United States. By the end of the year a new album, *In The Mix: Cocoon Club Ibiza*, was released. The album was taken from Väth's appearances at clubs on the island. In September 2001, the U.K. dance magazine *Ministry* gave away a CD, *Cocoon 2001*, on its front cover. The release was another album that focused on the music made by artists involved with Väth's Cocoon organization, and it was mixed by Väth himself. In December he released a version of Serge Gainsbourg and Jane Birkin's classic 1960s hit, "Je t'aime," replacing the laid-back, jazz-style backing track with a solid, melodic beat while retaining the whispered vocals of the original. As Cocoon continues to be Germany's leading agency, Väth continues to be the country's most influential deejay, a position he has held for over a decade.

References

www.sven-vaeth.de
DJ Culture 1995 by Ulf Poschardt (Hamburg: Quartet Books). ISBN 0704380986

Velasquez, Regine (Philippines)

Regina Encarnacion Velasquez was born on April 22, 1970, in the Philippine capital, Manila. Influenced by her mother, who sang in a choir, and encouraged by her father, Velasquez entered her first singing competition at age six. During the following years she entered over 200 competitions all over the country, winning over sixty of them. Prizes varied from bags of cash to bags of rice, but it wasn't until she entered a competition screened on TV that her big break came.

Appearing under the nickname Chona, she won the 1984 Ang Bagon Kampeon with a version of U.S. artist George Benson's "In Your Eyes." The prize was a recording contract with the Octo Arts International label. Still singing under the name Chona, she released a single, "Love Me Again," but the bland ballad failed to win her any notice. Undaunted, she was invited to appear on the popular TV show "Penthouse Live" by her friend and fellow singer **Pops Fernandez**. The program's co-host, singer **Martin Nievera**, decided that the name Chona sounded "too provincial" and altered her real Christian name to Regine. After her performance on "Penthouse Live," the show's producer, Ronnie Henares, offered to manage her and she accepted. Henares immediately sent Velasquez to a series of voice coaches and performance workshops to develop her vocal power and projection. After assembling a number of "easy on the ear" pop tunes, the resulting album *Regine*, released in 1986, after Velasquez turned professional, sold over 20,000 copies to become gold.

In the following year Velasquez performed her debut professional show at the Manila Midtown Hotel. Over the next seven years she released a string of albums, all featuring a mix of saccharine, piano-based ballads and dance numbers. The albums, released in the Philippines, included *Regine Special Edition* (1990) and *Nineteen 90* (1990) (both double platinum) and *Reason Enough* (1993) (platinum). During the same period her stunning looks led to film producers signing her to a series of motion pictures (*Pik Pak Boom* (1988) and *Elvis and James 2* (1990) among them in which she played the love interest of the male hero); in musicals, TV dramas and sitcoms, and commercials. She also performed at sold-out concerts, including the Asia-Pacific song festival, where she won grand prize in 1989. After her success the press began calling her "Asia's Songbird."

Although she was now a major star in the Philippines, it wasn't until 1993, when Velasquez moved to the Polygram label, that her music began to get a wider audience across Asia. Her first song for the label was a duet, the balled "It's Hard to Say Goodbye," with U.S. star Paul Anka. The subsequent album,

Listen without Prejudice (1994) featured more middle-of-the-road ballads and sold over 250,000 across Asia, including turning platinum (after just seven days) in Taiwan. To capitalize on her popularity in Taiwan she recorded a duet with one of the "Four Singing Kings," **Jacky Cheung**. A second Asian album, *My Love Emotion*, was released in 1995. Although she was nominated for best new act and best performance categories, she failed to win either.

Velasquez filled her schedule with live shows. These included many performances in the United States, playing to audiences during November 1994 at the Universal Amphitheater in Los Angeles, the Cow Palace Auditorium in San Francisco, and the Beacon Theater in New York. In April 1996 she celebrated her tenth year in music by playing at the Sunken Garden in Manila. In October of the same year her third Asian album was released: *Retro*, an unimaginative collection of her previous material re-recorded, reached the top of the Asian charts. Thereafter Velasquez released more records, still showing little variation musically on the formula that had won her such success, and continued her touring. Reality then seeped into the movies, as she appeared in *Kailangan Ko'y Ikaw* playing a pop star exhausted with life as a pop star. By August 2000 another formulaic album, *R2K*, became another chart topper, selling over 500,000 copies around the world, helped by her tours of Europe and North America. A live album of popular songs, *Songbird Sings the Classics* (2000), was recorded during a show at the Western Philippine Plaza. Then, in December, she appeared on MTV's "Fabulous Divas" show.

In February 2001, Velasquez was ranked #4 in the men's style magazine *FHM Philippines* in the "Asia's Hottest Babes" category as she appeared in another movie, *Pangako, Tayong Dalawa* as a girl who falls in love with a man in a coma in hospital. The romantic comedy was a huge hit. In September, she again played shows in the United States under the banner "Flying High," where Velasquez soared above a delighted audience on invisible wires as she presented nearly two decades of hits.

In June 2002 she performed in Los Angeles and San Francisco with a show titled "Regine at the Movies." The concerts featured Velasquez singing tunes from blockbuster movies. During a question and answer session at a show in the Philippines, when a member of the audience asked if she was about to retire, as had been rumoured, she said she would in order to bring up a family but, as she has yet to marry, her career seems set to continue.

References

www.reginevelasquez.net

Vissi, Anna (Cyprus)

Born in Cyprus on December 20, 1957, Anna Vissi began her education at the Cyprus Conservatory when she was six years old. At age twelve she won first prize in a singing competition, which led to her mother relocating the entire family to Greece, convinced that it would give her daughter a better chance

in the music business. In 1977, Vissi won first prize at the Festival of Thessalonika with the song "As Kanoune Apopse Mia Archi."

Her first real taste of success was when she achieved fifth place for Cyprus in
the popular Eurovision Song Contest in 1980 with "Monai Agapi." It wasn't
until 1984, however, that she released her first recordings and became an instant
celebrity. *Nahes Kardia* set the standard for Vissi's music as its dramatic, theatrical songs lent a distinctly Eastern flavor to the rhythms and instrumentation.
Two more albums, *Kati Simvainei* (1985) and *I Epomeni Kinisi* (1986), made
Vissi a national star in both Cyprus and Greece as her powerful voice gave a
depth and quality to her ballads and dance numbers. As more albums were released, including *Tora* (1988), *Fotia* (1989) and *Lambo* (1992), Vissi began to
take on a more western backing rhythm. Although the loose percussive sound
of her traditional music was still evident, a more solid 4/4 drum beat was slowly
being introduced that gave her a music a firmer foundation and more modern
feel. The new basis to her music was evident on the 1993 live album, Live.
Alongside traditional instruments such as the bazouki (a small eight-stringed
triangular guitar) and extensive percussion, there was also a drum kit and bass.

As Vissi spent more time in Greece, there were accusations that she was losing touch with her home country, and in reply she released *O! Kypros* (1994).
The album was a collection of sentimental songs aimed at the Cypriot people
and re-affirmed her affection for the country. Her next album, *nClima
Tropikon,* continued Vissi's cocktail of solid backbeats with a "busy" percussion rhythm pushing the songs along. The album sold over 100,000 copies
within weeks of its release. To promote the album she embarked on a 40-date
tour that included a series of concerts in Athens, where a new theater had to be
built specifically for the shows to cope with the demand for tickets from fans.

In 1997 Vissi released *Travna.* The album included her first song in English,
released as a single in America in an attempt to expand her fan-base. Although
the album sold triple platinum in Greece and Cyprus, she could still only attract
mainly ex-patriot fans in the U.S. After one show, however, the L.A. Times published an article under the headline, "Greece Is The Word," and went on to de-
scribe her as a "combination of Madonna and Celine Dion" as well as "svelte
and elegant."

After returning home to record her next album, *Antidoton* (1998), she in-
tended to make a series of personal appearances in music shops across Greece.
But 5,000 fans gathered for the first date in Pireus and, after she was unable to
reach a store in Thessalonika due to the number of people who appeared, the
tour was cancelled.

Instead Vissi performed in concert halls across Greece and Cyprus. By the
end of the year she had won seven categories of the PopCorn Music Awards:
best female singer, best interpretation of a song, best live show, best album and
best album cover (both for *Antidoton*), and best song and most played song
(both for the single "Travna" that dominated the local charts after its release).

In February 1999 she appeared in London before crossing the Atlantic to
play some shows in the United States, visiting Los Angeles, Atlantic City,

Chicago, Boston, and New York as well as releasing *Epitihies* in Cyprus and Greece. During the tour she began recording material for an album that would eventually be her first release in the English language. The single "Everything I Am" (2000), from the album of the same name, was another success in Greece and Cyprus but failed to have much impact anywhere else in the world. It was the beginning of a busy period for Vissi, as she released two more albums in the same year, first in July with *Agapi Iperviliki* and then in November with the seven times platinum *Kravgi*. The record led to Vissi being named best singer at the 2000 PopCorn Awards. Later in the year she sang to a TV audience of millions as she appeared at the Miss Universe pageant that was being held in her native Cyprus. Vissi then began performing with Keti Garbi in a nightclub act, "Fever," that has played to sold-out audiences in the Greek capital since the start of 2001 (although the show had to be cancelled temporarily when Vissi contracted throat problems). Her theater work continued into 2001, when she appeared in her own show "2001 Peace Odyssey."

Vissi's profile in Europe seemed more widespread when she reached #1 in Holland with "Still in Love with You," and she also played a short series of concerts in Australia in May 2002. Vissi's popularity in Cyprus and Greece will continue, as she is due to perform at the Olympic Games in Athens in 2004.

References

www.annavissi.net

W

Waterman, Pete (England)

Between 1985 and 1989 writer and producer Pete Waterman had ten #1's in the United Kingdom with ten different artists; and every week from March 15, 1986, to October 20, 1990, he had at least one record in the top 75. Of the top 40 sellers in the United Kingdom for 1989, eleven could claim Waterman as writer, producer, or performer.

Born in 1947 in England, Waterman began his interest in music through American R&B records of the 1960s. Finding a niche in the music business promoter, he was an early champion of The Beatles, Eric Clapton, and Rod Stewart before becoming one of the country's top club deejays. His love of soul and pop lead him to America. In 1973 he moved to Philadelphia and found work in the studios of Gamble & Huff, where he began working with soul singers who later created the "Philly Sound." He formed Loose Ends, his first production company, in 1979, and at the onset of the 1980s Waterman found himself part of the most successful songwriting partnership in Britain.

In 1984 he teamed with Mike Stock and Matt Aitken to form Stock, Aitken, and Waterman (SAW), and in the following years they took numerous artists to the top of the charts either as writers, producers, or both. SAW's first hit came in 1985 with Hazell Dean's "What Ever I Do (Wherever I Go)." The "easy on the ear" disco number based around drum machines and synthesizers was the template for most SAW productions to come. In the same year they reached the top spot twice as a production team with Dead or Alive's "You Spin Me Round" and Bananarama's "Venus." This marked the beginning of a run of hit records that were all critically destroyed by the music press, which deemed the SAW formula just that: a formulaic production line of synthetic pop. Waterman replied that they "made records for people who buy them and not to please the critics." He was vindicated, as the public bought SAW records by the million. These included releases featuring artists like Rick Astley, Mel & Kim, Jason

Donovan, and Brother Beyond, as well as established acts such as Cliff Richard and Donna Summer. As a result many awards came SAW's way, including the Ivor Novello Award for songwriter of the year for 1987, 1988, and 1989. In 1988 SAW took the award for most performed works. In 1988, SAW recordings accounted for 6 percent of Britain's songwriting output as the group reached #1 for five weeks with "I Should Be So Lucky," sung by an Australian ex-soap opera actress called Kylie Minogue.

Yet heavy criticism continued to come SAW's way, as each successive release relied on a backing track generated by drum machines, synthesizers, and samplers with very little "live" input from musicians, the only difference in the tracks being who sang them. Critics suggested that all the songs were interchangeable with all the SAW artists. In 1989, as a reaction to the criticism, the team released a single, "Roadblock," anonymously. The record won huge acclaim as the critics pondered who the new geniuses might be. When it was announced that "Roadblock" was a product of SAW, the critics were left looking seriously foolish. Also in 1989, SAW released twenty-three singles, only one of which failed to reach the top 40. In a twelve-month period the team had seven #1's, four of which ran consecutively. It was, however, the beginning of the end for the SAW team, as music in the United Kingdom became dominated by "real" bands playing real instruments (such as **The Stone Roses** and others that developed the "Madchester" scene). The early 1990s produced a string of flops for SAW, and in 1993 Waterman left the partnership. During the years that followed he kept a low profile.

In 1996 Waterman found different musical projects to employ his time. The first fruits of these new labors, the boy/girl band Steps, released its first single, " . . . 5, 6, 7, 8," which went to the top five in Britain. The music had changed little from SAW's glory days and appealed to a pre-pubescent audience that bought the releases in huge numbers. Waterman continued to work with Steps and helped them become one of the biggest acts in Britain, as well as producing Irish boyband Westlife, which is in direct competition for the same market. In October 1999, Steps and Westlife were at #1 and #2, respectively, in the charts. Earlier, in March 1999, the British music industry finally acknowledged Waterman's career by presenting him with an outstanding achievement award. As Steps continues to reach the top of the U.K. charts with each successive release, in September 2001 Waterman was enlisted to be on the panel of the U.K. TV show *Pop Star,* which aims to find an unknown singer and turn him or her into the pop star of the show's title.

Waterman continues to write and produce records for a diverse number of artists, most of which reach the top ten in the United Kingdom.

References

www.pwl-empire.co.uk

I Wish I Was Me by Pete Waterman and Paul Mathur (London: Virgin Publishing, 2000). ISBN 1852279001.

Weller, Paul (England)

Paul Weller was born on May 25, 1958, in Woking, near London, England. He played his first concert as a duo with schoolfriend Steve Brooks at a working man's club in his hometown in 1972. Although the pair played mainly old rock and roll numbers, Weller was already beginning to experiment with songwriting. In the following year Weller and Brooks formed **The Jam** with friends Dave Waller and Neil Harris. At this time Weller became interested in the Mod scene that had flourished in England in the mid-1960s, led by bands such as The Who and Small Faces. Weller dressed his new band in suits and began writing material that was heavily influenced by Pete Townsend and Ray Davis.

After the band settled as a three-piece, with Bruce Foxton on bass and Rick Buckler on drums, the group secured a record contract with Polydor and released its debut single, "In the City," in 1977. *In The City*, the album, followed. Now the band began to win an audience that differentiated the group from the punks of the time—primarily because of their clothes and the proficiency of their musicianship, although the guitar-driven songs had all the energy and anger of punk. Although a second album, *This Is the Modern World* (1978), was not well received by critics who stated that it was lyrically naïve. *All Mod Cons* (1979), the band's third album, with its combination of mellow love songs and hard-hitting social commentary, reached #6 in the charts. By now The Jam was a major force in English music. Although the group's singles up to now had only reached the top twenty, "The Eton Rifles," a vicious attack on English public schools and the class system, taken from the *Setting Sons* album, reached #3. The follow-up single, "Going Underground," released in February 1980, entered the charts at #1, as did "Start!" in September. The band's fifth album, *Sound Affects*, was released at the end of the year; its sparse, empty sound propelled it to #2. At the end of the year The Jam topped music polls in established music papers like the *NME* and *Melody Maker*. Although now widely regarded as the most popular band in the United Kingdom, the group had tried and failed to make inroads into the U.S. market. Europe also showed little interest, but the band had a huge following in Japan. As the group prepared to release *The Gift* in April 1982, a single, "Town Called Malice," with its Motown bass line and newly acquired keyboard riff, entered the charts at #1, as did the album itself in the following month. By now Weller was becoming frustrated by the limitations of the band, and later in 1982 he announced that The Jam was splitting up. A live album, *Dig the New Breed*, was released in December as Weller began writing new material to be released under the name The Style Council.

The new band was basically a duo of Weller and Mick Talbot, a piano player whom Weller had known for some years. The band's first single, "Speak Like a Child," reached the top ten on the strength of Weller's loyal following, but his fans became increasingly puzzled by his new European outlook. This was embodied on the "à Paris" single that reached #3 even with Weller singing one track partly in French. The band's debut album, *Café Bleu* (1983)—an eclectic mix of pop sings that employed different singers, double basses and violins, and other instruments that Weller had previously shied away from—hit the top ten. The group's second album, *Our Favourite Shop* (1985), was a more coherent effort and gave the band a #1. As Weller reached into his political songbook once again, he took on subjects such as racism, unemployment, and the devastating miners' strike for the songs' lyrics. (The strike by British mine workers was a bitter struggle that divided communities and families as the government of the day, led by Margaret Thatcher, sought to break the strength of the United Kingdom's trade unions. It largely succeeded.) The group's next album, *The Cost of Loving* (1987), reached #2, but hit singles were becoming increasingly difficult to produce. The radical change of The Style Council from The Jam was losing Weller fans, and when *Confessions of a Pop Group* was released in 1986, featuring a collection of bland, unmemorable tunes, it barely reached the top twenty. By 1989 the band was no more, and Weller found himself without a record label.

He then began touring as The Paul Weller Movement, until in 1992 he signed with Go! Discs and released an eponymous debut solo album in September. The record had a folk style with wistful songs that were more concerned with love and living, as Weller appeared to have overcome his anger. The release was well received and gave Weller his first hit in five years, "Uh Huh, Oh Yeah," which reached #21 in 1992. In the following year he released *Wild Wood*; this album carried on where his debut began, as it employed more acoustic guitar and more personal songs rather than the polemics of Weller's youth. It reached #2 as critics once again spoke of Weller as the best songwriter of the past twenty years. As his stock as a solo artist continued to rise, he once again undertook a tour, but this time he was playing arenas because his 1995 album, *Stanley Road*, had given him his first #1 in ten years. The album was Weller's version of 1960s R&B and soul, more of an electric album than the acoustic work of his previous releases. By now the Britpop phenomenon was in full force, and Weller and The Jam were named by bands such as Supergrass and Ocean Colour Scene as a major influence.

Still touring Europe and the United States, albeit to smaller audiences, Weller continued writing. In 1997 he released *Heavy Soul*, which reached #2 in the U.K. charts. Considered by many to be a dour record (the title itself giving credence to the opinion), its medium-paced numbers still reflected the R&B sound that Weller loved. By now he was only playing occasional festivals around the United Kingdom and Europe. It wasn't until July 2000 that he released his fifth solo album, *Heliocentric*. The release had an upbeat feel of drive and purpose. It gave Weller another U.K. chart #1, and he toured the United Kingdom to promote it. In 2001 he recorded a number of programs for BBC Radio, playing records that had influenced him as a teenager (including records on the Motown and Stax label). In May 2001 he recorded a solo concert where he played songs by The Jam for the first time in almost twenty years. The show was the catalyst for Weller to embark on a series of sold-out, one-man, acoustic concerts across the United Kingdom, which resulted in the October release of a live album *Days of Speed*, Weller's fifteenth top ten album.

References

www.paul-weller.com
Paul Weller: My Everchanging Moods by John Reed (London: Omnibus Press, 2002).
  ISBN 0711988668.

Wet Wet Wet (Scotland)

In 1977 in Glasgow, Scotland, bassist Graeme Clark (b. April 15, 1965), drummer Tommy Cunningham (b. June 22, 1964), pianist Neil Mitchell (b. June 8, 1965) and vocalist Mark McLachlan (b. March 23, 1965) formed Vortex Motion. In 1983 McLachlan changed his name to Marti Pellow and the band changed its name to Wet Wet Wet, then headed to London in an attempt to secure a record deal. Although they found some interest, it was after their debut gig in Glasgow that the promoter of the show suggested they create their own label. Thus the Precious Organisation was formed, and a fifth member, Graeme Duffin (b. February 28, 1956), was invited to join as permanent guitarist, although he was never photographed as part of the band and Wet Wet Wet remained, to the public, a four-piece. Styling its music on 1970s American soul, the band went to Memphis in 1986 to record, but the band thought the songs were not released and the band returned to Britain. In April of the following year the single "Wishing I Was Lucky" did find a release, and it reached #6 in the charts. It was an upbeat song, and the video of the band on a sun-kissed beach gave it a feel-good quality that dogged the band in its later career as critics marked it a light pop band, while the members considered themselves a serious soul band. The group's next single, "Sweet Little Mystery," was identical in feel to the debut single and went to #5. By the end of the year the band's debut album had been released; after staying in the charts for fourteen weeks, *Popped In Souled Out* finally reached #1 after selling over 2 million copies.

The year 1988 began with a tour of Europe and Japan, where the group played in front of over half a million people in just over a month. In May the group released a cover version of The Beatles' "With a Little Help from My Friends" as part of BBC TV's Childline charity, and the single reached #1, selling 500,000 copies. During the summer the band played at Nelson Mandela's seventieth birthday concert in front of a TV audience of millions and subsequently was invited to join Elton John on his tour of America, during which the group played four dates at the Hollywood Bowl and five at Madison Square Garden. Also in 1988 the band won awards from various music organizations and pop magazines, including a best album trophy for *Popped In Souled Out*. The most prestigious presentation was the Nordoff Robins Music Therapy Award for best band. At the end of 1988 the songs recorded in Memphis in 1986 were released as *The Memphis Sessions*; the album reached #3 and became the group's second platinum-selling record. Wet Wet Wet kept a low profile during 1989 as they retired to the studio to concentrate on new material and released a third album at the end of the year: *Holding Back the River*, firmly entrenched in the 1970s U.S. soul sound, hit #2 (and was the fourth bestselling album of the 1980s in Britain). However, the band's single releases were beginning to be less successful. Although the band appeared at the John Lennon tribute concert in Liverpool in 1990, the group primarily kept out of the public eye, releasing two singles that only reached the lower reaches of the top sixty.

The band was back at the top of the charts at the beginning of 1992 when the album *High on the Happy Side* (1992) reached #1, as did the first single release, "Goodnight Girl." Although the songs were less uproarious than the group's early efforts, they still portrayed a band enjoying its music. Two more albums followed: *Live at the Royal Albert Hall* (May 1993) and a greatest hits compilation (November 1993). In May 1994 the band released "Love Is All Around" from the film *Four Weddings and a Funeral*; the single stayed at #1 for a record fifteen weeks and became the second biggest-selling single ever in Britain. Wet Wet Wet's next album, *Picture This* (1995), featuring more polished soul, also reached #1 (the fourth album to do so). In the following year the group received the Scottish Silver Clef for outstanding contribution to Scottish music, but the pressure was beginning to weigh on the band. More tours followed the release of *10* (1997), the band's eighth album, celebrating ten years in the music business. By the end of the year Cunningham had left and in the following year the band disappeared completely from public view as Pellow suffered from ill health.

In May 1999, Pellow announced he was leaving the band. Although Clark and Mitchell attempted to keep the band going, Wet Wet Wet officially broke up in 2000. Toward the end of the year Pellow undertook a solo tour of Britain, and in the summer of 2001 he released new material that produced a top ten hit with the single "Close to You." taken from the album *Smile* (2001). In November he was invited to appear in the popular U.K. soap opera *Emmerdale*. The rest of the band members continue to play music in their native Scotland.

References

www.wetwetwet.org.uk
Wet Wet Wet: Picture This by John Sandford (Music Sales Ltd.). ISBN 0711951748

Whigfield (Denmark)

Although Sannie Charlotte Carlson was born in Skaelskar, Denmark, on April 11, 1970, she spent the early part of her life in Africa, where her father worked as an engineer. She later returned to Denmark to complete her education. While in Denmark she sang with her brother's band; but after she finished her schooling she moved to Italy to study fashion design and later became a model. While in Italy she caught the attention of producer Larry Pignagnoli, who, after auditions to establish her singing ability, signed her to a record deal.

Carlson now changed her name to Whigfield (after a piano teacher she had studied under as a young girl) and released her first single, "Saturday Night," at the end of 1993 in Italy. The record was a catchy Europop number driven by synthesized drum beats and bright keyboard riffs that included an infectious chorus and a specially choreographed dance routine that was soon being imitated in the clubs across Europe. The single reached #1 and soon became a hit all over the continent, including #1 in Spain, a position it held for eleven weeks. In the United Kingdom it became the first debut single by any artist to enter the charts at #1 after selling over 750,000 copies within the first three weeks of its release. By the end of 1994 "Saturday Night" had become the second biggest-selling single in Europe, behind **Wet Wet Wet's** "Love Is All Around."

Whigfield's self-titled debut album, released in 1995, replicated the feel-good dance sound of her #1 single. The unchallenging, somewhat trite nature of the music helped the album reach silver in England, Italy, Germany, Holland, and Belgium; gold in Canada, India, and the Philippines; and triple platinum in South Africa. Three other top twenty hits came from *Whigfield*: "Another Day," "Think of You," and "Close to You." At the end of the year Whigfield released a cover version of "Last Christmas," originally performed by British artist George Michael's first band, Wham. The single was another hit in Europe and Scandinavia. In the following year, with a scarcity of new, original material, a re-mix version of the album was released under the title *Special Edition*, while a single, "Sexy Eyes," took Whigfield to #1 in Australia.

By 1997 an album of new, but not radically different, material, *Whigfield II*, was released. Although it repeated the sales figures of *Whigfield* in South Africa by going triple platinum, it failed to catch the imagination of the public to the extent that "Saturday Night" had, and it sold poorly elsewhere. Over the next two years Whigfield released two singles—"Givin All My Love" (1998), and a cover of U.S. girl band The Ronettes' 1960s hit "Be My Baby" (1999)—and an album of previously recorded material, *Megamixes* (1998), with a limited release in Scandinavia. During this time Whigfield also continued to perform at clubs across Europe.

At the start of 2000 Whigfield released *Whigfield III*. The album failed to break new ground musically but sold relatively well in Europe and Denmark, as did a single, "Doo Whop." Another single released in the following year, "Much More," again won only a small audience in Europe as Whigfield's apparent inability to grow musically meant she was still appealing only to a small core audience. The artist released *Whigfield III* in Asia in April 2001, as well as *Greatest Hits 2001* in Mexico and *Eurodance* in Canada. She then undertook a tour of small clubs in the United Kingdom in July. Whigfield's career will always be judged against the success of "Saturday Night," a hit she seems unlikely to repeat. A new single, "Gotta Getcha," was released in May 2002 in Italy while a new album of synth disco-pop, *Whigfield 4,* was released across Europe in June and was moderately successful in Scandinavia, Italy, and Germany.

References

www.whigfield.com

Wong, Faye (China)

A native of Beijing, China, Wong Jing Man was born on August 8, 1969, the daughter of an engineer father and a singer mother. During her school years Wong showed little inclination to be a singer, despite her mother's career. When Wong was sixteen her debut album, *Miss Charming*, was released to little notice. Within twelve months another two albums were on the market, but again the public showed little interest in the young singer's unchallenging pop music. When Wong was eighteen her family moved to Hong Kong; but after initially finding work as a model she soon lost interest in that career, and her father enrolled her at a singing school. With the approval of her singing teacher, Wong entered the 1989 Asian Golden Zither Pop Music Competition. Performing an original song, "Still the Old Sayings," she won third prize. Her teacher then introduced her to record producer Chan Tsiau Bao, who, impressed with her raw talent, gave her a contract with Cinepoly Records.

Renamed Wong Fei, when the Hong Kong record company felt that her name was "too introverted" she became Wong Chin Man. Because it was also common practice to give a new artist an English name, "Shirley" was added. Her first album for the new company, *Shirley Wong*, released in November 1989, featured synthesized pop dealing with love and loss. Within a year she released two other albums, *Everything* (June 1990) and *You're the Only One* (December 1990), focusing on similar material. Thereafter Wong, disappointed at the lack of interest her music was creating, moved to New York to stay with relatives and enrolled in singing and dancing classes.

Returning to Hong Kong in 1992, she was contractually obliged to make another album with Cinepoly before attending university. After a fourth and final name change to Faye (introducing the phenomena of "Fayenatics," as her fans soon began calling themselves), Wong released *Coming Home* in August 1992. A single from the album, "Easily Hurt Woman," was released separately. It became a huge hit in Asia and won a Jade Solid Gold award, although it displayed little change from her previous work. It was then that Wong gave up on her university career to concentrate on singing. Between the release of her debut album in 1989 and her winning the award for most popular Hong Kong female singer in 1994, Wong released eight albums. In 1994 she appeared as a romantic heroine in the movie *Chung King Express*, for which she won the best actress award at the Swedish Film Festival. In November 1994, Wong gave her first live performance in over five years in Toronto, Canada, before completing a tour of Asia as well as other shows in Canada and the United States. Wong was now writing more of her own material. In fact, in her final album for Cinepoly, *Exasperation* (1996), she was responsible for all the songs. Winning huge critical praise, the album contained three tracks that had no lyrics but, instead, just utilized Wong's voice. It was unlike any song ever heard in Hong Kong to that date, and it showed Wong as a thoughtful and maturing artist.

A very private person, Wong shunned the many TV and newspaper appearances that her peers craved. As a result, she caused something of a sensation when, in 1996, she announced that she was married and expecting her first child. The impending birth did little to diminish her popularity. In May 1997 she signed with EMI, through which, with the resources that were now behind her, she became instantly more accessible to the public. In the same year she won a Billboard award for most popular Asian singer and played a show in Taiwan to an audience of 20,000 fans.

In January 1998, Wong won the favorite female category at Taiwan's Channel V awards. As part of her new goal of winning wider recognition, in the same year she released *Sing and Play*. The album included some Wong compositions and introduced more ballads to her canon, as most of her previous releases had been unerringly jaunty pop numbers. She then undertook a tour of Japan that lasted for six months. Her nomadic lifestyle throughout this period made her one of the most widely recognized people in East Asia (*Asiaweek* magazine included her in a list of "50 people you should know in China"), but it began to have an effect on her private life. As a result of the work she was putting into her career, Wong's marriage dissolved. She separated from her husband in the summer of 1999, the same time that her face appeared across the continent on cans of Pepsi. In the following year Wong won five trophies at the RTHK Top Ten Awards, including best song for "Love Letter to Myself" and the nation's most popular woman artist. Her album *Fable*, released in October, began to focus on Wong's faith, as the first part of the album centered on the teachings of Buddhism.

In 2001, Wong, now enthralled by the Buddhist faith, began to focus on the Japanese market and in April appeared on the front cover of *Frau* magazine. By the summer she was singing "Separate Ways," the theme song to the popular Japanese TV drama *Usokoi,* and in October she performed live in the country for the first time. In the following month she was named Artist of the Month on MTVChina. She also released the "Buddhist" single in Hong Kong. In November a double release, *Loving, Kindness and Wisdom*, highlighted Wong's devotion to her newfound faith, as the first part of the album featured Buddhist chants. Later in November a "best of" album was released.

In May 2002 Wong won a place in the Guinness Book of Records as the best-selling woman singer of Cantonese music, selling nearly 10 million albums. Shortly after a new album of orchestrated ballads, *Chinese Odyssey,* was released and kept Wong at the top of the Asian pop charts. Her career has encompassed more than 20 albums as she continues to record material for future release.

References

www.faye.com

Y

Yello (Switzerland)

Dieter Meier (b. March 4, 1945) and Boris Blank (b. January 15, 1953) were both born in Zurich, the capital of Switzerland. The son of a millionaire banker, Meier drifted through school in the knowledge that he would never have to work for a living and became a law student, professional gambler, member of the Swiss national golf team, and performance artist. In 1978 he released a single, "Cry for Fame," on the small Periphery Perfume label. While Meier was experimenting with ways of living, Blank was experimenting with sound on homemade equipment in his Zurich apartment. Blind in one eye from a childhood accident with fireworks, Blank was a TV repairman and truck driver before his sound experiments came to the attention of Periphery Perfume. Before long, a meeting between this unlikely pair was suggested.

In the fall of 1979 Meier visited Blank's apartment, and the duo created a thirty-minute piece of theater that Meier called "Dead Cat." Ten days later the pair performed "Dead Cat" at the Forum Cinema in Zurich. The work was an avant-garde, electronic diaspora. Meier delivered the vocals in front of the film screen while Blank hid in the orchestra pit suffering from acute shyness. Meier later recalled that "people were shocked and surprised," but "[we] knew that we had given birth to something that was important." Meier and Blank subsequently christened themselves Yello.

During 1980 Blank, always seeking new sounds, met a fellow enthusiast at a car-crushing plant where they were both recording the noise of the machines. The new friend, Carlos Peron, took Blank to San Francisco, where he signed a deal with Ralph Records. Following the release of a single, "Bimbo," the first Yello album, *Solid Pleasure* (1980), was released in the United States, the United Kingdom, and Germany. The album was an amalgamation of experimental and hard mechanical sounds that made little impact, and after its release Yello returned to Zurich. In September, Ralph released another single,

Yello
Pictorialpress Ltd., London, UK

"Bostich," in the United States, soon thereafter Meier received a phone call telling him that "Bostich" was receiving heavy airplay on the New York radio station WBLS, which specialized in R&B, soul, rap, and hip-hop. "Bostich," with its heavy bass beat, had become a favorite in the clubs of the city and was also being used as the basis of early work by rap pioneer Afrika Bambaataa. Later, the Lee Cooper company used the song for a commercial that began a long relationship between Yello and commercial soundtracks. A second album, *Claro Qui Si* (1981), was released at the same time as "Bostich" was generating interest in the band, and Meier's unique vocal, a whispered mix of French and English, won the group new fans. A single from the album, "Pinball Cha Cha," released in October 1981, came complete with what was then the relatively new medium of video. Shot on 16mm, Meier's film was later featured in New York's Museum of Modern Art's Music Video Exhibition of 1985. Meier went on to win various awards for his visual work, including the Midem Music Video Award in Cannes in 1986 for "Desire" (from the album *Stella*), and the Diamond Award for Special Effects in Brussels in 1988 for "The Race" (from the album *One Second* (1987)).

As Yello's use of sound brought the group to the attention of fashion designers, its music was used as an accompaniment to catwalk shows in New York and Paris. When Meier recognized the danger that the band might become a victim of its own "fashionablity," the pair made a decision to remain in Switzerland.

This proved difficult for Meier, as in 1981 he released his first movie, *Jetzt Und Alles*, and had to relocate to New York to promote the film. However, he traveled back to Zurich whenever possible to find out what Blank had been creating while he was away. In 1983 the band's third album was released: *You Gotta Say Yes to Another Excess* featured simpler, more melodic music than previous works. Although the band had become celebrated in musical and artistic circles for its continued experimentation with sound, it had yet to taste commercial success in the pop charts. But two singles from the album brought a taste of pop stardom. "I Love You," released in the United Kingdom, reached the top twenty, and "Lost Again" repeated the feat in the United States. As the band now had a chart hit, a rare gig was arranged at the Roxy in New York in December. A sold-out audience of mainly black and Hispanic fans gave Yello a thunderous welcome. In the summer of 1984 a recording of the concert was released while the band worked on new material.

In January 1985 the group released *Stella*. The album was the most commercial to date, as Meier's melodies hovered gently over Blank's simpler backing tracks. The single "Desire," with its award-winning video shot in Havana, Cuba, found its way onto the soundtrack of the U.S. cop show "Miami Vice." Another single, "Oh Yeah," raced up the U.S. chart, helped on its way by its use on TV accompanying American football coverage, as well as appearing in commercials for cars and chocolate. Later the song was used in the motion pictures *Ferris Beuller's Day Off* and Michael J. Fox's *The Secret of My Success*. The success of the singles kept Meier traveling the world giving interviews, while Blank remained in Zurich writing music that Meier would eventually add lyrics to. An album of re-mixed versions of early songs, *1980–85: The New Mix in One Go*, was released in March 1986, but it wasn't until May 1987 that a new album was completed.

One Second (1987) featured collaborations with U.K. band Associate's vocalist, Billy McKenzie, and a specially written song, "The Rhythm Divine," for Welsh diva Shirley Bassey. As the acid house phenomenon began to hit the United Kingdom, Yello found that deejays were playing the band's back catalogue over new beats, exposing a new audience to the work of Meier and Blank. Later in 1987, Meier helped out two magician friends with an old, forgotten piece that the illusionists used behind their performance at the Magicians World Championship in New York. The pair, Tempest and Cottet, won against the odds, and Meier took the piece of music and reworked it into a song, "The Race." Released in the summer of 1988, the single became an international top five hit, giving Yello its highest chart placing to date.

The following album, *Flag*, released in October, was a delicate balance between the band's predilection for experimentation and its new commerciality. It sold over a million copies, making Yello one of the highest-selling Swiss pop acts ever. At the same time Meier moved to Poland to concentrate on a new film, *Snowball*, a "neo expressionist baroque opera kind of thing." In the following years Yello released a compilation album and wrote pieces for two British motion pictures, *She Devil* and the comedy *Nuns on the Run*, starring former Monty Python star Eric Idle. Although a new album, *Zebra*, was released in Germany in October 1994, the band had effectively removed itself from the pop arena. It was beginning to concentrate on writing for movies and did a re-working of the Christmas song "Jingle Bells" for the movie *The Santa Clause* in December 1995.

Pocket Universe was released in February 1997, but the band did little to promote the album of electronica and dance beats, concentrating instead on writing the music for the 1998 movie *Senseless*. By the end of 1999, Yello released its own album of "soundtrack" music, called *Motion Picture*. The single "Squeeze Please" (1999) has to date been the last release from the band. An exhibition of Meier's cinema work, "In the Picture," was held in May and June 2001 in New York but as yet there is no new material due for release.

References

www.yello.ch
The Rough Guide to Rock edited by Jonathan Buckley and Mark Ellingham (London: Rough Guides Ltd., 1996). ISBN 1858282012

Z

Zaragoza, Jessa (Philippines)

Born in Caloocan City in the Philippines on January 31, 1979, Jessa Zaragoza was a national star by the age of thirteen. Initially appearing in a commercial for soap in 1992, in the same year she joined *That's Entertainment,* a TV variety show, where she remained as part of the cast until 1994. While performing on "That's Entertainment," she also starred in the sitcom "Kool Iskul," appeared in other TV commercials, modeled clothes for magazines, and appeared in numerous movies, including her debut in 1992, *Mahirap Maging Pogi.*

In 1995 she won her first major role in the soap opera *Villa Quintana,* where she remained for the next two years. Although she appeared in both another soap opera, *Anna Karenina,* and a sitcom, *Ibang Klase,* in 1997, she signed with the Octo Arts label and released her first album in July, *Just Can't Help Feeling*. The album followed the formula of many Filipino pop stars, being a collection of ballads and dance numbers with an electronic backing. *Just Can't Help Feeling* turned eight times platinum, selling over half a million copies, and was named the highest-grossing album in the country during 1998. Zaragoza was also presented with the Young Professional Award for Entertainment. During this period she was still starring in movies. After being asked to appear in "bold" scenes for *Masamang Damo*, the singer/actress reportedly attempted suicide on account of the pressure she was under. Recovering from her ordeal, she was still contracted to appear in film and TV, and it wasn't until February 1999 that she performed live for the first time. When she appeared at the Cuneta Astrodome under the title "All My Love Jessa Zaragoza," the concert was a prelude to the release of her second album, *Phenomenal*, in March that continued her successful musical formula. Although it failed to reach the sales figures of her debut album, it still earned her a platinum disc as she was named best female entertainer of the year and Jukebox Queen, as well as winning an award for excellence from the mayor of the town of Binangonan. At this time she also won her first starring role in the soap opera "Di Ba't Ikaw." In November 1999, Zaragoza played her first show outside the Philippines, visiting Bahrain, Dubai, and Japan.

In 2000 she became the host of a TV comedy show, "Oops," and released a third album, *S'ya Ba Ang Dahilan*. Similar in sound and content to her previous two albums, it reached gold and enabled Zaragoza to appear on the cover of *Philippines Cosmopolitan*. After the release of *S'ya Ba Ang Dahilan*, the singer encountered rumors that she was going to leave her record company, Octo Arts. Although Zaragoza denied this, on September 12 it was announced that she had joined the rival Star Records, and by December a new album, *Ibigay Mo Na*, was released. The change of record company did not signal a change of style, however, as the album's content repeated her former formula for success. At the end of the year Zaragoza won the Awit award for best country ballad and was named sensational recording artist of the year. In February and March 2001, Zaragoza joined fellow Filipino singing star **Martin Nievera** on a U.S. tour before returning home to begin more recording. The results of the recording included a cover version of a song by popular Filipino singer Ding Dong Avanzado, "Maghihintay Sa Yo," and a duet with the singer, "Glory of Love." Soon thereafter Zaragosa and Avanzado were married. In September, Zaragosa toured the United States with a group of other Filipino artists.

References

Members.tripod.com/musikpriend

Zucchero (Italy)

Adelmo Fornaciari was born in the village of Roncocesi, in the Emilia Romagna region of Italy, on September 25, 1955. As a child he learned to play the organ in his local church before being introduced to soul, blues, and R&B by an American student when he was thirteen. Already known as Zucchero ("Sugar"), the nickname he received from a teacher while still at junior high school, he performed with various bands between 1970 and 1978, traveling throughout Italy and playing the blues. In 1981 he won a competition, the Castrocaro Festival, and in the following year he entered the San Remo festival competition. Encouraged by the positive reviews of his performance there, he entered again in 1983 and won with his own composition, "Nuvola." His debut album, *Un po' di Zucchero*, which reflected his love of the blues, followed soon thereafter.

Invited to San Francisco by the producer Corrado Rustici, he met bass player Randy Jackson and, with Jackson's help, formed a blues band that returned to Italy in 1985 and subsequently released *Zucchero and the Randy Jackson Band* (1985). He appeared for a third time at the San Remo festival, where his song "Donne" was placed second to last but won good reviews and earned the singer radio play. The following album, *Rispetto* (1986), began to show more soul and R&B influences and featured well-known guest artists such as Brian Auger and

Narada Michael Waldon. The album reached the top of the charts in the week of its release. It wasn't until 1987, however, that Zucchero became a household name.

His fourth album, *Blues* (1987), became the biggest-selling Italian album ever at the time, with over 1,300,000 copies sold in Italy alone. A sold-out tour of Italy followed. Then, in 1988, the rest of mainland Europe had the chance to see him play as he completed another sold-out run of concerts. As a result of these shows, the filmmaker Tinto Brass invited Zucchero to write the score for the movie *Snack Bar Budapest*. The album *Ora Incenso E Birra* (1989) was then re-recorded with English lyrics, and in 1990, to promote the record, Zucchero undertook to tour Europe with Eric Clapton. In the following year he recorded a duet, "Senza Una Donna," originally a track on the *Blues* album, with the English singer Paul Young. The song was a departure from Zucchero's usual style; the heartfelt ballad took him to #2 in the U.K. charts and #4 in the United States, as well as topping the charts across Europe. Zucchero was then asked to contribute Italian lyrics for Sting's *Soul Cages* (1991) album and was personally invited by Brian May, former guitarist in the rock band Queen, to perform at the Freddie Mercury tribute concert at Wembley Stadium in London on April 20, 1992. Although his music was still influenced by the blues, Zucchero's sixth album, *Miserere* (1992), began to show a more pop sensibility and was his first to gain a simultaneous release in both the Italian and English languages. The record reached #11 in the U.K. chart. Also in 1992 he began a series of benefit concerts with the Italian tenor Luciano Pavarotti. In 1993, Zucchero was presented with a seven times platinum disc for sales of *Miserere* and was named most successful Italian singer of the year at the World Music Awards.

In 1994, Zucchero released his first Spanish-language album, *Diamante*, and traveled to South America to tour for six weeks. In September, he was back in the studio working on *Spirito DiVino*. The album was recorded in New Orleans, as Zucchero attempted to capture the authentic feel of the blues that had been his earliest musical passion. The album was released in 1995 and remained in the Italian chart for a record seventy-five weeks. Zucchero's first world tour to promote the album ended with a Christmas show at the Palasport in the Italian town of Parma. The concert was recorded and subsequently shown on Italian TV on December 26, 1995.

Zucchero's first show of 1996 closed the traditional Labor Day festivities in Rome, where over 400,000 people attended. Later that month he was presented with the prize for the world's bestselling Italian artist for 1995 by the Italian music industry. The year ended with the release of a "best of" album, *Zucchero Sugar Fornaciari's Greatest Hits*, that raced to #1 in Italy, where it stayed for seven weeks, and went eleven times platinum. It also reached #1 in France, #2 in Switzerland, #4 in Portugal, #5 in Belgium, #7 in Austria, #10 in Germany, and #15 in Holland.

It wasn't until November 1998 that Zucchero released a new album, *Blue-sugar*, still following the blues route that had been his inspiration at the outset of his career but showing the commerciality that had begun with "Senza Una Donna" over seven years earlier. The album was the catalyst for a world tour that began with thirteen sold-out shows in Italy and lasted until December 1999. The tour took in the Imst Festival in Austria, where Zucchero performed between Bryan Adams and The Rolling Stones to over 200,000 fans, and the Michael Jackson & Friends charity show in Munich, where he performed with Mariah Carey as well as Jackson himself. During 1999, Zucchero released two new albums; although both *Overdose D'Amour the Ballads* and *Bluesugar & Whitechristmas* were far more pop than blues, his fans bought each copy in huge numbers. The year ended with a Millennium show in Milan to over 200,000 people.

During the early part of 2001, Zucchero retired to his farmhouse, Louisiana Soul, and began preparing material for a new album. *Shake* was released in Europe in September and in the United States in October. A single, "Baila (Sexy Thing)," was the first release off the album. Zucchero promoted the album with a thirty-date tour of Italy and Europe in February and March of 2002 and then took part in European festivals in May and June before embarking on a world tour, also called "Shake."

References

www.zucchero.it

Appendix A

Entries Listed Alphabetically by Country

ARGENTINA
Soda Stereo

AUSTRALIA
Conway, Deborah
Go-Betweens, The
Kelly, Paul
Powderfinger
Silverchair

AUSTRIA
Falco

BELGIUM
Axelle Red
Front 242
Hintjens, Arno
Soulsister

BRAZIL
Mercury, Daniela

CANADA
Crash Test Dummies
I Mother Earth
Moist

CHILE
Tiro De Gracia

CHINA
Cheung, Jacky
Cui Jian
Lai, Leon
Wong, Faye

CYPRUS
Vissi, Anna

DENMARK
Whigfield

ENGLAND
Beautiful South, The
Blur
Delirious?
Gray, David
Jam, The
Madness
New Order
Smiths, The
Stone Roses, The
Waterman, Pete
Weller, Paul

FINLAND
Bomfunk MC's
Hanoi Rocks
HIM

Leningrad Cowboys, The
Nylon Beat

FRANCE
Bashung, Alain
Belolo, Henry
Daho, Etienne
Farmer, Mylene
MC Solaar
Murat
Paradis, Vanessa

GERMANY
Bohlen, Dieter
Die Prinzen
Guano Apes
Nena
Väth, Sven

GREECE
Garbi, Keti

HOLLAND
Doe Maar

HONG KONG
Cheng, Sammi
Kwok, Aaron
Lau, Andy
Lee, Coco

ICELAND
Morthens, Bubbi
Sugarcubes, The

INDIA
Chinai, Alisha
Jassi
Mehndi, Daler

INDONESIA
Anggun

REPUBLIC OF IRELAND
Enya

ISRAEL
Haza, Ofra
Noa
Rita

ITALY
Ligabue, Luciano
Pausini, Laura
Ramazotti, Eros
Rossi, Vasco
Zucchero

JAPAN
Chage & Aska
Dragon Ash
Dreams Come True
Glay
Hikaru, Utada
Naime, Amuro
Puffy
Tamio, Okuda
Thee Michelle Gun Elephant
Unicorn

MALAYSIA
Majid, Sheila

MEXICO
Mana
Trevi, Gloria

NEW ZEALAND
Dobbyn, Dave
Mutton Birds, The
Runga, Bic
Spilt Enz
Stellar*
Strawpeople

NORWAY
Abel, Morten
A-Ha
Lind, Espen
Marlin, Lene
Rein, Trine

Sissel

PAKISTAN
Hassan, Nazia
Junoon

PHILIPPINES
Cruz, Donna
Fernandez, Pops
Nievera, Martin
Velasquez, Regine
Zaragoza, Jessa

PORTUGAL
Silence 4

RUSSIA
Aquarium
Kirkorov, Philip
Pugacheva, Alla
Shevchuck, Yury

SCOTLAND
Deacon Blue
Run Rig
Wet Wet Wet

SLOVENIA
Laibach

SOUTH AFRICA
Botha, Piet
Clegg, Johnny
Springbok Nude Girls
Trompies

SOUTH KOREA
Fin.K.L
Seo Taiji & Boys

SPAIN
Arbelo, Rosana
Casal, Luz
Ella Baila Sola
Heroes Del Silencio
Mecano

SWEDEN
Ace of Base
Gyllene Tider
Roxette

SWITZERLAND
Yello

TAIWAN
A-Mei

THAILAND
Bazoo
Raptor

TURKEY
Aksu, Sezen

WALES
Manic Street Preachers
Stereophonics, The

Appendix B

Awards

These awards are all presented annually and acknowledge a significant contribution to the country's music industry for a given year. All the countries represented have other awards but the ones listed here are considered among the most prestigious by both the media and the public.

ARIA

Presented by the Australian Record Industry Association (ARIA), the awards celebrated their fourteenth year in 2001.

www.aria.com.au

AWIT

First presented in 1988, the Awit is organized by the Philippine Association of Recording Industry and the Organisation of Filipino Composers.

www.mb.com.ph/entr/1999-12/en120203.asp

BRIT AWARDS

Awarded by the British Phonographic Industry.

www.brits.co.uk

CASBY

Voted for by the Canadian public, Casby is an acronym for Canadian Awards Selected By You.

CASH

Awarded by the Composers and Authors Society of Hong Kong.

CHANNEL V AWARDS

Often viewed as the most important awards in India, partly owing to the support of the Indian Music Industry (IMI).

ECHO
Formed in 1992, the Echos are awarded by the Phono-Acadamie of Germany.
www.gema.de/eng/public/n161/echo

EMMA
Often referred to as the "Finnish Grammy."
www.emmaawards.com

GOLDEN DRAGON
Presented in Taiwan for achievement in the film industry.

IFPI PLATINUM EUROPE AWARDS
Launched in 1998 by the International Federation of the Phonographic Industry, the awards are presented to artists from any part of the world in recognition of album sales of over a million copies in Europe.
www.ifpi.org/platinum

IVOR NOVELLO
Born in Wales, Ivor Novello (1893–1951) was a silent film star, playwright, and composer. The awards, first presented in 1955, acknowledge outstanding contributions in music by British artists.
www.britishacademy.com/ivornovello

JADE SOLID GOLD
Awards presented in Hong Kong by the countries largest broadcasting organization, TVB.

JUNO
Organized by the Canadian Academy of Recording Arts and Sciences.
www.juno-awards.ca

KATHA
Established in 1990 in the Philippines, the Kathas are in competition with the Awits.
www.mb.com.ph/entr/1999-12/en120203.asp

MUCHMUSIC
MuchMusic is a Canadian radio station. The first awards were presented in 1990.
www.muchmusic.com

NRJ AWARDS
A relatively new organization, the NRJs have been presented in France since 2000.

PREMIOS AMIGOS

Commonly known as the "Spanish Grammy."

PREMIOS ONDAS

First presented in Spain in 1953, the Premios Ondas recognize achievement in music, TV, and radio.

ROCKBJÖRNEN

The "Swedish Grammy," the Rockbjörnen is distinguished from other awards in that the trophy is a toy teddy bear.

SAMA

The South African Music Awards.

SCREEN VIDEOCON

Viewed in India much like the Oscars are in the West, the Screen Videocon awards were first presented in 1994.

SPELLEMANSPRIS

The "Norwegian Grammy."

TAMUZ

Presented by the Israeli Music Industry.

TENCO

Luigi Tenco (1938–1951) was an Italian singer who was shot in an Italian hotel room, though whether by accident, suicide, or homicide was never determined. The awards are presented in Italy and are dedicated to his memory.

TIGRA

Presented in Germany.

VICTOIRES DE LA MUSIQUE

Since 1985, members of the French music industry have voted for the Victoires De La Musique.
www.lesvictoiresdelamusique.mcity.fr

WORLD MUSIC AWARDS

Under the patronage of Prince Albert of Monaco, the awards are based on sales figures and are presented to artists from across the globe. The awards ceremony is held in Monte Carlo.
www.worldmusicawards.com

Appendix C

Silver/Gold/Platinum Sales Requirements
(number of units sold per country to qualify for a silver, gold, or platinum disc)

	SILVER		GOLD		PLATINUM	
	Album	Single	Album	Single	Album	Single
Australia	—	—	15,000	50,000	—	—
Austria	—	—	25,000	100,000	—	—
Belgium	10,000	50,000	25,000	100,000	50,000	—
Canada	—	—	50,000	75,000	100,000	—
Denmark	25,000	25,000	50,000	50,000	—	—
Finland	—	—	15,000	10,000	—	—
France	—	—	100,000	500,000	—	—
Ireland	—	50,000	—	100,000	—	—
Germany	125,000	500,000	250,000	1,000,000	500,000	2,000,000
Italy	500,000	—	1,000,000	1,000,000	—	—
Holland	10,000	50,000	25,000	100,000	50,000	250,000
Norway*	20,000	250,000kr	40,000	50,000kr	—	—
Spain	—	—	100,000	100,000	—	—
Sweden	—	50,000	25,000	100,000	50,000	—
U.K.	60,000	250,000	100,000	500,000	300,000	1,000,000

* In Norway the presenting of silver and gold discs is based on the amount of Danish krona the discs earn, not the number of unit sales.

Bibliography

Aizlewood, J., A. Collins, and B. Prince. *The Q Book of Punk Legends*. Enfield: Guinness Publishing, 1996.

Bergman, B. *African Pop: Goodtime Kings*. Poole: Blandford Press, 1985.

Clifford, M. *New Illustrated Rock Hand Book*. London: Salamander Books, 1988.

Ewens, G. *Africa U-Ye! A Celebration of African Music*. Enfield: Guinness Publishing, 1991.

Friedlander, P. *Rock and Roll: A Social History*. Boulder: Westview Press, 1996.

Gambaccini, P., T. Rice, and R. Rice. *Guinness Hits of the 80s*. Enfield: Guinness Publishing, 1990.

Gregory, H. *A Century of Pop: A Hundred Years of Music That Changed the World*. London: Hamlyn, 1998.

Haslam, D. *Manchester, England: The Story of the Pop Cult City*. London: Fourth Estate, 1999.

Hogg, B. *All That Ever Mattered: The History of Scottish Rock and Pop*. Enfield: Guinness Publishing, 1993.

Hounsome, T. *New Rock Record*. Poole: Blandford Press, 1982.

Larkin, C. *The Virgin Encyclopedia of Dance Music*. London: Virgin, 1998.

McAleer, D. *Chart Beats*. Enfield: Guinness Publishing, 1991.

———. *The Omnibus Chart Book of the 80's*. London: Omnibus Press, 1989.

———. *The Warner Guide to U.K. and U.S. Hit Albums*. London: Carlton/Little, Brown, 1995.

Moore, A. F. *Rock: The Primary Text*. Buckingham: Open University Press, 1993.

Murrells, J. *Million Selling Records from the 1900s to the 1980s: An Illustrated Directory*. London: Batsford, 1984.

Osborne, B. *Twenty Years of Loving It: The A–Z of Club Culture*. London: Sceptre, 1999.

Prendergast, M. J. *Irish Rock: Roots, Personalities, Directions*. Dublin: O'Brien Press, 1987.

Rawlings, T. *Mod: A Very British Phenomenon*. London: Omnibus Press, 2000.

Redhead, S. *The End of the Century Party: Youth and Pop towards 2000*. Manchester: MUP, 1990.

Rees, D., and L. Crampton. *The Guinness Book of Rock Stars*. Enfield: Guinness Publishing, 1991.

Reynolds, S. *Blissed Out: The Rapture of Rock*. London: Serpent's Tail, 1990.

Ryback, T. W. *Rock Around the Bloc*. New York: Oxford University Press, 1990.

Stapleton, C., and C. May. *African All Stars: The Pop Music of a Continent*. London: Paladin, 1987.

Sweeney, P. *The Directory of World Music*. London: Virgin, 1991.

Troitsky, A. *Back in the U.S.S.R.* London: Omnibus, 1987.

Index

Main articles and their page numbers are in **Bold**. Album titles, TV Programs, and films are in *Italic*. Single songs are in "Quotes." Album titles and songs are followed by the artist in (Parentheses).

About the Author

Stan Jeffries is a music critic and radio show host. He has worked as venue manager at Newcastle University and entertainment manager at Hallam University. He was a contributor to *The Rough Guide to Rock*.